Lecture Notes in Computer Science 7547

Commenced Publication in 1973
Founding and Former Series Editors:
Gerhard Goos, Juris Hartmanis, and Jan van Leeuwen

Francisco Cipolla-Ficarra   Kim Veltman
Domen Verber   Miguel Cipolla-Ficarra
Florian Kammüller (Eds.)

Advances in New Technologies, Interactive Interfaces and Communicability

Second International Conference, ADNTIIC 2011
Huerta Grande, Argentina, December 5-7, 2011
Revised Selected Papers

 Springer

Volume Editors

Francisco Cipolla-Ficarra
Miguel Cipolla-Ficarra
ALAIPO and AINCI, HCI Lab.
Via Tabajani 1 - Suc. 15 (CP 7), 24121 Bergamo, Italy
E-mail: ficarra@alaipo.com, ficarra@ainci.com

Kim Veltman
Virtual Maastricht McLuhan Institute
Europalaan 73, 6226 CN, Maastricht, The Netherlands
E-mail: kim_veltman@hotmail.com

Domen Verber
University of Maribor, FERI Insitute of Informatics
Smetanova Ulica 17, Maribor, Slovenia
E-mail: domen.verber@uni-mb.si

Florian Kammüller
Middlesex University London, Department of Computer Communications
Rm T 109, Townhall The Burroughs, Hendon London, NW4 4BT, UK
E-mail: f.kammueller@mdx.ac.uk

ISSN 0302-9743   e-ISSN 1611-3349
ISBN 978-3-642-34009-3   e-ISBN 978-3-642-34010-9
DOI 10.1007/978-3-642-34010-9
Springer Heidelberg Dordrecht London New York

Library of Congress Control Number: 2012949335

CR Subject Classification (1998): H.4, H.5, C.2, H.3, D.2, I.2

LNCS Sublibrary: SL 3 – Information Systems and Application, incl. Internet/Web
and HCI

Typesetting: Camera-ready by author, data conversion by Scientific Publishing Services, Chennai, India

Printed on acid-free paper

Springer is part of Springer Science+Business Media (www.springer.com)

Preface

In the evolution of computers, software has always lagged behind hardware. Microcomputing joined to telecommunications is generating at a dazzling speed new paradigms in social communication through computers. However, interactive design is still governed by static communication models, especially with text. In the current creative process of content for interactive communication with these computers, for instance, the computer animation, educational video, radial publicity, etc., usually starts with pencil and paper.

Thus, in the new millennium with new information and communication techniques, human beings constantly return to the early stages of writing. It is here that the wit and creativity of the fundamental structures of new content must draw powerfully the attention of millions of potential users in the least possible time, among different cultures and mindsets. This is why the content of these works must have a minimal triad of quality attributes, i.e., originality, simplicity, and universality.

The second decade of the new millennium is laying the foundations of new ways of working which were already tested at the end of the twentieth century and early twenty-first century. The results were very positive, along with the team work for three-dimensional design of industrial components, for instance; work that can be performed from home (telework) and with members of the group scattered all around the planet. This simple example of interactive design on-line, which formerly was seldom used, is today the common denominator for this kind of computer-made activity.

Interactive design and the human factors are key in the development of the current interactive hypermedia systems. In the era of expansion of interactive communicability, it is important to have a compass to advance steadily in the right direction. An advance that must be shared by all the participants in the generation of new interactive systems of microcomputing, such as multimedia phones, e-books, PC tablets, videogames, etc. These interactive products of the new millennium are based on the functional balance of computer science, electronics, and telecommunications.

A balance that must be shared by everyone involved in the design, planning, production, implementation, quality control, the correction of eventual mistakes, and in the attention to the potential users and/or clients, etc. Each individual who participates in the stages of the evolution of the product and/or service makes up the source of the human factors. That is, factors which sometimes are invisible but are vital for the success or the failure of new services and products.

As a rule, these novel products and/or services entail a long time of research and development. Knowing the human factors and software tools, improving the design of the interactive systems, icreasing ergonomics, etc. are basic tasks to avoid agents that slow down or make it difficult to reach the maximum levels of quality, in the least possible time and with the lowest cost.

The Program Committee of the Second International Conference on Advances in New Technologies, Interactive Interfaces and Communicability (ADNTIIC 2011) consisted of Albert, C. (Spain), Anderson, S. (USA), Barazzetti, L. (Italy), Bleecker, J. (USA), Bonanno, P. (Malta), Bonilla, L. (Costa Rica), Buzzi, M. (Italy), Cáceres-Díaz, A. (Puerto Rico), Carré, J. (Curaçao), Casas, S. (Argentina), Chih-Fang, H. (Taiwan), Chorianopoulos, K. (Greece), Cipolla-Ficarra, M. (Italy and Spain), Colorado, A. (Spain), Brie, M. (Malta), Dalmasso, M. (Argentina), Darmawan, R. (Indonesia), Demirors, O. (Turkey), Edison, D. (Canada), El Sadik, A. (Canada), Fekonja Peklaj, U. (Slovenia), Fidelibus, M. (Argentina), Fotouhi, F. (USA), Flores, S. (Spain), Fulton, P. (Canada), Garrido-Lora, M. (Spain), Griffith, S. (Jamaica), Grosky, W. (USA), Guarinos-Galán, V. (Spain), Hadad, G. (Argentina), Ilavarasan, V. (India), Imaz, M. (UK), Jen, W. (Taiwan), Kammüller, F. (UK), Kratky, A. (USA), Kirakowski, J. (Ireland), Lau, F. (China), Lebrón-Vázquez, M. (Puerto Rico), Liudmila, P. (Russia), Marcos, C. (Argentina), Milrad, M. (Sweden), Moreno, I. (Spain), Mori, G. (Italy), Možina, K. (Slovenia), Pargman, D. (Sweden), Ramirez-Alvarado, M. (Spain), Read, T. (Spain), Salvendy, G. (China), Scolnik, H. (Argentina), Silva-Salmerón, J. (Canada), Stanchev, P. (USA), Styliaras, G. (Greece), Tamai, T. (Japan), Varela, L. (France), Verber, D. (Slovenia), Veltman, K. (The Netherlands), Vidal, G. (Argentina), Vilches-López, I. (Spain), who supported the preparation of the conference.

I would like to thank all of the authors and speakers for their effort as well as the referees for their kind collaboration. Finally, a special thanks goes to Alfred Hofmann (Springer), Anna Kramer (Springer), Ingrid Beyer (Springer), Christine Reiss (Springer), Maria Ficarra (ALAIPO and AINCI), various individuals and local authorities, and all those who financially supported the international conference.

November 2011   Francisco V. Cipolla-Ficarra

Acknowledgments

Table of Contents

The Argentinization of the User Centered Design 1
  Francisco V. Cipolla Ficarra, Miguel Cipolla Ficarra, and
  Jacqueline Alma

Integrated Synergy for Cultural Contents Recursivity in *e-Culture*
System 15
  María M. Clusella, María G. Mitre, María A. Santillán,
  Adriana Generoso, and Paola D. Budàn

Federation and Security Aspects for the Management of the EHR
in Italy 26
  Maria Claudia Buzzi, Francesco Donini, Abraham Gebrehiwot,
  Alessio Lunardelli, Cristian Lucchesi, and Paolo Mori

Are Smartphones Really Useful for Scientific Computing? 38
  Juan Manuel Rodríguez, Cristian Mateos, and Alejandro Zunino

Ontology and Rule Based Inferring on Project Teams 48
  Vili Podgorelec

Simulation on Cloud Computing Infrastructures of Parametric Studies
of Nonlinear Solids Problems 58
  Elina Pacini, Melisa Ribero, Cristian Mateos, Anibal Mirasso, and
  Carlos García Garino

New Technologies of the Information and Communication: Analysis
of the Constructors and Destructors of the European Educational
System 71
  Francisco V. Cipolla Ficarra, Valeria M. Ficarra, and
  Miguel Cipolla Ficarra

A Multi-agent Model That Promotes Team-Role Balance in Computer
Supported Collaborative Learning 85
  Rubén Fares and Rosanna Costaguta

A Memetic Algorithm for Collaborative Learning Team Formation in
the Context of Software Engineering Courses 92
  Virginia Yannibelli and Analía Amandi

Empirically Derived Guidelines for Audio-Visual E-mail Browsing   104
  Saad Alharbi

Intelligent Analysis of User Interactions in a Collaborative Software
Engineering Context   114
  Alejandro Corbellini, Silvia Schiaffino, and Daniela Godoy

Motivation for Next Generation of Users versus Parochialism in
Software Engineering   124
  Francisco V. Cipolla Ficarra and Valeria M. Ficarra

Group and Students Profiles to Support Collaborative Learning in a
Multiagent Model   134
  Rosanna Costaguta and Elena Durán

Teaching Scrum to Software Engineering Students with Virtual Reality
Support   140
  Guillermo Rodríguez, Alvaro Soria, and Marcelo Campo

Security of the Automatic Information On-Line: A Study of the
Controls Forbid   151
  Francisco V. Cipolla Ficarra and Andreas Kratky

Communicability and Usability for the Interface in e-Learning   165
  Leda B. Digión and Mabel Sosa

Towards Software Architecture Documents Matching Stakeholders'
Interests   176
  Matías Nicoletti, J. Andrés Diaz-Pace, and Silvia Schiaffino

An Architecture for Resource Behavior Prediction to Improve
Scheduling Systems Performance on Enterprise Desktop Grids   186
  Sergio Ariel Salinas, Carlos García Garino, and Alejandro Zunino

Discrete Sequences Analysis for Detecting Software Design Patterns   197
  Juan Francisco Silva Logroño, Luis Berdún,
  Marcelo Armentano, and Analía Amandi

A Programming Model for the Semantic Web   208
  Marco Crasso, Cristian Mateos, Alejandro Zunino, and
  Marcelo Campo

Combining Semantic Web Technologies and Rule-Based Systems
for Building Advanced Medical Applications   219
  Vili Podgorelec and Mitja Gradišnik

Designing ABA-Based Software for Low-Functioning Autistic
Children   230
  Silvia Artoni, Maria Claudia Buzzi, Marina Buzzi, Fabio Ceccarelli,
  Claudia Fenili, Beatrice Rapisarda, and Maurizio Tesconi

What Are Your Children Watching on YouTube? 243
  Marina Buzzi

Can Your Friends Help You to Find Interesting Multimedia Content on
Web 2.0? 253
  Alejandro Corbellini, Daniela Godoy, and Silvia Schiaffino

Author Index 263

The Argentinization of the User Centered Design

Francisco V. Cipolla Ficarra[1,2], Miguel Cipolla Ficarra[2], and Jacqueline Alma[3]

HCI Lab. – F&F Multimedia Communic@tions Corp.
[1] ALAIPO: Asociación Latina de Interacción Persona-Ordenador
[2] AINCI: Asociación Internacional de la Comunicación Interactiva
[3] Electronic Arts, Canada

c/ Angel Baixeras, 5 – AP 1638, 08080 Barcelona, Spain
via Tabajani, 1 – S. 15 – CP 7, 24121 Bergamo, Italy
ficarra@alaipo.com, ficarra@ainci.com, jacqueline_alma@yahoo.com

Abstract. The current study presents an analysis of the degree of circulation of traditional colours of the villages, whether it is in the internet or in the emerging digital communication media. A diachronic study of the colours azure or light blue, white, yellow and red allows to detect how the use of these colours has spread in the most varied environments of multimedia contents of the current technological decade. Further some communicability keys to detect the presence or absence of human and/or social factors in the global diffusion of certain colours and user-centered design in our days are presented.

Keywords: Interactive Systems, User Centered Design, Internalization, Human Factors, New Media, Communicability, Diachronism, Evaluation.

1   Introduction

In the evolution of the design of on-line and off-line interactive systems many professionals have been involved in this process coming from the varied disciplines of the formal and factual sciences [1]. Depending on the environment and the format in which they worked, an endless number of simple or compound terms have been generated which were intended to determine aprioristically the conceptual and/or practical fields. However, in this process the limits among the different fields (audio-visual, art, industrial engineering, etc.) are not exact, but rather ambiguous, due to the greater or lesser degree of affiliation of these professionals with the computer science field, and therefore their ability to occupy key positions in the process of product development and/or services. Disparities were such that in Southern Europe, for instance, a designer in Barcelona in the mid nineties got a higher pay to implement a new audiovisual product on CD-ROM than the programmer and systems analyst. At that time the word "usability" was related to the computer context, and the design notion in fine arts and/or audiovisual. Consequently, in Spain, the user-centered design, appeared as the exclusive domain of psychologists and not designers. Something similar happened with pervasive usability, where anyone coming from the formal sciences (mathematicians, engineers, physicists, etc.), regarded membership to

F.V. Cipolla-Ficarra et al. (Eds.): ADNTIIC 2011, LNCS 7547, pp. 1–14, 2012.

that field as something that they naturally owned. Now if we talk of design in countries of the American south cone, that is, Argentina, Uruguay and Chile in the 90s, it was a field of knowledge of the faculties of architecture and/or industrial design in certain public or state universities. The university-based mercantilism of Southern Europe in the 90s boosted the elimination of borders among the different disciplines, thus generating professionals experienced in the use of design oriented commercial software [2] but not in its theoretical bases, such as it can be acquired in an industrial design faculty. In this latter field for instance the user was always the focus of the creation of products.

In the early 90s Jacob Nielsen set down the guidelines of usability engineering leaving aside a major issue such as the measurement of the five stated criteria: easy to learn, efficient to use, few errors, easy to remember, and subjectively pleasant [3]. Later on, Ben Shneiderman and Jacob Nielsen approached the system acceptability issue separately. In this work the notion of usability appears as a part of "usefulness", that is, with the following components [4]:

- Efficiency: Once users have learned the design, how quickly can they perform tasks?
- Errors: How many errors do users make, how severe are these errors, and how easily can they
- recover from the errors?
- Learnability. How easy is it for users to accomplish basic tasks the first time they encounter the design?
- Memorability: When users return to the design after a period of not using it, how easily can they re-establish proficiency?
- Satisfaction: How pleasant is it to use the design?

In this work the first intersection between design and use of the interactive systems takes place. However, we leave the communicability component aside, which is present in everything that is designed in the interaction between computers and users. Usability engineering had its momentum in the 90s, coinciding with the democratization process of the Internet, and the spread of the personal computers in millions of homes in Southern Europe. Besides, it coincides with the era of software quality [5]. However, in the new millennium we are under the communicability era, and in the current decade in the communicability expansion era [1], having left behind the usability stage of the interactive systems in the personal computers.

Now in this design process the presentation component of the contents still remains a key element, whether it is on the traditional computer screen, or in the new microcomputing and telecommunications multimedia devices. That is, the communicability of the elements of the interface, plays an essential role for the potential users of on-line and off-line interactive systems. One of the elements that make up the interfaces is the colour of the dynamic and static component elements of the interfaces, that is, typography, pictures, graphics, background, lines, etc. All of these elements require a correct combination of the contents visible on the screen for better acceptance by the users, regardless of the place where it is found and the purpose of the interaction with the contents of the interactive system.

The best designers of 2D and 3D computer animations systematically resorted to the traditional colours of the place where the enculturation and transculturation process of the new users has started [6]. In those images were always present the colours of the flag, with which the number of spectators of the TV network increased, as the viewers identified with that television network. That is, colours play an essential role in the identification and the feeling of belonging to a community. Now in the Spanish and Italian case, to mention just two examples, one has to take into account that a city hall of a Mediterranean city may have as many as four flags on the portal of its main entrance and their offices: European, Spanish/Italian, autonomous region, and the city flag. Lately, and in an implicit way, there may also be the colours of the club that represents the club that has more followers in the city.

2 The Colours of the Argentina Flag: Analogical Design and Digital Design Online

In the following figure 1 we have the main colours of the flag of Argentina. As we can see, there are two values of the colours for digital reproduction: in hexadecimal and in RGB. The listing is completed with other analogical means, such as paper or cardboard, canvas and plastic.

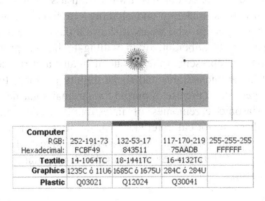

Computer				
RGB:	252-191-73	132-53-17	117-170-219	255-255-255
Hexadecimal:	FCBF49	843511	75AADB	FFFFFF
Textile	14-1064TC	18-1441TC	16-4132TC	
Graphics	1235C ó 11U6	1685C ó 1675U	284C ó 284U	
Plastic	Q03021	Q12024	Q30041	

Fig. 1. Flag of Argentina –colours and the different codes used in regard to the support that is used

Conceptual evolution of colours in relation to the field of study (psychology, art, etc.), use (industrial design, fashion, publicity communication, etc.), and transformation of meanings with the passing of time. Lüscher and Jung [7] [8] have a first analysis of the meaning of these colours (reflections and conclusions) from several points of view (cultural, artistic, etc.) is as follows [9–13]:

- *White:* A white fabric suggests values of pureness, innocence, cleanness, lightness, brightness. Rudolf Steiner writes about light-white: "When we try to approach to white we must say that, first of all, we are taken, through white, towards light as such". Simultaneity, Vasilij Kandinsky writes about white as an interval [8]: "white acts on our psyche as a long silence, that is absolute for us. It has an interior sound that is actually an absence of sound and corresponds quite well to the pauses that, in the music, break only temporarily the development of a sentence or a content and are not its final conclusion".

- *Light blue:* A light blue fabric appears to be light, soft, delicate and gentle. This colour is associated with sweetness, spirituality and kindness. Kandinsky writes: "Light blue has an indifferent nature and places itself far from the audience, like the light sky. The lighter it is, the least sonorous it is, until you reach a dumb calmness, the white".

- *Yellow:* A yellow fabric is bright, light, joyful, warm, cheerful, and lively, it conveys extroversion and youth. "People who love yellow, desire it and wear it, they want to transmit the solar aspect that is inside them, the most external and extrovert, open towards others and to novelties. People who prefer this colour thirst for life and experience [...] they express the desire to feel cheerful and expand into social life" [Ass you have been using other quotes, maybe if would be useful to restate Lüscher/Jung?]. Action: instability, change. Purpose: freedom. Temporality: future. Sensation: hope.

- *Red:* A red fabric conveys heat, brilliance, sensuality, and has a strong and important presence. "This colour has always been associated with sexual desire [...] and is – in tattoos, make-up and clothing – a signal of appeal. As red is a boasting colour, the person who wears it shows a passionate and young image of himself, energetic and exuberant, often willing to be the protagonist and have power. In the past it represented the colour of luxury and richness, of power and sovereignty, of hierarchical status and social dignity for long: today a memory of this symbolism persists in the use of purple for cardinal's garments, for magistracy, for royal or Masonic ceremonies of investiture, besides theatre that, taking possession of these historical references, made it the colour of false-luxury". Action: to provoke an effect, to buy. Purpose: conquest. Temporality. Present. Sensation: Success. Historicity: sacrifice, royalty, corruption, popular and socialist, playful consumerism.

The reader who is interested in the meanings of the colours and their correct use in the generation of interfaces may widen the current notions in the following bibliography: [14]. Without going into the historical aspects through which the creator of the flag of Argentina (Manuel Belgrano [15]) combined those colours and their disposition, currently and in the interactive design, these colours have reached a great acceptance by the users of interactive systems. That is, the combination of the colours in the flag has a very positive connotation in a great part of the world population. A proof of this statement is the spread of its use in the most varied contents of the different on-line information supports, for instance. Perhaps one of the reasons has to do with the elements of nature it depicts, that is, sun, sky, clouds. Elements which are to be found all across planet Earth.

2.1   Cultural Aspects and Internalization of the Inferfaces

The current context of analysis, including the cultural aspects, had its origins in the 90s with the internalization of the interfaces design. In this regard there was an attempt to generate several design guidelines in relation to the operating system being used: Microsoft or Macintosh. The same happened with the graphic arts which from paper support had to be taken to the CD-ROM support, in the last decade of the past century there was a great wealth of knowledge which had to be transferred quickly to the new global communication media that were starting to work thanks to the Internet. In some cases adaptability studies were made to the new emerging media [16–19]. In other cases, designers only resorted to a straight transfer. Whatever the used methodology was in this knowledge transfer, the cultural meanings of the colours do not change quickly, unless there are factors alien to computer science, such as the political parties that seize key colours to gain adepts in the least possible time, and resorting to emotional factors, rather than rational in their campaigns. We have an example with the orange colour in Spain and the Netherlands and its sportive meaning, whereas in the Ukraine today it has a revolutionary connotation. Another colour is the green, which in the Hispanic world means hope and that in the Italian Alps is the colour of a political party that has bred hopelessness among its voters. That is, sometimes the diachronic cultural meanings are changed by the social synchronism of reality inside a certain community. In the following figure 2 we see how the main colours of the Argentina flag of figure 1 are used in a propaganda banner related to work issues, by a Spanish political party, when in fact the colours it should use are those of its national flag (red and yellow) or the combination of both, that is, orange. These latter examples are social factors which have been excluded from the current work and we leave it as a matter of study for the future.

Fig. 2. An example of the described phenomenon with political purposes in other places of the Earth (Spain) www.elpais.es –11.05.2011

Resorting to the notions deriving from the factual sciences and following Mario Bunge's [20] enunciations, we will try to give an answer with hypothesis and plausible realities to the following rhetoric question: How can it be that the colours of the Argentinian flag have spread in Southern Europe, especially in Spain and Italy? In the inventory of the main characteristics of the factual science presented by Mario Bunge [20] we find that this science is analytical, that is, it approaches the described problems, one by one, and tries to decompose all of it into elements. It tries to understand a whole situation in the terms of its components. Besides, it tries to find the elements that make up every total, and the interconnections that explain its integration. Research starts by decomposing its objects with the purpose of understanding the internal mechanism responsible for the observed phenomena. However, this disassembly process of the "mechanism" does not stop when the nature of its parts has been researched. The next step is the study of the interdependence of the parts and the final stage is the intention of rebuilding the whole in terms of its interconnected parts. Science does not ignore synthesis, what it rejects is the irrational pretension that the synthesis can be apprehended by a special intuition, without a previous analysis.

In 1996 a project to generate the first off-line interactive systems for a virtual campus in Catalonia –Open University of Catalonia [21], carried out in a record time, and with a resounding success, made apparent several main elements in giving response to the rhetoric question we have posed. In the first place, the preferences of the colours among the different peoples of the world, including countries such as Argentina, Brazil, Canada, Japan, etc. at the time when the importance of the colours we are analyzing was already established. In the second place, the percentages with which the users grasped the multimedia contents in relation to the different senses, and in an autonomous or combined way. The work held other important conclusions, which the interested reader may look up in [21]. It was in that research that the main elements that made up the off-line and on-line multimedia systems were presented, with which the quality of an interactive system could start to be evaluated. That is, that work meant an important synthesis not only as a work tool for the college education oriented multimedia systems, but also as lines of future research inside the software quality sector.

A way to eclipse a research work which may be considered as pioneering or revolutionary, due to the reached results even without having access to big sums of money (the techniques and methods used do not require labs, specialized staff, technological instruments, etc.), consists in what we would currently call "scientific stalking". Scientific stalking has its genesis in those individuals who deny the importance of the works which are made by the professionals in an autonomous, anonymous, modest and honest way. The conclusions reached are systematically plagiarized, through the use of the said references in similar works, but without ever quoting the source of the pioneering work. Besides, the clones of the pioneering professional spring up. Clones who thanks to the European social communication media occupy the privileged places in the scientific and/or academic community, eclipsing for ever those honest workers without financial subsidies, who daily take charge of scientific issues. It is these clones and their followers who will discredit for decades all the results reached by those who undergo scientific stalking. A way to do it is publishing in the printed press or other commercial magazines, associations or organizations allegedly devoted to the same issues, etc., those conclusions of the scientific pioneers so that to the eyes of the reader, viewer, listener, etc., the results reached look like just another banality. That is, every conclusion or work he makes is no good, or scientifically has a value equal to zero. When in reality it is the very opposite, that is, it is a real breakthrough in the sector of the formal and/or factual sciences if we refer to multimedia interactive systems issues. This stalking is easily detectable since mid 95' in the university environments of Autonomous University of Barcelona, Polytechnic University of Catalonia, Pompeu Fabra University, University of Zaragoza, etc. and it branches out on the other side of the Atlantic, if that pioneer has his/her roots in the American continent, for instance. The reasons for this persecution are due to the lack of knowledge and/or experience of the academic staff that sought to take quickly the steady university posts in the late 20th century and beginning of the new millennium in Southern Europe. Posts that were related to design, usability, multimedia, virtual reality, the Internet architecture, audiovisual, cognitive psychology, the degrees in computing and systems, software engineering, etc. We have an example in the following figure, where in the shape of a funnel we have all those professionals of Southern Europe who allegedly today define themselves as software engineers.

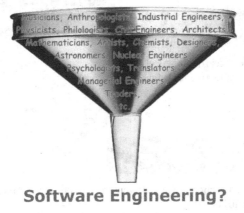

Software Engineering?

Fig. 3. Funnel of the alleged professionals in software engineering in Southern Europe

The consequences of these distortions have a direct influence in the drop of the college educational quality and the millions of unemployed in Southern Europe. The professionals who had the knowledge and/or experience were systematically excluded from the university working system in Southern Europe for political reasons (especially the Catalan or Lombardian universities) and the eternal Latin university endogamy [1] [22].

Now from some university departments of the Spanish Mediterranean coast it is easy to see how they promote scientific stalking in their on-line publications. An example in this regard are the colours they use in the digital versions of their newspapers, allegedly global for linguistic reasons. For instance, instead of using the red, yellow and orange colours, etc. currently the newspaper "El País" (www.elpais.com –second semester, 2011) resorts to the azure and the white in the news. Besides, in the upper side of the title of the newspaper appears a dynamic advertisement banner with the flag of Brazil. Something unthinkable in the on-line interactive design of the 90s. However, perhaps because of social and economic motives, it is something that is frequently done in the second decade of the new millennium. Next some examples about this from the newspaper "El País" – www.elpais.com.

Fig. 4. The title of the Saturday magazine is a clear example of the phenomenon we are describing (El País –www.elpais.com, 10.01.2011)

Fig. 5. In the international section are also present the colours of the Argentina flag (El País – www.elpais.com, 09.30.2011)

Fig. 6. In the advertisement of the rounding-up of 2010 with the poster Spain soccer world champion 2010 (El País –www.elpais.com, 09.30.2011)

Example from an Italian newspaper with dynamic advertisement banner:

Fig. 7. Banner advertisement (Il Giornale, www.ilgiornale.it –08.06.2011)

Fig. 8. In the advertisement of the phone services firm of the Italian newspaper are all the colours of the Argentina flag (Il Giornale, www.ilgiornale.it –08.06.2011)

3   Learned Lessons and Future Works

The user-centered design or pervasive usability changes from country to country, where its principles are put into practice sometimes in a correct way and other times they just copy and paste the conclusions of the scientific works, excluding their sources (see Annex #1). This is the main reason why the human and social factors may distort the scientific reality in the short term. However, in the long term the economic factor of these disorders affects the whole community where they take place. An example of this statement is the high number of unemployed in Southern Europe. A reality that denotes that the R&D university sector (public and private) which has received millions and millions of subsidies in the university field has not been able to develop systems and structures to prevent such a reality. Besides, the digital gap between the population has widened with that existing in the emerging countries. Consequently there is a tendency to homogenize these conjunctures and a way to do it is through the design of the analog and digital media. Obviously, the

Internet plays an essential role in the globalization of communication. That's why the digital media enclose as slogan the global character of the information they offer, resorting not so much to the local colours, but rather to the international where they aim to expand. That is, the strategy used in the audiovisual media of the 90s with satellite TV is repeated, that is, getting the higher possible number of viewers all around the planet in the least possible time. The colour of the design is a resort that triggers the essential elements of UCD of a web site, such as the accessibility of the visual contents and the communicability of the information in the interface, just to mention two examples.

In the current work we have focused on a visual aspect of the press digital media, such as colour. However, we are working on the TDTV (digital terrestrial television) and digital radio, especially, when they broadcast negative European news related to the financial, sports or social fields. For instance, the use of metropolitan music – "tango", that represents the identity of the peoples which are over 11,000 km beyond the European borders, and who have nothing to do with those negative factors, which is constantly used as background music of the dynamic or static images, in the daily programming of the multimedia contents to go with the negative news in Spain, Italy, France, and Portugal.

4   Conclusion

The use of the analyzed colours has expanded exponentially since the early 90s to our days. That is, colours that have boosted the usability and the communicability of the on-line and off-line multimedia systems. However, the social factors that are usually currently linked to them may put an end to the meanings they have had since their origins and even from the point of view of international culture. Their strength lies in the fact that three of them make up common elements of nature such as the sun, the clouds, the sky, etc. Consequently, we are in the face of a phenomenon of Argentinization of user-centered design. This phenomenon can be regarded as positive from the local cultures. However, this positive sign can turn to negative when they are used to go with detrimental contents, such as are the cases of financial corruption broadcast by the terrestrial digital television in Southern Europe that we are analyzing in these moments.

Acknowledgments. The authors would like to thank to Maria Ficarra, Sonia Flores, Pamela Fulton, Mary Brie, Doris Edision, Carlos, Andreas Kratky (University of Southern California) for helpful comments.

References

1. Cipolla-Ficarra, F., et al.: Quality and Communicability for Interactive Hypermedia Systems: Concepts and Practices for Design. IGI Global, Hershey (2010)
2. Cipolla-Ficarra, F., et al.: Computational Informatics, Social Factors and New Information Technologies: Hypermedia Perspectives and Avant-Garde Experiences in the Era of Communicability Expansion. Blue Herons Editions, Bergamo (2011)

3. Nielsen, J.: Usability Engineering. Academic Press, London (1993)
4. Nielsen, J.: The Usability Engineering Life Cycle. IEEE Computer 25(3), 12–22 (1992)
5. Potts, C.: Software Engineering Research Revisited. IEEE Software 10(5), 19–28 (1993)
6. Rosebush, J.: Historical Computer Animation: The First Decade 1960-1970. In: ACM Siggraph, New York (1992)
7. Riedel, I., Farben, M.: Gesellschaft, Kunst und Psychotherapie. Kreuz Verlag, Sttugart (1999)
8. Alison, F., et al.: Colours of Life. La Stampa, Torino (1995)
9. Gage, J.: Color and Meaning: Art, Science, and Symbolism. University of California Press, Berkeley (2000)
10. Brown, D.C., et al.: Evaluating Web Page Color and Layout Adaptations. IEEE Multimedia 9(1), 86–89 (2002)
11. Fernandes, T.: Global Interface Design: A guide to Designing International User Interfaces. Academic Press, Boston (1995)
12. Shneiderman, B., et al.: Designing the User Interface: Strategies for Effective Human-Computer Interaction. Addison Wesley, New York (2010)
13. Murch, G.: Color graphics: Blessing or ballyhoo? Computer Graphics Forum 4, 127–135 (1985)
14. Cipolla-Ficarra, F., Cipolla-Ficarra, M.: HECHE: Heuristic Evaluation of Colours in HomepagE. In: CD Proc. Applied Human Factors and Ergonomics, Las Vegas (2008)
15. Giménez, O.: Vida, época y obra de Manuel Belgrano. El Ateneo, Buenos Aires (1993) (in Spanish)
16. Gillmor, D.: Imagining Tomorrow's News. Interactions 11(2), 58–59 (2004)
17. Sellen, A., et al.: Reflecting Human Values in the Digital Age. Communications of ACM 52(3), 58–66 (2009)
18. Fidock, J., Carroll, J.: Why Do Users Employ the Same System in So Many Different Ways? IEEE Intelligent Systems 26(4), 32–39 (2011)
19. Olson, G., et al.: New Missions for a Sociotechnical Infrastructure. IEEE Computer 43(11), 37–43 (2010)
20. Bunge, M.: The science: your method and your philosophy. Buenos Aires, Siglo XXI (1981)
21. Cipolla-Ficarra, F.: Evaluation and Communication Techniques in Multimedia Product Design for On the Net University Education. Multimedia on the Net. Springer, Vienna (1996)
22. Peñalva, J.: Corrupción en la Universidad. Ciudadela, Madrid (2011)

Annex #1

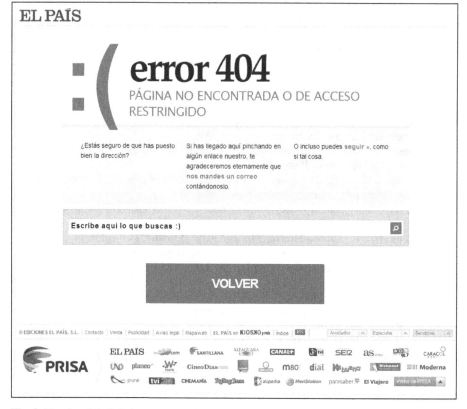

Fig. 9. The Spanish digital newspaper: El País –www.elpais.com and the Argentinization of the mistake 404

The Argentinization of the user centered design phenomenon has been included in some European digital papers, imitating other newspapers in Argentina.

It is a phenomenon fostered by pressure groups made up by fine arts graduates in Spain, who never quote their sources, since they follow the famous "copy and paste".

Something which is very usual in the computer art in Spain (figure 10), since even in the animated or static pixel festivals plagiarism is fostered as a common practice from Catalonia or Majorca in Spain (see text below of the Art Futura blog: "copy is not theft" –figure 10).

Nowadays these very same shapes and style created for Acuarinto (designer: Javier Mariscal) are to be found in many shops in the Balearic Islands. As a rule, the love of plagiarism may be part of the associations which protect copyright and it will even be tutored through the copyright of a part of these figures, such as can be creating cyclopean characters (figure 11), but instead of using a circle, resorts to a ellipsis, divided by a vertical line and two dots as eyes inside the big eye.

In few words, the appearance of a Argentinization phenomenon in European-Mediterranean region is due to pressure groups devoted for decades to style plagiarism and prompted by the clerical premise: "Nobody can hurt us". That is, they are above the laws and the copyrights. Examples, from Catalonia (figure 10), and Majorca (figure 11).

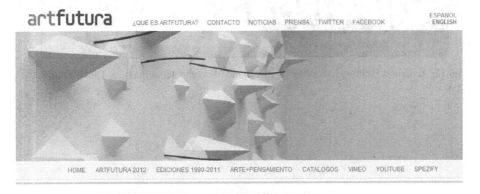

Fig. 10. Art Futura (http://www.artfutura.org/v2/blog/?p=4287&langswitch_lang=es)

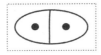

Fig. 11. Cyclops or thief's mask

Fig. 12. Acuarinto (author: Javier Mariscal) 2D and 3D computer animation. This is an original work.

Integrated Synergy for Cultural Contents Recursivity in *e-Culture* System

María M. Clusella[1,2], María G. Mitre[1], María A. Santillán[1],
Adriana Generoso[1], and Paola D. Budàn[1,3]

[1] International Institute Galileo Galilei
[2] Universidad Católica de Santiago del Estero
[3] Universidad Nacional de Santiago del Estero
mercedes.clusella@ucse.edu.ar,
{asantillan.ccs,gabriela.mitre.presidente}@fundaringenio.org.ar,
pbudan1@gmail.com

Abstract. This paper presents the results obtained by the International Institute Galileo Galilei a research unit of Fundaringenio, within the framework of the research project *An interactive information system for e-culture*. It aims at designing a web interactive information system for e –culture in order to promote and spread worldwide the cultural heritage of a northwestern region of Argentina for future generations. The research hypothesis is based on a new design of Simbionomic System. Culture as a complex phenomenon, is studied from the Systemic Paradigm. The methodic process consists of the systemic modelling process and the retroprospective methodology. The Method/technique of Syntegration by recursion allows the generation of distinctive cultural features. The selection and application of this interactive processing technique foster integration, cohesion and synergy of multiple topics and perspectives of cultural contents. The process, that is being tested- allows the different aspects of a central problem to be examined in parallel.

Keywords: *e-culture* System, Retroprospectivation, Syntegration, Simbionomic System.

1 Introduction

This work is carried out within the framework of the research project presented at an International Scientific Meeting in 2010 [1]. This research aims at developing interactive information systems that can promote and disseminate world cultures, including Santiago del Esteros`s culture (the culture of a northwestern region of Argentina). Currently, a prototype of the e-culture system of Santiago del Estero is the main product expected. This prototype can be applied by analogy to other cultures and will contribute to spread cultural identity for academic, sports, business and touristic purposes.

Culture can be identified as a hypercomplex phenomenon which involves an epistemic process [2] for the construction of identity. This process covers the origins

F.V. Cipolla-Ficarra et al. (Eds.): ADNTIIC 2011, LNCS 7547, pp. 15–25, 2012.
© Springer-Verlag Berlin Heidelberg 2012

of native people and endogenous changes produced by new cultures that are received through physical, intellectual or virtual immigration. As a hypercomplex process, culture is studied by means of systemic paradigm and methodology, and taking into account informatics and new systemics techniques. From the systemic perspective, culture can be studied using a retrosprospective methodology [3]. This process begins with the conception of the Meta Model to be achieved: the e-culture Model corresponding to an interactive web information system for the promotion of Santiago's culture. The Existed Model is built in relation to its past, history. After that, Existing Model is developed in relation to its present. From these, an Operating Model is being designed and adapted. In this case an e-culture web information system is built. Since it is based on a formal abstraction it is possible to apply it to different cultures [4]. Thus, as a multidimensional and circular sequence it could be repeated recursively. Such sequence is identified as from part to whole and from whole to part until it becomes an acceptable and satisfactory scenario. To sum up, it is a process of synergy and recursion.

In this case study the modeling process that allowed the definition of the existing model as a system and the outline of the ideas in a more concrete way is presented. The Existing Model is addressed with more details in the light of the initial Meta Model. The Meta Model of Santiagueñidad involves twelve topics as interrelated elements that represent distinctive cultural features. The structure technique known as Team Syntegrity Model –TSM [5] was applied in an adapted way to delineate the Existing Model more accurately. The process consists of an exercise that tests 4 of the 12 topics of the Meta Model (Feelings-Dancing and Knowing-Doings). The process will continue to test the other topics until an e-culture Model of santiagueñidad is achieved.

This paper presents a first version of the Existing Model which is the result of the activities carried out by two of the four groups of researches (called Beta Node and Delta node) from multidisciplinary perspectives. The Beta Node deals with the cultural contents from the philosophical, epistemic, conceptual, theoretical and methodical point of view, while the Delta Node brings the technical support that allows innovation through paradigmatics and evolutionary changes.

Next sections are structured as follows: Section 2 presents basic concepts related to e-culture, and the Existing Model of Santiagueñidad is proposed and better defined from the process of integrated synergy. Then, the TSM method is briefly commented. At the same time, the simulation of syntegration process for obtaining new knowledge by recursivity of the main topics of that culture is set out in Section 3. Section 4 discusses the results obtained. Finally, the conclusions and future work are presented.

2   Framework

The first ideas generated by the researchers and presented at scientific conferences [5] gave rise to a Binational Science Project in order to co-participate in the scientific exchange governmental program between Austria and Argentine. Despite being considered of national interest the project did not get funding. The objective of the

IIGG group and of the collegues at Vienna University was to study two significant cultural phenomena by different methods and then compare them.

The local Group which comprises 18 researchers divided into four nodes of different multidisciplinar perspectives continued with local research. The Alfa Node perspective is oriented to the productive language, communication and infonomics.

The Gamma Node deals with multimedia formats and prototyped capabilities. Beta and Delta Nodes have been described before. It is a systemic strategy to analyze in parallel the object of study from different perspectives in order to achieve knowledge management or the generation of new knowledge from a shared global view.

The following subsections will briefly mention the main concepts that contextualize the results presented in this communication.

2.1   Santiago del Estero Culture

On the basis of the conceptualizations elaborated by prestigious researchers on systemic studies [6-7] and of the work done by IIGG [8-11], culture can be defined as a complex phenomenon that involves the adaptation of a group of values and norms by a numerous group of people which tends toward the creation of a dynamic, stable entity that persists by itself for a considerable period of time in history. Santiago del Estero culture is the product of an uninterrupted cultural construction over the centuries. This culture is strongly symbolic with a special artistic wealth that possesses material, procedural, and spiritual elements which confer it an identity of differentiating power [12-14]. To sum up, the culture of Santiago del Estero allows unique perceptions, representations and ways of thinking and acting.

2.2   E-Culture

Currently, the New Technologies of Information and Communication provide tools to facilitate knowledge and enable people to share the most important aspects of cultural identities [15]. E-culture is understood as the culture manifested and referenced by electronic devices [16]. The development of an Interactive Information System for e-culture, through web applications allows mass access by people of different cultures [17-18]. The user interaction should allow efficient communication and cultural diffusion for which the premises of emotional systems design [19] for the web application is taken into account.

2.3   Integrated Synergy

The Team Syntegrity Model (TSM), created by Stafford Beer, is an effective and scientifically developed management method to address complex issues [20]. The procedure allows that different aspects of a central issue can be examined in parallel to achieve a consensus. The process helps the participants to put aside the disciplinar boundaries of their own differences, placing them in a broader context and facilitating the achievement of a consensus. Starting from an initial matter the participants choose the topics that make up the different approaches to the problem, and will be themselves who, exercising different roles, generate a circular process of information dissemination that will result in a global vision shared by all [21] thereby achieving an integrated synergy. In more general terms this is a mode of representing a system in a way that the parts include general information about the whole.

Based on an icosahedron arquitecture, which is the most complex of Platonic solids; this structure is especially suitable to fostering synergetic communication. The 12 vertices of an icosahedron represent differents topics to discuss, giving a whole overview. One color is assigned to each topic [22]. In the investigation these 12 elements represent the cultural features identifying the people of the province of Santiago del Estero. These features are described using nouns derived from verbs or nominalized verbs. The 30 edges represent a team member, referred to in this research as qualified informants (disciplinary specialists) who adopt a position in this structure and influence one another on the 12 topics (see Fig. 1). Through this process regulated distribution of information among all the subjects is acquired in a self-regulated way. From the point of view of the interconnection and information exchange it is the most effective way of managing complexity through a group process.

Based on these concepts an exercise was designed to allow the generation of cultural contents. The electronic syntegration fostered optimal communication and the subsequent achievement of a synergetic interaction among topics and participants. The flow of information allowed a maximum distribution of intelligence and Know-how of the participants in a short period. The purpose of that interaction is an integration of multiple topics and perspectives towards a shared body of knowledge and the emergence of new knowledge in the process. In sum, integrated synergy can be understood as the amount of knowledge fostering by the alignment of individual and topis.

3   Developments

The Meta Model of culture can be considered as a meta-metaphor since it involves groups of metaphors proposed by Flood and Jackson [23] to describe knowledge. According to his latest works [24] we can say that the use of metaphor in the conception presented here brings together the efforts of the scientific world to characterize the systemic knowledge in the world. Andriessen [25], for example, argues that in order to describe the metaphors that characterize knowledge, verbs or nouns can be used as lexical units, and that metaphors can be used as thinking devices that establish how we think and talk about knowledge. With this we are referring to culture as a Complex-Pluralist System, according to the TSI; a complex system that encompasses a wide variety of complex subsystems (dancing, living styles, feelings and talking, among others), characterized by highly compatible common values, interests and beliefs. Therefore, these arguments consent to describe the culture through the 12 nominalized verbs.

Thus, the Meta Cultural Model of Santiagueñidad is a systemic model [26] that involves twelve elements or cultural features. These features are described using 12 nouns derived from verbs or nominalized verbs. They are: {1}*believing* (beliefs), {2}*speaking*, {3}*singing*, {4}*dancings* (dances), {5}*story-telling*, {6}*ways of thinking* (patterns of thought), {7}*practical knowledge* (alternative popular medicine), {8}*doings* (traditional craftwork), {9}*feelings* (popular religiosity),{10}*living* (ways of living),{11}*fighting* (heroic epics), {12}*perceiving* (perception patterns and its infuence in the construction of reality). The results are depicted in Fig. 1.

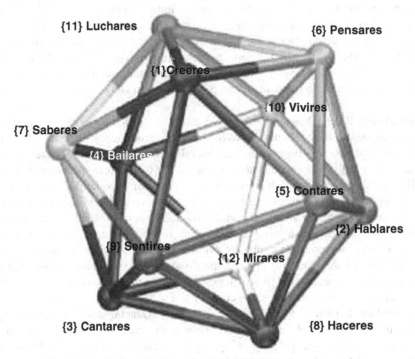

{11} Luchares   **{6} Pensares**
{1}Creeres
{10} Vivires
{7} Saberes
{4} Bailares
{5} Contares
{2} Hablares
{9} Sentires
{12} Mirares
{3} Cantares   **{8} Haceres**

Fig. 1. Meta Cultural Model of Santiagueñidad based on sintegration

Figure 1 reveals that each vertice of the icosahedron represents a topic expressed as a nominalized verb or metaphor used to describe or characterize culture "santiagueña". At the same time, five edges lead to each vertex. That is, there are five participantes in each team. Thus altogether the 30 edges (participantes) enable the sharing of information so as to foster cohesion about all topics (autopoiesis). The result obtained by consensus as consolidated statements of importance can be defined as arguments (according to the concept taken from Artificial Intelligence). An argument is understood as the reasons given to support or criticize an assertion that is questionable or open to doubt [27]. They are evidence of the refinement of the Operating Model during the pre-design process in 2012.

The simulation process carried out methodically responds to a hypothetical deductive premise which through the process of integrated synergy obtains empirical evidence allowing the adjustments in the systemic modeling process by recursion.

3.1   The Simulation Process

The developed exercise was a search experience on the disciplinary issues raised in the virtual space as part of the empirical research. The results obtained in this first simulation allowed the adjustment of the procedure for training the 30 participants (qualified informants), required by the applied technique. Such procedure will be carried out to survey the empirical evidence of features in the Existing Models of 2011 culture Santiagueña in order to contrast the initial hypothesis of the Meta Model represented by the ontic topics diagram, in current evaluation and review. This will be guided by the Existed Model for the design and systematic construction of the Operating Model. This will be done by retroprospectivation of the Meta Model System "e-culture Santiagueña" and at the same time the evaluation of all activities will provide guidance to refine the initial design of this model.

- **Regarding Roles.** Differents roles were assigned to each participant (experts). In this experience, they "simulated" to be qualified informants, critics and observers. The informants are those academic discipline referents who generate contents through synergy. They write statements specifing the features of the local culture. The Critics coordinate dialogues and iteractions among qualified informants to indicate contents (synergy-recursion). The observers supervise the process / product with dynamic and timely intervention. In summary, each participant takes three different roles, is a member of the team in two subjects, and is critic in two issues and observer in four subjects. On the other hand, the moderators (guiding team) control the platform, manage the flow records, and issue reports. All the processes are documented in real time, including action plans developed for all participants to build the essence of change.
- **Regarding Topics.** The four "topics" ("Feelings-Dancing and Knowing-Doings) formulated as cultural features were chosen in order to improve their initial definition during the process of synergy / recursion and of distillation and decanting the minimum conceptual contents. The steps followed in the exercise to aquire the syntegration process were the following steps:

  - *Opening:* the general topic was defined as an opening question, e-culture system Santiagueña. Participants (experts with the role of informants) which made up the team were selected according to their knowhow, experience and role.
  - *Generation of Agenda*: by means of a decanting process 4 of the 12 topics to be addressed - technically called "consolidated statements of importance"- were defined and expressed as nominalized verbs.
  - *Topic Auction* and *outcome Resolve*: On the one hand, the four topics were selected because each participant has to study and discuss only two topics represented by the edge in the icosahedron structure. In turn, each participant shares the vision of each topic with four different people at a time. On the other hand, the individual teams explore their respective topic several times by iterations and writes up a summary of its results. The fact is that the same issue with its different but interconnected aspects is continually and iteratively processed according to its "meaning" gathering an important composition which

implies exemplifications as strong reverberations. This leads to a self-organized process with high levels of knowledge integration.

- **Regarding Platform.** A free software platform was designed and used for the electronic simulation of syntegration. The functions, training access and usage rules recommended were explained taking into account the role of each participant through digital conversations. A procedure Handbook was developed to test the technique in a given period to generate the initial instance of Systemic Modeling.

4   Discussion

The multipurpose exercise designed served as a testing and trial tool to carry out the corresponding adjustments to the structure, content, rules, guides, and so on, tending to its final implementation with 30 informants. From the perspectives of the Beta and Delta Nodes (such as bridges between content and participatory techniques) all records were evaluated. On that assessment, the individual and joint roles carried out were evaluated and set out the relevant aspects related to the interactions / content.

The processed results allowed the performance reevaluation for the selection of informants in successive runs of syntegration process. The developed schematic was based on a sequence of synergy and recursivity to foster the process of decanting and distillation with the aim of improving the definition of the topics raised. That is, the improvement of their characteristics and types in order to better expand and describe what was expressed in the initial description of the topics was achieved.

4.1   Evaluation from Beta Perspective

The results obtained regarding *content parameters* confirm that different aspects of a central problem were examined in parallel. Such is the case of popular religion that was examined from the cultural, psychological and medical perspectives. It is observed that there were efforts in the nonlinearity interconnected through discussions over many aspects of a central problem. The exemplifications were oriented to determine the possession of current features. The outputs of interconnected dialogues are seen as attempts to pose country/city costumes as sub-cultures. The citations / references presented were oriented towards specific re-elaborations of what happens today. Active participants were aware of being related, accepting that they can learn from one onother.

As a conclusion, there was evidence that working together is essential to the formulation of recommendations in order to improve the response given, due to the complexity of the problem. Moreover, the participants showed efforts to break through the boundaries of their own disciplinary differences.

A self-regulatory coordination of the topics in sentences or phrases, according to Besnard and Hunter [28] are arguments that reflect the best knowledge of the participants concerning the initial question during an important cognitive process that allows us to treat the information under quetion by means of the generation and / or comparison of the arguments [27].

Regarding the results obtained in relation to *Sintegrity Profiles* it was found that the themes were selected by the participants regardless their different approaches. In some cases a good circular process was achieved from their different roles. The profiles, that is, the function and mission of the roles should be adjusted to make the interaction and iterations among the participants and topics more efficient so that the dissemination of information results in a global vision shared by all. It is clear in the process that the answers are relevant because they evolve within the group and accompany the broader vision of the possibilities and constraints of the group.

The process of "reverberation" is observed in the topic exchanges posed around the decision-making system, in such expressions as "I will research about it", "I will go into it in depth", "I will find it out", and "I will ask about it". This shows that during the process there has been learning and mutual understanding among all participants from the point of views of their peers to overcome their own barriers and abandon habitual patterns of thought.

The results determine which aspects over roles and sentences are neccesary to adjust for the final process. It is also clear from the experience that the method of sintegration was better understood. This will tend to effective networking among the participants so that syntegration can operate as a think tank of ideas that participants generate.

It is also possible to define causal circuits between the elements and conjectures which may be understood as dynamic features for the development of "semantic elements" to be integrated in the communicational languages to foster audiovisual intelligence. Reagrding prototyping of the operate model in particular, formats / media / modes might be selected. Finally, as a result of the modelling experience, the elements and self-regulated dialogues among participants allow us to predict that following the appropriate adjustments it could be possible to obtain the constituent elements of e-Culture System.

4.2   Evaluation from Delta Perspective

The purpose was to evaluate the technical process, participation, interaction and flows of meanings of the participants. The results obtained during the testing of the virtual platform "e-SOCONCHO" were satisfactory. The selection of the forum technique was appropriate to record and verify iterations of the model in question at the moment. Moreover, the results were evaluated and this allowed delimitation of the guidelines for the next experience in order to improve the techniques applied.

Regarding platform control, improvement is oriented toward a better description of the usage of platform / forum for user training. As for the moderation of dialogues, the improvement is aimed at strengthening the roles of dialogue facilitators, while the evidenced need to re-design the tutorial and put more emphasis on training.

In this type of experiments, a motivation function is necessary. The success / failure of the sub-processes of Synergy-Recursivity depend on the degree, in quantity and quality, of the involvement of qualified informants, their dialogues and written statements /post. The approach aims to fostering improvement and diminishing the impossibilities in technical access. The role assumed by the moderator has the function of co-evaluation, to rescue successes and failures and to detect and consider enhancements that serve as criteria for the final experience to work with the 30 informants with the total 12 topics, leading to the generation of the specific contents of culture "santiagueña".

5   Conclusion

Undoubtedly, the experience provided significant results. Besides those already mentioned, the characterization of the Existing Model is worth noticing. It was agreed on the definition that determines the new features and that the Existing Model is the recipient of the empirical evidence collected from informants. The criterions for the selection of the qualified informants were also determined, as well as the receptors of the Operating Model that is guided and sustained by the Meta Model.

The systemic definition according to Joel de Rosnay [26] that characterizes the new features of the existing model is innovative in terms of hypothesis / thesis: "A set of 'n' elements interrelated in spatio-temporal dynamics inter-related, which are informants qualified (by genus and specific difference) chosen according to well-defined criteria such that integrated cultural content resources obtained by recursion and integrated synergy so that determines the cultural System in a restroprospective way.

Dimensions and typology were defined and these allows be applied to other cultures. They are classified with a range of 1 to 5 for each qualified informants to

- Cognitive Class / Type: magic, wise, enlightened, elected
- Affective Class / emotional, voluntary, festive
- Productive Class: manual, interactive, folklore, cultural for being other, range 1-5

The definition of the criteria for the selection of the final qualified informants was achieved. They are criteria of accessibility, sustainability, inmediacy, specificity (reference), meta-awareness (able to look at yourself), be prosumer (cultural produced and consumed, in order to Marina´s concept [29]) with minimum interactive capacity, reachable in philosophical / conceptual / epistemic area. Those are selection rules that will enable decision making for the selection of informants in the two topics involved in the edge.

6   Future Work

Given the Existing Model obtained for four topics is possible to extend the treatment of the twelve topics defined in the Meta Model with the participation of the 30 qualified informants required by the technique of Syntegration. The Existing Model is enrich with the defined rules to the selection of participants, and the Existed Model is complemented.

It will be the starting point for the requirements for transmedia formats that meet the technical possibilities of Argumented Reality [30] for the operating Model profiled in terms of requirements for prototipation [31] which include the emotional interactivity, intelligence-related audiovisual [29] and that in turn respond to the New Communication Strategy [32].

Finally, this product will be in a book called: "Santiagueñidad Siglo XXI", a communication of FundArIngenio seeking the attention of the young "digital natives" who are interested on the Culture "santiagueña", retroprospectivation and systemic process. The research will start 2012.

Acknowledgements. We would like to thank the members of IIGG, researchers and scholarship holders who, with their contribution, made these results possible.

References

1. Herrera, S.I., Clusella, M.M., Mitre, M.G., Santillán, M.A., García, C.M.: An Interactive Information System for *e – Culture*. In: Cipolla Ficarra, F.V., de Castro Lozano, C., Pérez Jiménez, M., Nicol, E., Kratky, A., Cipolla-Ficarra, M. (eds.) ADNTIIC 2010. LNCS, vol. 6616, pp. 30–43. Springer, Heidelberg (2011)
2. Clusella, M., Luna, P., Ortiz, E.: Systemic Epistemology: A synthetic view of the Systems Science Foundations. In: First World Congress of IFSR. IFSR Press, Kobe (2005)
3. Rosnay, J.: El Hombre Simbiótico: Miradas sobre el tercer milenio. Ediciones Cátedra, Madrid (1996) (in Spanish)
4. Luna, P.A.: Cursos Sistémica y Metódica. Cátedra FCEyT, UNSE, Santiago del Estero (2002) (in Spanish)
5. Schwaninger, M.: A cybernetic model to enhace organizational intelligence. In: Systems Analysis Model Simul., vol. 43(1), pp. 53–65. Taylor & Francis, London (2003)
6. Bunge, M.: Social Systems: Foundations & Pholosphy of Sciences. Mc Graw Gill University, Montreal (1997)
7. Francois, Ch.: International Encyclopedia of Systems and Cybernetics. Munchen (2004)
8. Clusella, M.: La sistémica, como ciencia de sistema, requiere asumir una postura ética para servir mejor a las culturas, sus comunidades y personas. ALAS 2, Ibagué (2007) (in Spanish)
9. Clusella, M.: Organizational changes in catching-up countries context. In: 19th European Meeting of Cybernetics Systems. IFSR Press, Vienna (2008)
10. Ortiz, E., Clusella, M.: Civilization-Culture Context as Sistemic Background. In: Proc. 50th Annual Meeting ISSS. ISSS Press, California (2006)
11. Santillán, M.A.: Tesis sobre aproximación sistémica a los Mitos y Leyendas Santiagueñas. Coloquios Universitarios, Termas Río Hondo (2006) (in Spanish)
12. Colombres, A.: Teoría transcultural del Arte. Ed. del Sol, Buenos Aires (2003) (in Spanish)
13. Austín, M.T.: Hacia una visión sistémica de la sociedad y de la cultura. Ed. del Sol, Buenos Aires (2000) (in Spanish)
14. Isajiw, W.: Entender la diversidad. Thompson Pub., Toronto (1999) (in Spanish)
15. Maier, A.: Complete Beginner's Guide to Interaction Design, http://www.uxbooth.com/blog/complete-beginners-guide-to-interaction-design
16. Ronchi, A.: eCulture: Cultural Content in the Digital Age, 91 p. Springer, Heidelberg (2009)
17. Interaction Design Asociation. IxDA, http://www.ixda.org

18. Colorado, A.: Perspectivas de la cultura digital. Universidad Complutense, Madrid 15(28), 103–115 (2010) (in Spanish), http://www.ehu.es/zer/zer28/zer28-06.pdf
19. Norman, D.: Emotional Design. Perseus Books, New York (2004)
20. Schwaninger, M.: The evolution of organizational cybernetics. In: Proc.: Scientae Mathematicae Japonicae online, e-2006 (2006)
21. Schwaninger, M.: What can cybernetics contribute to the conscious Evolution of organizations and society? In: System Research and Behavioral Science, Syst. Res., vol. 21, pp. 515–527. John Wiley & Sons, New York (2004)
22. Schwaninger, M.: Optimal Structures for Social systems. In: Proc. Complexity Theory and Philosophy Workshop, Rio de Janeiro (2004)
23. Flood, R., Jackson, M.: Creative Problem Solving. Total Systems Intervention. John Wiley, London (1991)
24. IFSR. The Official Journal of International Federation System Research. Marzo-Abril, Mayo-Junio- Julio-Agosto, Septiembre-Octubre (2011)
25. Andriessen, D.: Metaphors in Knowledge Management. The Official Journal of the International Federation for Systems Research 28(2) (2011)
26. Rosnay, J.: El Macroscopio. AC, Madrid (2011)
27. Walton, D.: Fundamentals of Critical Argumentation. Cambridge University Press, Cambridge (2006)
28. Besnard, P., Hunter, A.: Argumentation in Artificial Intelligence. In: Rahwan, Simari (eds.) Argumentation Based on Classical Logical. Springer, Berlin (2009)
29. Marina, J.: Conferencias sobre inteligencia audiovisual. Colegio Monserrat, Madrid (2009) (in Spanish), http://www.think1.tv
30. Luna, P.D., Palavecino, M.L., Leguizamón, H.: Enmarque en inteligencia audiovisual por sistemas infonómicos "e-culture". In: XV Jornadas Nacionales de Investigadores en Comunicación, Río Cuarto (2011) (in Spanish)
31. Herrera, S., Zuain, S., Gallo, F., Avila, H.: Emotion and Communicability in e-culture Applications. In: Proc. HCITOCH 2011, Huerta Grande, Córdoba. Springer, Heidelberg (2011) (in printer)
32. Pérez Gonzáles, R., Massoni, S.: Hacia una nueva Teoría General de la estrategia. El cambio de paradigma en el comportamiento humano, la sociedad y las instituciones. Editorial Ariel, Madrid (2009) (in Spanish)

Federation and Security Aspects for the Management of the EHR in Italy

M. Claudia Buzzi, Francesco Donini, Abraham Gebrehiwot, Alessio Lunardelli,
Cristian Lucchesi, and Paolo Mori

CNR-IIT, Pisa, Italy
{Claudia.Buzzi,Francesco.Donini,Abraham.Gebrehiwot,
Alessio.Lunardelli,Cristian.Lucchesi,Paolo.Mori}@iit.cnr.it

Abstract. The Electronic Health Record (EHR) or Electronic Patient Record is a collection of electronic health information about a patient, created to increase personal safety through more accurate evidence-based decision support. Healthcare organizations, especially in different regions/local governments, can have different architectural solutions and procedures, and thus different access control policies. The requirement of compliance with previously developed architectural solutions binds them to using a single Federated infrastructure model. Since data stored in the EHR Infrastructure concerns the health status of patients, they must be considered critical and their confidentiality and integrity must be protected by proper security support. In this paper we will present the analysis of federation and security aspects and issues for the management of the Electronic Health Record in Italy, suggesting a possible solution.

Keywords: eHealth, Electronic Health Record, SOA, Federation, Security.

1   Introduction

The Electronic Health Record (EHR) is a collection of electronic health information about a patient, created to increase personal safety through more accurate evidence-based decision support. It may be composed of laboratory test results, radiology images, vital signs, personal stats such as age and weight, and other information that can be distributed to different Health Care Organizations (HCOs). Some healthcare agencies also provide a patient summary containing all relevant information such as blood group, allergies, vital medicines and others; the patient summary is very useful in emergencies or to describe the general health conditions of a patient. Different health care organizations may follow different procedures, and thus direct various access control policies [1]. To facilitate the creation of the Electronic Health Record by reassembling data maintained in different health care organizations, the Italian Ministry for the Public Administration and Innovation is supporting the process of building an interoperability framework for EHR management; this framework will allow all citizens and authorized health professionals to access the EHR wherever they are located. The health information will be available for primary uses such as emergency   assistance   or   evidence-based   decision   support,   but   also   for

F.V. Cipolla-Ficarra et al. (Eds.): ADNTIIC 2011, LNCS 7547, pp. 26–37, 2012.

epidemiological studies, administrative purposes and government. There are many requirements for the technological infrastructure of the interoperability framework: it should be compliant with the architectural solutions previously developed by the different regions/local governments; this requirement binds to use a single federated infrastructure model. The technological infrastructure needs to be consistent with Italian law regarding the Public Connectivity System (SPC), which specifically regulates the rules for the Public Administration communication. Furthermore, since data stored in the EHR Infrastructure concern the health status of patients, they must be considered critical and their confidentiality and integrity must be protected by proper security support; thus, access control in EHR systems poses many challenges: the information is sensitive and highly confidential but it may be necessary to access it (for instance, in emergencies) [1]. Moreover, Italian guidelines for privacy in managing electronic health records [2] are based on patient consent: each patient can choose his/her access control policies, e.g.: if the EHR should be created and for how long, who if anyone may access a specific document of the EH records, and the time interval when he/she can have access.

In this paper we will describe the analysis of federation and security aspects for managing the infrastructure for Electronic Health Records in Italy, suggesting a possible solution. The paper is organized into seven parts. Section 2 presents related work, Section 3 briefly illustrates the interoperability framework of the Italian Public Connectivity System (SPC) and Section 4 presents an interoperability framework for Electronic Health Record (EHR) systems proposed in the OpenInFSE[1] project. Section 5 introduces a short discussion on federated identity management aspects and issues, also proposing a possible solution. Section 6 briefly describes security issues and the management of the security policy. Section 7 ends the paper with conclusions.

2   Related Work

Creation and management of the Electronic Health Record (EHR) is widely discussed in the literature, but to the best of our knowledge few papers are specifically related on infrastructure aspects. In 2006 Eyers et al. proposed a prototype for secure, scalable, access control infrastructure for management of the EHR in United Kingdom. The system was based on an OASIS open architecture for secure interworking services, using the CASSANDRA language to express role-based access control policies with the distributed model PERMIS. Our proposal is similar but we use XACML (eXtensible Access Control Markup Language, [3]) for access control policies [1]. Bergmann et al. presented a survey of architectural approaches for EHR architecture, proposing a model for a virtual shared EHR that combines a patient-centered integration policy with provider-oriented document management and developing a system prototype [4]. A dated paper (2002) discusses priorities and trends in development of the EHR infrastructure, describing the implementation of the infrastructure for the regional health information network of Crete, Greece [5].

---

[1] http://ehealth.icar.cnr.it

Data protection is a main concern in the adoption of EHR in a real scenario. Several studies have been performed to determine the security of the solutions adopted to implement EHR in several countries. As an example, in 1995 the British Medical Association (BMA), asked R.J. Anderson to analyze the main threats to the system developed by the UK National Health Service (NHS) to manage personal health information. In [6, 7], he reported some issues in the NHS threat model, security policy and architecture, and he defined a new security policy model by "translating the traditional ethics of the profession into a concise set of rules that would provide a clear and unambiguous basis of communication between patients, clinicians and policy makers on the one hand, and computer system builders on the other". In 2005, K.T. Win [8] investigates whether current information security technologies are adequate for protecting medical data. In particular, he compares the security requirements defined by the legislations of the United States of America and of Canada with the available technologies for information security, concluding that there is still room for improvement. Also D. Acharya, in [9], presents an overview of the security threats in pervasive healthcare applications, and analyzes some open issues. Instead, B. Hewitt, in [10], investigates how the security features affect the use of EHR and proposed a model that incorporates into a hybrid Technology Acceptance Model a set of security measures including biometric authentication, Multiple Access Systems, and Single Sign On systems, to explore whether these measures influence the healthcare organization decision to use the Electronic Patient Record. Finally, guaranteeing secure access to clinical information is the main issue of [11], where the authors formally specify access control policies in clinical information systems by means of temporal linear first-order logic.

3   The Italian Interoperability Framework

The legal framework for the Italian e-Government strategy is the Code of Digital Administration (CAD) which regulates the creation, management, preservation and transmission of electronic documents used by the Public Administration and promotes the reutilization of public information systems. The Code also introduces the Public Connectivity System (SPC), i.e., the connectivity infrastructure for Italian PAs, and the Public Connection and Cooperation System (SPCoop), the infrastructure for the interoperability and cooperation between Public Administrations. The SPCoop model is that of a "light SOA" based on three pillars:

- Formalization of service agreements, which makes it possible to define interfaces, behaviors, service level agreements (SLA), security requirements and links with domain ontologies.
- Definition of a federated identity and its access management system.
- Definition of metadata, semantics and domain ontologies.

The SPCoop cooperation model is realized through the supply and use of application services, that are offered by a PA through a unique (logic) element belonging to its own information system, called Domain Gateway. In this way the complete autonomy of the administration is guaranteed, as far as the implementation and management of the provided application services, since they can be based on any application platform supplied through the Domain Gateway (which handles the routing of the application requests of a node -- administration or structure -- towards the SPCoop infrastructure). The fruition of the application services is carried out through the exchange of messages, whose format is formally specified in the Italian standard referred to as e-Gov Envelope. Such a standard is basically an extension of SOAP and represents the data structure used for the interactions between the domains, also ensuring all the principles of security.

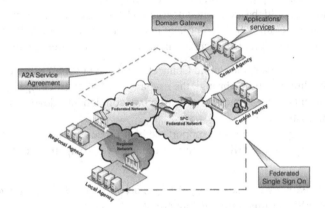

Fig. 1. SPC high-level architecture (© CNIPA[2])

The ICAR[3] project is an Italian e-Government initiative that addresses the establishment of SPCoop infrastructure for central and local governments. The ICAR initiative (ICAR stands for "Infrastructure for Application services Cooperation among Italian Regional authorities") is setting up and testing the shared technical infrastructure for delivering interoperability (IO) and applications cooperation (AC) services among Italian regional authorities, following the national standards defined for the development of SPC. Since in Italy the management of electronic identities and security policies is left/delegated to the Regions, the ICAR initiative is trying to implement an interregional Federated Authentication System.

4   Openinfse Interoperability Framework

The OpenInFSE project aims to implement an operational infrastructure to support interoperability for the management and the recomposition of electronic health records (EHR): indeed, medical documents relating to the same patient could be stored in different Italian health care organizations and each organization could have

---

[2] http://archivio.cnipa.gov.it/HTML/docs/SPCoop-Introduzione% 20ai%20Servizi%20SICA% 20V_1.0.pdf

[3] www.progettoicar.it/

different architectural and organizational systems. The infrastructure of the EHR must operate at a national level and allow the localization and propagation of health information scattered in the territory, by integrating all healthcare organizations involved in the production or consultation of events related to a patient.

The logic interaction between HCOs is made with infrastructure components developed ad hoc and localized in the Regions and the HCOs (all or just one for administrative district), depending by the Region interoperability policies. The architectural model of the EHR, based on decentralized and distributed architecture, is then composed by first-level nodes (Regional nodes) and second-level nodes (local nodes, the HCOs: hospital, laboratory test agency, pharmacies, etc.). At least each first-level node should be connected to the EHR infrastructure through a Domain Gateway, in order to allow SPC-compliant inter-regional communications.

The EHR model is SOA (Service Oriented Architecture) based on three levels:

1. Connectivity Layer: the Public Connectivity System (SPC) used for cooperation among administrations through the exchange of "eGov Envelope"
2. Component Layer: specific infrastructure components developed ad hoc for EHR infrastructure
3. Business Layer: services to support medical processes, such as "ePrescription". Services can be identified as part of the actors participating in the information process.

The Components layer extends partly the SPC architecture; the components proposed by the OpenInFSE for this infrastructure are:

Access Interface (AI). Present in each node (regional or local). The AI represents the access point of the infrastructure and receives all the requests made by regional actors (e.g., health care professionals or paraprofessionals, administrative staff, but also patients, who can access their EHRs) or by an AI of other regions. The AI interacts with other infrastructure components to fulfill the request by notifying the event to the broker nodes and the registers.

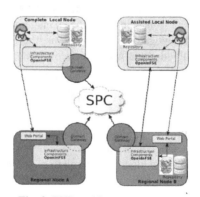

Fig. 2. EHR architectural model

Document Manager (DM). Stores documents associated with health events in a persistent, reliable and secure way. Each node of the infrastructure, local and regional, can interact with one or more repositories through one or more components of the Document Manager. The Document Manager is able to process medical documents structured according to the standard HL7 CDA Rel-2.0, but could be also compatible with other formats of documents.

Federated Index Registry (FIR). Acts as an index of documents and index of services. It is an index of documents because it stores information (metadata) related to medical records present in the repositories in order to facilitate searching and localization. Moreover, it is an index of services because it stores service addresses represented by metadata (e.g., URIs) enabling the location of the services that expose local nodes. Registered members of the federation are aligned with each other through a notification mechanism based on publish/subscribe paradigm events in order to manage the redundancy of metadata.

Hierarchical Event Manager (HEM). Manages routing and notification of health events to all stakeholders. To make management and event notification more efficient, a hierarchical model for classification of events using of a publish/subscribe model based on a broker is used.

Security Manager (SM). Implements the security support of the EHR framework. Since data stored by the EHR infrastructure are critical, proper security support is required to protect them. The Security Manager is based on the security as a service model (commonly in object oriented architectures), and it controls the Federated Authentication and the Authorization process. The SM is indicated and is a unique component but it includes some other components that will be described in the following.

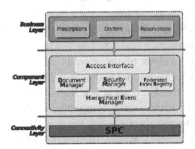

Fig. 3. OpenInFSE layers

5   Federated Identity Management in Openinfse

Identity management is a broad administrative area that deals with identifying individuals in a network and controlling access to resources in that system by placing restrictions on the established identities of the individuals. Federated identity management is the means of linking a person's electronic identity and attributes, stored across trusted multiple distinct identity management systems.

The OpenInFSE identity management architecture is compliant with the reference implementation for Identity management released by the ICAR initiative (in the following referred as ICAR INF-3); reuse of the reference implementations is one of the requirements of the OpenInFSE project to better guarantee the integration with the Regions infrastructures. At the moment, ICAR INF-3 implementation supports only the Web Single Sign On (Web SSO) profile, so compliance is possible only on this profile. Instead, the federated identity management in OpenInFSE should use two SAML profiles: Web SSO and also Web Services. In the following, we will describe OpenInFSE requirements for the implementation of a federated identity management model, based on the distinct existing identity management systems of the Italian Regions. Furthermore, the interaction of the ICAR INF-3 components for the WEB SSO profile and a solution to extend the Web Services profile for the ICAR INF-3 reference implementation will be presented.

5.1   The OpenInFSE Identity Management Constraints

Each Italian Region is responsible for the healthcare of citizens residing within their region. In some cases, they have already implemented heterogeneous identity management infrastructures. A requirement of the OpenInFSE project is to maintain the already deployed infrastructures and to implement an interoperable federated identity management system between the various regions using the SAML2 standard protocol. The constraints are the following: 1. The identity of an individual is managed by the Italian Region where a citizen/patient resides; 2. Individuals are identified by an Identity Provider (IDP) using an authentication mechanism that is decided by the Region; 3. An authenticated user is identified by various attributes such as: first name, surname, date of birth, citizenship, sex, municipality of residence, stature, eye color, etc.; 4. The role of the authenticated user is identified by various Attribute Authorities (AA) using attributes such as: general practitioner, emergency room doctor, patient, nurse, professional organization membership, administrative employee of a hospital, pharmacist, etc.; 5. The electronic identity of an individual is composed of the aggregate values of the identity and the role of the subject. The aggregation is managed by an additional authority called the Profile Authority (PA).

The services offered by the Federation are distributed among the various Italian Regions health care organizations using components called Service Providers (SP). Access to services is managed through federated authentication and authorization mechanisms. For federated identity access, the internal SPs within a particular region appoint the Local Proxy (LP) to authenticate and retrieve the appropriate profile of a user belonging to the Federation. The local proxy implements a Discovery Service (DS) to locate the origin of the user Profile Authority. The interaction between the common infrastructure components SP, IDP, AA, PA, LP and DS uses the SAML2 standard protocol.

5.2   Interaction of OpenInFSE Components for the Web SSO Profile

This part presents an example of interaction for the Web SSO profile. A Web browser of a user coming from Region B tries to access a protected resource (an item of the HCR) by a Service Provider (SP) in Region A using his federated identity.

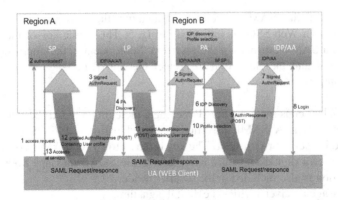

Fig. 4. Interaction of OpenInFSE components for the Web SSO profile

The SP will redirect the web browser to a Local Proxy (LP) belonging to the same Region. The SP does not have the knowledge of the complexity of the Italian federated identity management system. It simply forwards every authentication and attribute request to the LP. Subsequently, the LP forwards the authentication request to the proper PA and the PA will also forward the request to the appropriate IDP: only at this point, the user will be authenticated. Individuation/selection of both the PA and the IDP generally require the interaction of the user. Once the user is authenticated the Web browser containing the user's identity will be redirected back to the SP. Details of the interaction are described in Fig. 4.

5.3   Interaction of OpenInFSE Components for the Web Services

The OpenInFSE Web Services infrastructure is implemented using the OASIS Web Services Security (WS-Security) profile with the objective of providing authentication, data integrity, and confidentiality of SOAP messages. The federated identity management architecture for Web Services is shown in Fig. 5:

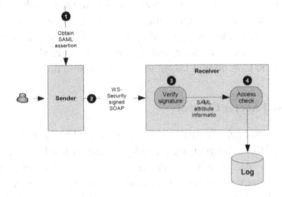

Fig. 5. Typical Use of WS-Security with SAML Token [12]

Recovery of the SAML assertions containing the user profile is previously obtained through Web SSO, as indicated in Fig. 5. The public key of the "sender" is included as a SAML attribute in the assertion. Subsequently, the interaction between the Front End and the Back End to protect the SOAP message is describe in the following steps:

1. The "sender" constructs the SOAP message, including a SOAP header with a WS-Security header. A SAML assertion is placed within a WS-Security token and included in the security header. The key referred to by the SAML assertion is used to construct a digital signature over data in the SOAP message body. Signature information is also included in the security header.
2. The message receiver verifies the digital signature.
3. The information in the SAML assertion is used for purposes such as Access Control and Audit logging.

6   Authorization

Data protection is fundamental in infrastructure architecture for the management of the EHR since stored data includes sensitive information that is highly confidential. Obviously, health data are critical and must be properly protected. Metadata (i.e., pointers to health data/records) could also be considered critical, since they could reveal that certain treatments or tests have been carried out on a patient, providing indirect but clear information about his/her health status. Moreover, the need for an advanced and flexible security support that provides an effective protection of the patients' data is also stated in the Italian guidelines for the EHR management [2] issued by the Italian data protection authority.

The authorization is the decision process that determines the right of a given subject to access one of the components of the EHR infrastructure to read or even modify the stored data. The authorization process is performed after authentication, in which the identity of the subject requesting the access has been verified, and the SAML assertions representing the attributes the subject wishes to exploit in the authorization process have been collected. The attributes collection is a very important step, because the security policy will exploit those attributes to determine the access rights. Hence, these assertions must be added to the access request messages sent to the Component Layer services to enable the authorization process.

6.1   Role Based Access Control

The Role Based Access Control model (RBAC) [13] allows assigning roles to subjects. In the EHR Infrastructure, the role represents the function of subject in the healthcare system. As mentioned in Sec. 5.1, examples of roles are: general practitioner, emergency room doctor, patient, administrative employee of a hospital, pharmacist, etc. The RBAC model can be adopted in EHR management because it allows defining access control policies where rights are paired to roles instead of being assigned directly to subjects. Hence, an example of policy might be: data of a patient (health and personal data) can be read by subjects who have the role "Emergency Doctor"; a patient's personal data can be read by subjects with the role "Reservation Agent"; Health data of a patients can be modified by the subject who wrote them.

6.2   Architecture

From an architectural point of view, the authorization process requires the integration of some new components in the EHR Infrastructure defined for the OpenInFSE project; the most relevant are the Policy Enforcement Points (PEP) and the Policy Decision Point (PDP). The PEPs are in charge of intercepting the access requests that are relevant from a security point of view, to trigger the authorization decision process. An important feature of PEPs is that they must be non-bypassable, i.e., they must be invoked every time that security-relevant actions are executed. PEPs extract the assertions submitted by the user that represent his attributes from the access requests, and embed them in the request for the PDP. PEPs invoke the PDP and wait for the result of the decision process before performing the real access. If the right is granted, the PEP resumes the execution of the access request, otherwise the access request is deleted and the access is not executed.

A PEP must be embedded in each critical component of the OpenInFSE Infrastructure. Hence PEPs will be embedded in the following Component Layer services: Federated Index Registry, Hierarchical Event Manager, and Document Manager, as shown in Fig. 6. The technique used for the integration depends on the component's implementation, that could be different in distinct Italian regions. Some components could be already prepared for the integration of PEPs. As an example, the standard OASIS ebXML Registry 3.0 [14], that could be adopted for the implementation of Federated Index Registry can be configured to invoke the PDP. If the component is implemented as a web service, the PEP could be implemented exploiting the Inflow Handler Chain. In this case, a new handler that invokes the PDP is added to the original chain. This handler is invoked every time that a request message is received, and if the PDP response does not allow the execution of the request, the handler simply deletes the request message and returns an error to the requestor. Another solution for integration of the PEP in components of the EHR infrastructure is to develop a wrapper service that is invoked instead of the original one. The wrapper service invokes the PDP, and then invokes the original service only if the PDP response is positive.

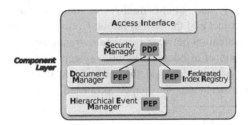

Fig. 6. Integration of PEPs in the EHR architecture components

The PDP is the component of the architecture that performs the access decision process to determine whether a given subject has the right to perform the access he/she required. At first, the PDP obtains the security policy from a repository, managed by the Policy Administration Point (PAP), and it builds its internal data structures for the policy representation. Next, it receives the access requests from the PEPs embedded in the EHR Infrastructure components. A PDP can be paired with more than one PEP. Communication between the PEPs and the PDP can be performed exploiting the SAML protocol [15], and should be secure to protect both the integrity and the confidentiality of the requests and responses. Since the Security Manager is implemented as a web service, the SOAP Message Security standard defined by the OASIS consortium [16] can be adopted to secure the interactions between PEPs and PDP. Before evaluating the security policy, the PDP checks the validity of the attribute assertions received in the access request (e.g., the validity of the signature of the issuer, and the expiration date). The security policy is expressed exploiting the XACML language [3], which is a well-known and widely used standard that naturally allows the use of roles in the authorization process [17]. The XACML language is adequate for expressing the security policies required for protecting EHRs because it allows to represent roles for subjects and to assign rights to roles, to exploit attributes to perform the decision process, and it is flexible enough to express also specific access restrictions required by the patients. The PDP could invoke a further component of the architecture, the Policy Information Point (PIP), when the attributes required to perform the decision process are not included in the set that has been submitted by the requestor. Hence, the PIP is in charge of retrieving the fresh values of the missing attributes. Some free implementation of the XACML PDP is currently available, such as the one released by SUN[4], that currently supports the XACML version 2.0. Axiomatics[5], instead, provides a commercial version of the XACML framework that implements the full Policy Life Cycle Management for XACML policies, from editing to enforcement.

7   Conclusion

This paper describes the infrastructure defined by the OpenInFSE project to support interoperability between the various organizations operating in the Italian healthcare scenario for the management and recomposition of Electronic Health Records. There are many crucial requirements, among these the compliance with previously developed local architectural solutions and with the Italian laws, the distributed architecture, criticality and confidentiality of data managed. After a general presentation of the project and the Italian Public Connection and Cooperation System for managing communication between healthcare organizations, in this paper we have focused on the adoption of a federated identity system and a proper security support for preserving the confidentiality and the integrity of data stored in the Electronic Health Records. Furthermore, the paper proposed a possible solution for the

---

[4] http://sunxacml.sourceforge.net/
[5] http://www.axiomatics.com/products.html

implementation of federated authentication and authorization in the OpenInFSE infrastructure, based on the ICAR INF3 project and the OASIS XACML standard for the RBAC model. The next step of the OpenInFSE project will be the test of the described components with three Italian Regions, in order to verify and tune the architecture.

Acknowledgments. This work was supported by the joint project CNR-Presidenza del Consiglio dei Ministri: Infrastruttura Operativa a Supporto dell'Interoperabilità delle Soluzioni Territoriali di FSE nel Contesto SPC.

References

1. Eyers, D., Bacon, J., Moody, K.: OASIS Role-based Access Control For Electronic Health Records. In: IEEE Proceedings on Software, vol. 153(1), pp. 16–23. IEEE (2006)
2. The Italian Data Protection Authority, Linee guida in tema di Fascicolo Sanitario Elettronico (FSE) e di dossier sanitario – 16 luglio 2009 (G.U. n. 178 del 3 agosto 2009)
3. OASIS, eXtensible Access Control Markup Language (XACML) v.3.0 (April 16, 2009)
4. Bergmann, J., Bott, O., Pretschner, D., Haux, R.: An e-consent-based shared EHR system architecture for integrated healthcare networks. International Journal of Medical Informatics 76(2-3), 130–136 (1973) ISSN 1386-5056, doi:10.1016/j.ijmedinf.2006.07.013
5. Tsiknakis, M., Katehakis, D., Orphanoudakis, S.: An open, component-based information infrastructure for integrated health information networks. Int. Journal of Medical Informatics 68(1-3), 3–26, http://www.sciencedirect.com/science/article/pii/S1386505602000606
6. Anderson, R.: A Security Policy Model for Clinical Information Systems. In: IEEE Symposium on Security and Privacy, pp. 30–42 (1996)
7. Anderson, R.: Security in Clinical Information Systems, Computer Laboratory University of Cambridge (1996)
8. Win, K.: A review of security of electronic health records. Health Information Management 34(1), 13–18 (2005)
9. Acharya, D.: Security in Pervasive Health Care Networks: Current R&D and Future Challenges. In: Mobile Data Management, pp. 305–306 (2010)
10. Hewitt, B.: Exploring how security features affect the use of electronic health records. Healthcare Technology and Management 11(1/2), 31–49 (2010)
11. Sohr, K., Drouineaud, M., Ahn, G.: Formal specification of role-based security policies for clinical information systems. In: SAC: Security Track, pp. 332–339. ACM (2005)
12. Security Assertion Markup Language (SAML) V2.0 Technical Overview Committee Draft 02 (March 25, 2008)
13. Sandhu, R.S., Coyne, E.J., Feinstein, H.L., Youman, C.E.: Role-Based Access Control Models. IEEE Computer 29(2), 38–47 (1996)
14. OASIS, ebXML Registry Services and Protocols Version 3.0, OASIS (May 2, 2005)
15. OASIS, SAML 2.0 profile of XACML v2.0, OASIS Standard (February 1, 2005)
16. OASIS: Web Service Security: SOAP Message Security 1.1 (WS-Security 2004) OASIS Standard incorporating Approved Errata (November 1, 2006)
17. OASIS, XACML Profile for Role Based Access Control (RBAC) (February 13, 2004)

Are Smartphones Really Useful
for Scientific Computing?

Juan Manuel Rodríguez[1,2], Cristian Mateos[1,2], and Alejandro Zunino[1,2]

[1] ISISTAN Research Institute, UNICEN University, Tandil, Buenos Aires, Argentina
[2] Consejo Nacional de Investigaciones Científicas y Técnicas (CONICET), Argentina
azunino@exa.unicen.edu.ar

Abstract. Smartphones are a new kind of mobile devices that allow users to take their office anywhere and anytime with them. The number of smartphones is rapidly growing. Most of the time their capabilities are underused, therefore several authors have studied how to exploit smartphones for assisting scientific computing. Yet, as far as we know, there is no study aimed at determining whether smartphones can do a significant contribution to this area as resource providers. This paper shows that smartphones are not that slow when compared to standard mobile devices, such as notebooks. Furthermore, a notebook running on battery only performed 8 times more work than a low-end smartphone before their batteries run out. However, the low-end smartphone is 145 times slower than the notebook, and the smartphone battery has less capacity than the notebook battery. Since smartphones can execute large amount of work running on battery, we think that smartphones can have a major role in building the next-generation HPC infrastructures.

Keywords: Smartphones, Android, Scientific Computing, Benchmark, Linpack, SciMark.

1 Introduction

Mobile devices have recently evolved from simple mobile phones and Personal Digital Assistants (PDAs) to small "computers" with everywhere Internet access using wireless technology, such as 3G or 802.11 wireless LANs (commonly called WiFi). In addition to this evolution, mobile devices are probably the commonest form of technological device in the world with more than 2 billion people owning at least one of them. Furthermore, people in established markets frequently own two or more mobile devices [12]. Nowadays, mobile devices have a remarkable amount of computational resources that allows them to execute complex applications, such as 3D games, and to store large amounts of data. Besides, the capability of mobile devices to be connected everywhere makes it possible to do on-the-way tasks that traditionally required a desktop computer, like checking and sending e-mails. This kind of mobile devices that, aside from placing phone calls, allow users to access the Internet, play games, and listen to music, among other features, are known as smartphones. Another kind of mobile devices focused on gaming and Internet browsing are called tablets. Tablets have similar computational capabilities to

F.V. Cipolla-Ficarra et al. (Eds.): ADNTIIC 2011, LNCS 7547, pp. 38–47, 2012.

smartphones, but bigger screens to improve the user's experience. However, smartphones and tablets can be treated as equal concerning the goal of this paper.

Due to their new capabilities, which are not present in traditional devices, emergent research lines have aimed at integrating smartphones and other mobile devices into traditional distributed computational environments, such as clusters and Grids [14]. Since smartphones have a wide variety of sensors, such as GPS, microphone and accelerometer, they are usually seen as providers of a new kind of context-dependent information, which was previously unavailable [1]. Another common role of smartphones in distributed computational environments is as resource consumers. Offloading computational work to fixed servers and accessing the results through smartphones allows end users to perform complex computational tasks without draining their smartphones' batteries [7].

Although the capabilities of smartphones have increased at an exponential rate [11], little research has been carried out to study the viability of using them to contribute to solve computational problems from the engineering or scientific communities. This is because practitioners tend to disregard smartphone capabilities [14] because they are very limited when compared to desktop computers or servers. However, they somehow fail to consider the stunning amount of smartphone currently available that together can represent an interesting pool of resources.

This work studies the viability of using smartphones as resources of scientific clusters and Grids by presenting a comparison among different Android-based smartphones/tablets and Linux netbooks/notebooks in terms of their computational capabilities. In addition, this work analyzes how different types of operations typically used in scientific computing, such as integer and floating-point arithmetic and array management, perform in several devices. This analysis goal is to have preliminary hints for which scientific applications smartphones might run effectively. We have two main reasons for choosing Android as the base for our study:

- There are plenty of available Android-based devices. According to Google I/O 2011 announcements[1], there are 310 Android-based smartphone models produced by 36 manufacturers.
- Android is an open platform that does not restrain developers from using any available feature, such as multi-tasking [2]. This makes the platform suitable for solving scientific computational problems.

The rest of the paper is organized as follows. Section 2 surveys previous works aiming at integrating smartphones and traditional mobile devices into distributed systems. Section 3 discusses the motivations behind our vision of using smartphones in HPC scientific computing. Section 4 presents an experimental comparison of different devices in terms of their computing capabilities. Finally, Section 5 concludes the paper and delineates future research opportunities.

2   Background

From the beginnings of the mobile Internet, mobile devices have been seen as administrative tools for distributed computing infrastructures [6]. This idea is

---

[1] Google I/O 2011 announcements:
http://www.google.com/events/io/2011/announcements-archive.html

followed even in recent approaches, like [7] in which the authors discuss a fluid simulator implemented on a super-computer that offers a result visualizer application that runs on Android. When the simulation completes, a user can access the results through his smartphone. Although this work shows that Android smartphones can be used to access the results of this kind of applications, no scientific computation runs on the device. Furthermore, this particular work does not provide empirical evidence about battery consumption when accessing to simulation results.

Other recent study [14] has proposed using mobile devices as partial or full members of Grid Computing infrastructures. Several roles for mobile devices in distributed computing were analyzed, which vary from sensors to nodes that perform computations. These new roles were proposed because today's mobile devices have more features, and their hardware capabilities have increased at an exponential rate [11]. Yet, this is not the case with energy density in batteries. As a result of the disparity between computational power and energy density increase rate, most existent research is focused on minimizing battery use.

As suggested, some works have tried to integrate mobile devices as working nodes in Grids. In particular, several researchers [5, 9, 13, 14] have studied task scheduling algorithms for mobile Grids. In this context, a large computational problem is split into several parts, which are computed independently by using many mobile devices. In particular, both [9] and [5] propose scheduling algorithms in which assigning resources to tasks involves solving large equations systems with variables that are difficult, if not impossible, to determine. In contrast, the work presented in [13] uses simple equations and easily estimable variables. Although these works have their differences, these schedulers have not been evaluated with real mobile devices. Instead, all of them have been evaluated through simulated experiments, thereby there is no real assessment of using mobile devices for HPC computing viability.

3   Smartphones for Scientific Computing

Traditionally, research efforts based on conceiving mobile devices as being part of an HPC environment have been focused on moving expensive computations from devices to fixed servers, thus saving energy at the expense of potentially having greater communication costs. In this sense, computational offloading [8] has been recently proposed as a way of running resource intensive computations originated in a mobile device (e.g. a rendering algorithm integrated with the camera) to a Cloud infrastructure. Once the computation is done, the associated results are transferred back to the device. Particularly, this work addresses Clouds but is arguably also applicable to other distributed environments.

Alternatively, there are a number of research efforts that conceive mobile devices as an active processing element within a distributed environment [14, 10]. Under this approach, devices do not only harness the computational power offered by fixed computing infrastructures such as super-computers, clusters and Clouds, but also act as resource providers. However, works in this line are still under development, since there are in principle two important open questions that need to be answered before materializing this approach: a) Do real smartphones have appropriate resources to be exploited for executing computing intensive tasks? b) If so, what are the best techniques for scheduling tasks on real smartphones?

With respect to the former issue, particularly, the amount of CPU cycles that can be delivered and eventually donated by a single device intuitively depends on its battery availability. This latter is in turn subject to smartphone usage profiles. For illustrative purposes, Table 1 shows the fraction of time spent by four real smartphones in performing common activities. Collected data spans over several months[2]. Clearly, although generalization is not possible, the data suggests that there is a fraction of resources available in everyday smartphones that remain unused.

Table 1. Real-life smartphone activity (in percentage with respect to total usage time)

	Star A3000	Samsung I5700	Samsung I5500	Nexus One
Running	50.8%	13.5%	8.3%	23.2%
Screen on	8.3%	7.5%	5.1%	2.3%
Phone on	0.2%	0.6%	0.4%	0.5%
WiFi on	93.3%	55.0%	66.7%	100%
WiFi running	33.2%	26.2%	19.1%	32.3%

In addition, even when smartphones still have limited hardware capabilities, they are very energy-efficient. Therefore, we believe that answering this issue boils down to determining whether smartphones individually provide the necessary computing capabilities. Our main hypothesis is that smartphones offer a good balance between the computing capabilities and battery depletion rate tradeoff inherent to mobile devices making them suitable for HPC computing. In the following paragraphs we focus on providing empirical evidence to test this hypothesis. Methodologically, the followed experimental approach consisted in comparing smartphones and standard mobile devices, namely netbooks and notebooks, in terms of hardware capabilities by employing classical scientific benchmarks. As mentioned earlier, the experiments targeted smartphones running Android 2.2 (codenamed "Froyo").

It is worth mentioning that answering the second question is out of the scope of this paper. Nevertheless, several authors [5, 9, 13, 14] have pointed out that adapting and modifying traditional distributed scheduling algorithms to make them battery-aware might be a good starting point for answering this question.

4   Experimental Results

To assess the computing capabilities versus energy capacity tradeoff of Android-powered smartphones compared to traditional mobile devices, we have used a notebook, a netbook, a tablet that has similar hardware compared to a high-end smartphone, a mid-end smartphone, and a low-end smartphone. Table 2 specifies the devices used during this evaluation, which were selected because they are good referents of currently available mobile devices and smartphones. Note that the benchmarks were implemented in a single thread for fairness reasons.

---

[2] Data was collected by using the Android System Info application, which is available at
http://www.appbrain.com/app/android-
system-info/com.electricsheep.asi

Table 2. Devices features

Device Name	CPU	RAM	Storage	Battery
Dell Inspiron	Intel Core i3 M-380 (2.53 GHz)	4 GB	250 GB	6 cells 4600 mAh
Samsung N150	Intel ATOM processor N270 (1.60 GHz)	1 GB	160 GB	6 cells 5900 mAh
ViewPad 10s	NVidia Tegra 250 T20 (1 GHz)	512 MB	512MB + 32GB	Lithium Ion 3300 mAh
Nexus One	Qualcomm QSD 8250 Snapdragon (1 GHz)	512 MB	512MB + 32GB	Lithium Ion 1400 mAh
Samsung I5500	MSM7227-1 ARM11 (600 MHz)	256 MB	170MB + 16GB	Lithium Ion 1200 mAh

To compare the computational capabilities of the different devices, we executed several well-known scientific benchmarks in every device. We selected benchmarks written in Java because the notebook and the netbook can run Java applications, and the base programming language for Android applications is also Java. However, Java-based Android applications are compiled/run via a different virtual machine, called Dalvik, which is optimized for smartphones. Thus, before executing the experiments, we compiled the benchmarks using either Java compilers to ensure fairness.

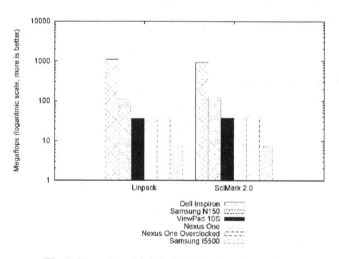

Fig. 1. Linpack and SciMark 2.0 benchmarks results

Firstly, we compared the different devices by using the Linpack [4] and the SciMark 2.0 [3] benchmarks, which are very popular within the HPC community and provide an estimation of the number of Megaflops (million of operations per second) a machine can perform.

Figure 1 depicts the results of the benchmarks executed in the different devices. The Linpack benchmark results indicate that the netbook, the ViewPad 10s, the Nexus One, and the Samsung I5500 are 10, 31, 36, and 145 times slower than the notebook, respectively. In contrast, the SciMark 2.0 benchmark, which emulates real-life numerical applications, resulted slightly better for the smartphones. In this case, the

ViewPad 10s performed 24 times slower than the notebook, while the Nexus One and the Samsung I5500 performed 26 and 127 times slower, respectively. Finally, we executed the benchmarks using the same Nexus One with its CPU overclocked to 1.113 GHz. Although it performed marginally better, this configuration resulted in a battery overheating. Consequently, we were unable to complete the experiments.

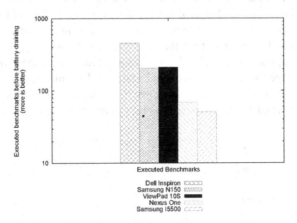

Fig. 2. Executed benchmarks

Secondly, we compared the power consumption from resolving various complex computations. To do the associated experiment, we selected five benchmarks of the JGrande section 2 [3]:

- EPBench: Is a Java implementation of the NAS Embarrisingly Parallel benchmark, which generates pseudo-random numbers with a Gaussian probability distribution.
- PrimeBench: Verifies whether a large number is prime.
- FFTBench: Is a Java implementation of the NAS Fast Fourier Transform (FFT) benchmark, which computes both a 3D FFT and inverse FFT. FFTs are commonly used in scientific computations, and require extensive floating-point arithmetic and data shuffling.
- HanoiBench: Solves the 25-disk Tower of Hanoi problem, which is a well-known combinatorial sorting puzzle.
- SieveBench: Calculates prime numbers using the Sieve of Erasthosthenes. It consists in integer arithmetic operations with a lot of array accesses.

The experiment consisted in executing the five benchmarks in a round robin fashion repeatedly until the battery of each individual device was empty. Basically, the idea was to measure how many computational tasks could be completed using the standard battery. To ensure fairness, this experiment was performed with all the devices connected to the Internet through a WiFi network. However, the benchmarks did not need Internet access, and no standard system application that requires Internet was deactivated, such as update managers.

Figure 2 presents how many benchmarks were executed by each device before they run out of battery capacity. Basically, the notebook executed 2.22, 2.14, 6.50, and 8.90 times more benchmarks than the netbook, the ViewPad 10s, the Nexus One, and the Samsung I5500, respectively.

Although both Linpack and SciMark 2.0 benchmarks pointed out that these smartphones are considerably slower than the notebook, the amount of work they can perform using only one full charge of battery power does not depend lineally on their computational capabilities. Despite being slower and having less battery, the ViewPad 10s executed more benchmarks than the netbook. This suggests that any smartphone can execute complex computational calculations even when they are running on battery, which is the most likely smartphone state [8]. In contrast, this extrapolation is sound since the Samsung I5500 is an entry-level smartphone which is very less powerful and power-efficient compared to other smartphones available in the market.

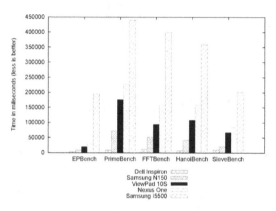

Fig. 3. Average benchmark time

In addition to measuring how many benchmarks were performed before battery depletion, we also measured the average time that each benchmark took to run. Figure 3 presents the result of these measurements. From this Figure, it is possible to observe that the different benchmarks performed quite different in the employed devices.

Table 3. Average benchmark execution times with respect to a notebook

	Samsung N150	ViewPad 10s	Nexus One	Samsung I5500
EPBench	3.34	7.61	12.04	72.99
PrimeBench	8.40	20.49	26.38	51.07
FFTBench	4.46	8.17	13.64	34.69
HanoiBench	5.84	15.10	21.89	50.01
SieveBench	2.10	6.95	8.74	20.62
Average	**4.83**	**11.66**	**16.54**	**45.88**
Std. deviation	**2.42**	**5.92**	**7.33**	**19.63**

In this regard, Table 3 presents a comparative result regarding how slower the different devices, including a notebook, a tablet, and two smartphones, executed the benchmarks compared to the notebook. This table shows that there are noticeable differences among the benchmarks' slowdown within the same device. These variations can be appreciated in the obtained standard deviations that are significant with respect to the average in each case. For example, the largest standard deviation is for the Samsung I5500, which is 42% w.r.t the average. Since the implementation used in the different benchmarks was the same, the difference in these results suggests that the devices performed some operations faster than others. This does not contradict the results obtained when executing Linpack and SciMark 2.0 because both benchmarks consist in two similar sets of operations, mostly related to floating point operations and loops. In contrast, the JGrande section 2 benchmark has algorithms that solve inherently complex problems, thereby they execute other operations, for example object creation or array manipulation.

The final experiment therefore consisted in analyzing the performance differences of several common statements, such as adding integers, creating objects or arrays. To do this, we used the JGrande section 1 benchmark, which measures the performance of these micro-operations. We have used the following micro-benchmarks: *Arith* (execution of arithmetic operations), *Assign* (variable assignment), *Create* (creating objects and arrays), *Math* (execution of commonly used mathematical library functions), and *Method* (method invocation in the same or another class/object).

There are some other micro-benchmarks in JGrande section 1, but we did not use them for different reasons. The benchmarks designed to measure casting, looping and exception throwing did not provide useful information because the notebook performs these operations too fast and the benchmark informs that the notebook can perform infinite operations of this kind. Another benchmark that were left out of the analysis was the serialization benchmark because it needs a lot of memory, which Android applications cannot request without using native code.

As a result of this experiment, we have empirically confirmed that, comparatively, some operations performed better than others in the smartphones. For example, the notebook can perform approximately 4 times more integer additions per time unit than the Nexus One, but the notebook, according to the benchmark results, could create 62,051 more java.lang.Object objects per time unit than the Nexus One. This does not necessarily implies that the Nexus One is 62,051 times slower than the notebook when creating one object because, when many short-lived object are created, the garbage collector is forced to run intensively, which is not the case when creating only one object or even few objects. Therefore, the garbage collector is probably introducing an important noise in this case. Since the test consist in creating thousands of objects, it is likely that the garbage collector in Android is launched many more times than the garbage collector in standard Java because Android applications have rigid memory constraints. Despite this, creating a large number of short-lived objects is not a good practice for Android applications.

Table 4 shows how slower, in average, the different used micro-benchmarks were processed in the netbook and the smartphones compared to the notebook. The slowdown of an algorithm mostly depends on the necessary operations or how it is implemented, thereby using Android smartphones for scientific computing might require to slightly re-write the algorithms to minimize the associated slowdown.

Interestingly, the micro-benchmarks shows that the ViewPad 10s is faster than the Nexus One for Arith, Assign and Create, but the ViewPad 10s is slower than the Samsung I5500 for calling methods. However, the benchmarks are designed to evaluate the performance of a single-thread, single-process application and the ViewPad 10s has a dual-core processor. Therefore, it is expectable the ViewPad 10s to perform better when executing parallel applications.

Table 4. Comparative operation performance

	Samsung N150	ViewPad 10s	Nexus One	Samsung I5500
Arith	3.45	6.43	9.07	134.07
Assign	87.79	154.19	164.14	454.11
Create Object	7575.30	420009.04	90931.63	114570.52
Create Array	3.95	221.87	435.31	526.79
Math	8.34	36.02	36.87	134.47
Method (same)	189.93	23983.98	9362.91	14532.00
Method (class)	1490.04	33002.55	14546.75	20852.60

Another result of the experiment is that different operations of the same kind have different behavior depending on where they are executed. For instance, adding two long values in the notebook is almost (takes 0.006% more time) as fast as adding two integers, but, in the Nexus One, adding two longs takes 33% more time than adding two integers. Hence, data type selection might not affect the performance in some platforms, while in others the impact on performance is significant.

5   Conclusion and Future Work

In this paper, through a number of rigorous experiments, we have empirically shown that smartphones are able to execute complex computational tasks even when their implementations have not been specifically adjusted to smartphone resource restrictions. Moreover, these experiments have also shown that, when smartphones are running on battery, they can perform an interesting amount of computing intensive code before the depletion of their batteries takes place.

In addition to this, preliminary results beyond this paper point out that optimizing a code for the Android platform might better exploit smartphones' capabilities when performing scientific computations. Improving code efficiency not only decreases response time, but also might improve battery usage. Therefore, scientific source code optimization for the Android platform is a prominent research line.

In future research, we aim to study the performance of multi-thread and multi-process applications. This is vital because current smartphone CPUs have multi-core capabilities. Another research line is analyzing the performance of Android platforms when using native code. Although native code is popular in the scientific community, it requires special cares to properly deploy it. For instance, native code usage can introduce memory leaks. Therefore, we are analyzing several benchmarks written in Android native C to reproduce our findings using native Android application codes.

Although Android smartphones might not be suitable for all scientific computational problems, this paper provides evidence about smartphones utility for solving computing intensive computational problems. We think that if the problems are carefully chosen and implemented, Android smartphones can be considered as useful processing elements. For instance, Android smartphones would be helpful for solving iterative algorithms with preponderance of integer operations. In contrast, Android smartphones would not be useful if the algorithms are recursive or require a lot of double operations. All in all, Android smartphones might the future resources' source of large distributed systems. In this sense, we are developing a battery-aware task scheduler for smartphones clusters and Grids.

Acknowledgments. We acknowledge the financial support of ANPCyT (grant PAE-PICT 2007-02311).

References

1. Anokwa, Y., Hartung, C., Brunette, W., Borriello, G., Lerer, A.: Open source data collection in the developing world. Computer 42(10), 97–99 (2009)
2. Blom, S., Book, M., Gruhn, V., Hrushchak, R., Köhler, A.: Write once, run anywhere – a survey of mobile runtime environments. In: International Conference on Grid and Pervasive Computing, pp. 132–137. IEEE Computer Society, Los Alamitos (2008)
3. Bull, J., Smith, L., Westhead, M., Henty, D., Davey, R.: A benchmark suite for high performance Java. Concurrency: Practice and Experience 12, 375–388 (2000)
4. Dongarra, J., Luszczek, P., Petitet, A.: The LINPACK benchmark: Past, present and future. Concurrency and Computation: Practice and Experience 15(9), 803–820 (2003)
5. Ghosh, P., Das, S.: Mobility-aware cost-efficient job scheduling for single-class grid jobs in a generic mobile grid architecture. Future Generation Computer Systems 26, 1356–1367 (2010)
6. González-Castaño, F., Vales-Alonso, J., Livny, M., Costa-Montenegro, E., Anido-Rifón, L.: Condor grid computing from mobile handheld devices. ACM SIGMOBILE Mobile Computing and Communications Review 7(1), 117–126 (2003)
7. Huynh, D., Knezevic, D., Peterson, J., Patera, A.: High-fidelity real-time simulation on deployed platforms. Computers & Fluids 43(1), 74–81 (2011)
8. Kumar, K., Lu, Y.-H.: Cloud Computing for mobile users: Can offloading computation save energy? Computer 43, 51–56 (2010)
9. Li, C., Li, L.: Energy constrained resource allocation optimization for mobile grids. Journal of Parallel and Distributed Computing 70(3), 245–258 (2010)
10. Murray, D., Yoneki, E., Crowcroft, J., Hand, S.: The case for crowd computing. In: 2nd ACM SIGCOMM Workshop on Networking, Systems, and Applications on Mobile Handhelds, pp. 39–44. ACM Press, New York (2010)
11. Paradiso, J., Starner, T.: Energy scavenging for mobile and wireless electronics. IEEE Pervasive Computing 4(1), 18–27 (2005)
12. Rice, A., Hay, S.: Measuring mobile phone energy consumption for 802.11 wireless networking. Pervasive and Mobile Computing 6(6), 593–606 (2010)
13. Rodriguez, J.M., Zunino, A., Campo, M.: Mobile grid SEAS: Simple Energy-Aware Scheduler. In: Proc. 3rd High-Performance Computing Symposium - 39th JAIIO (2010)
14. Rodriguez, J.M., Zunino, A., Campo, M.: Introducing mobile devices into Grid systems: A survey. International Journal of Web and Grid Services 7(1), 1–40 (2011)

Ontology and Rule Based Inferring on Project Teams

Vili Podgorelec

University of Maribor, FERI, Institute of Informatics, Smetanova ulica 17
SI-2000 Maribor, Slovenia
Vili.Podgorelec@uni-mb.si

Abstract. A task of automatic identification of potential project team members based on project requirements and personal competence profiles is a complex one. It requires a good knowledge base together with an adequate knowledge processing engine, capable of inferring on the knowledge available. In this paper, we study and present an approach to implement a knowledge management system with the use of semantic web technologies in combination with a declarative production rule-based system. We used ontologies to represent the needed knowledge and rule-based expert system to infer on the knowledge and to provide the requested results. In this manner we developed a prototype system that should assist in project team building activities.

Keywords: Semantic Web Technologies, Ontology, Rule-based Systems, Team Building Approach.

1 Introduction

With modern transportation, communication, and business connections, distances are becoming narrower and competition tougher. Therefore, successful companies nowadays need to adapt to changes in environment more rapidly than they used to. Besides ever rapidly changing environment, an organizational shift towards customer has been noticed. For the last ten years or so there has been a steady international move towards changing the way customer services are delivered, financed and regulated, with the main purpose being the improvement of efficiency so that more customers could receive better service more quickly without reducing (and possibly increasing) the quality.

Many a time it has been proven that the proper use of proper knowledge is the best way of optimizing work processes. As the evolution of information technology and software design progresses the possible solutions to the optimization of work processes could be knowledge management and web-based software services. Based on our experiences in developing software solutions, it is our belief that semantic web technologies (SWT), properly combined with alternative existing solutions wherever the stack of SWT is somewhat deficient, could solve this task. In this manner, we propose a new approach to solving the inferring part of semantic web application. Due to lack of inferring technologies promised by the semantic web designers, we decided to use a non-procedural rule-based programming language Clips, mainly used

F.V. Cipolla-Ficarra et al. (Eds.): ADNTIIC 2011, LNCS 7547, pp. 48–57, 2012.
© Springer-Verlag Berlin Heidelberg 2012

for the development of production rules based expert systems, to implement the inferring system.

This particular combination allowed us to develop an effective prototype system that is able to propose project team members based on their personal profiles and the requirements of a specific project.

2   Semantic Web Technologies

The idea behind semantic web is fairly simple. According to Passin [1], the vision of semantic web is that computers would be able to find, read and understand the meaning of data. Tim Berners-Lee sees semantic web as "web of data" compared to web of documents as we know world wide web today [2].

Semantic web technologies (SWT) are based on XML language that enables them to be platform and program language independent. They are built in layers, where each upper layer provides additional functional aspects and is based on the lower one, with which is fully compatible (http://www.w3.org/2001/sw/). The layers, from bottom up, include URI, XML and namespaces, RDF as the core technology for the semantic annotation of data [3,4], RDFS and OWL being languages for describing ontologies [5,6], SparQL as a language for querying semantic data and RIF as a rule interchange format for describing logical rules of the data being semantically described [7]. The two top most technologies (trust and proof) are not supported yet.

The central part of a semantic web application is an ontology that describes some knowledge domain using notions of concepts, instances, attributes, relations and axioms [8]. It is a useful way to organize and share information while offering means for enhanced semantic search in distributed and heterogeneous information systems.

In order to adopt the SWT for supporting the knowledge management in a specific domain (for example in team building), there is a key field that needs to be addressed: domain knowledge that we want to integrate within the domain. For this purpose the ontology needs to be defined, which will then allow all further actions, like semantic annotation of data (in accordance with the ontology), integration of data resources, advanced searching and inferring on the data.

3   Team Building Overview

For a technical project, let's say in software engineering, to be successfully implemented there is a need for bright, skilled individuals with good technical skills and exceptional attention to detail. However, the real world projects nowadays normally require more than just good individuals. Even a group of great individuals is not enough, what we really need is a team – a team of cleverly selected individuals, who will combine their personal technical skills with their teamwork skills in order to achieve the project goals. What we need to compose great teams is a proper team building approach and a supporting technology to implement the approach. It is our believe that adopting the SWT for describing a personal skill record, consisting of technical skills profile and teamwork skills profile, using an ontology, is a good and valid approach to project teams building.

Team building is an effort in which a team studies its own process of working together and acts to create a climate that encourages and values the contributions of team members [9]. Their energies are directed toward problem solving, task effectiveness, and maximizing the use of all members' resources to achieve the team's purpose. Sound team building recognizes that it is not possible to fully separate one's performance from those of others.

Team building will occur more easily when all team members work jointly on a task of mutual importance. This allows each member to provide their technical knowledge and skills in helping to solve the problem, complete the project, and develop new programs. During this process, team building can be facilitated as members evaluate their working relationship as a team and then develop and articulate guidelines that will lead to increased productivity and team member cooperation. Team performance can best be evaluated if the team develops a model of excellence against which to measure its performance.

4   Semantic Web Based Team Building Approach

In general, available knowledge management tools usually suffer from the following limitations for designing knowledge management (KM) systems [10]:

- Information searching is mainly based on keyword searches that may retrieve irrelevant information due to term ambiguity, and omit important relevant information when it is stored under different keywords.
- Manual methods such as browsing and reading are the main methods to extract relevant information from textual or other representation.
- Maintaining large repositories of weakly structured information remains a tough and time-consuming task.

It is our belief that a semantic web technologies offer the answer to those problems. The semantic portal serves as an entry point to our information solution in project team building. Semantic web portals enable users to find relevant sources for the problem at hand and provide knowledge resources for resolving it. In our case, the semantic web portal supports one in building project teams effectively and efficiently. The architecture of the portal is presented in Figure 1.

This architecture provides a mean to manage both members' and projects' profiles through a web server by members themselves, by project leaders and by project administrators. The inference engine uses the profiles together with previous projects' data in order to propose members for any new project regarding the requirements. The system's inferring capabilities can be improved by managing the skills matching database which is used to reveal the hidden skills of members, not provided directly by them or the project leaders.

During the project cycle the portal should not be used too frequently. If we would push users to use it over and over again, we would disturb project activities and waste team's energy. However, we want results from the portal – so we designed it to be used only on beginning and ending of a project (Figure 2). If project team uses information support for their project activities, portal should integrate their existing data, so no changes in work are necessary. When using some groupware to support project work, the data could be gathered automatically.

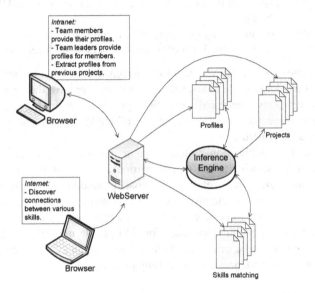

Fig. 1. Architecture of semantic web portal for project team building

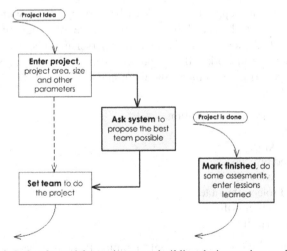

Fig. 2. Role of portal for project team building during project cycle

4.1   Ontology-Based Personal Skill Management

An overview of the related work in ontology-based personal skill management is presented in [11]. Already [12-13] promoted the idea of ontology-based modelling of personnel skills and job requirements – as part of comprehensive, workflow-oriented enterprise modelling. There, the following potential applications of ontology-based skill profiles are listed:

- Skill gap analysis – at the enterprise level, as a part of strategic HR planning.
- Project team building.
- Recruitment planning – again a part of strategic HR planning.
- Training analysis – at the level of individual personnel development.

Those approaches were mainly technology-driven and were – to our knowledge – never realized in a large-scale industrial environment. Nor have they been accepted by the HRM departments, translated into HRM people's terminology, embedded into more comprehensive models and procedures of HRM people, and integrated with existing software infrastructures.

After those first publications, there were a number of interesting technology-oriented researches which showed that in particular skill matching can benefit from interesting technological approaches, such as background knowledge exploitation. For instance, [14] employs declarative retrieval heuristics for traversing ontology structures. In [15] authors derive competency statements through F-Logic reasoning and developed a soft matching approach for skill profile matching. Colucci [16] and others use description logic inferences to take into account background knowledge as well as incomplete knowledge when matching profiles.

4.2   Personal Skills and Project Team Ontology

There have been many approaches to describe personal skills within an ontology. They included both technical skills (like knowledge of programming languages, development methods, specific tools) and inter-personal skills (like communication skills, affableness, teamwork). Based on the team building theory and our own experiences from performed projects the main items that have to be included in such ontology should be:

- Formal and informal education.
- Experiences.
- Practical skills.
- Performed projects.
- Preferred tasks.
- Preferred role within a team.
- Communication skills.
- Teamwork spirit.

As far as we could find within the recent literature, there have been some approaches to describe project teams with an ontology. However, they have not been used for project teams building. For this purpose the existing project team ontologies, which include basic information about team members, resources, purpose of the project, etc., should be extended with the following information:

- The priorities of the project.
- The importance of specific phases (regarding the current stage).
- Complexity of the project (regarding the previous ones).
- The technical type of the project (prototype, research, production, etc).
- Special knowledge requirements.
- Preferred personnel.
- The type of the product/service being developed.
- The relation with other (especially previously successfully performed) projects.

The resulting ontology is presented in Figure 3 – only classes and object properties are shown. Ontology is used in portal to help reasoner use metadata and construct the proper team for performing the project.

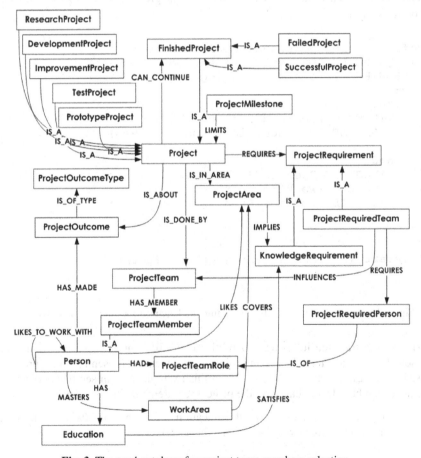

Fig. 3. The used ontology for project team members selection

4.3   The Use of Non-procedural Inferring

The project team building system prototype is implemented mainly in Java programming language using open source Jena semantic web development library [17]. It provides us with a straight-forward development system, very appropriate for semantic web portal application. The most important deficiency is the lack of an efficient inferring engine, which can be easily integrated within an existing application and would easily scale up to the real-world requirements. As such a technology is not available in this moment, for the inferring part of the prototype we chose CLIPS programming environment [18], a production rule-based programming system mainly used for developing expert systems. CLIPS is a productive development and delivery expert system tool which provides a complete environment for the construction of rule and/or object based expert systems. As it turned out, it enabled us with powerful inferring possibilities on semantic data. Additionally, it is very easy to execute CLIPS rules within Java applications using open source libraries such as JClips [19], what further enables one to integrate the inferring rules within an information system.

```
(defrule selectPersonBasedOnRequirements
  (IS_DONE_BY ?project ?projectTeam)
  (REQUIRES ?project ?knowledgeReq)
  (or
    (and
      (HAS ?person ?education)
      (SATISFIES ?education ?knowledgeReq)
    )
    (and
      (MASTERS ?person ?workArea)
      (COVERS ?workArea ?projectArea)
      (IMPLIES ?projectArea ?knowledgeReq)
    )
  )
=>
  (assert (HAS_MEMBER ?projectTeam ?person))
)
```

Fig. 4. An example rule in a CLIPS programming language for inferring on the ontology

To demonstrate the inferring capabilities of CLIPS, an example rule that selects persons for a project team based on project requirements is presented on Figure 4; it is based on the main ontology (Figure 3). In this example we can see that project team members can be selected based on the project requirements in two ways:

a) using the information about education of a person (which knowledge requirements are covered by some education), and

b) using the information about work areas mastered by a person (a work area covers several project areas and a project area implies several knowledge requirements).

In this way a team member can be automatically selected based on the requirements of a project. Note that an IS_A relation between knowledge requirement and project requirement has been implicitly used in this example. The knowledge base for the CLIPS program is induced directly from the ontology and/or the corresponding database (Figure 6).

As shown in Figure 5 the system itself does not consist of several different technologies, which is in our belief good. As mentioned before, fundamentals for the system lies in J2EE platform and XML enabled database (we used the Oracle 10gR2 database).

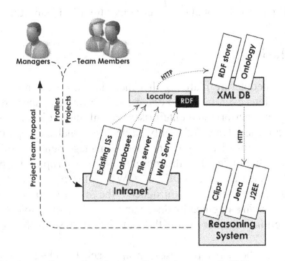

Fig. 5. Technologies used to develop the project team building portal

First vital component, called "locator", is responsible for collecting as many internal data in RDF as possible. It extracts data from existing systems, web pages, databases and file systems. Collected RDFs and presented ontology are persistently stored in XMD database and prepared for analyze with reasoning system, based on J2EE, Jena and CLIPS.

On Figure 6 there is an excerpt of data, automatically collected by the locator and transformed from RDF into CLIPS facts set to be used by the developed inferring engine. CLIPS facts represent the initial knowledge base for the CLIPS production rules. Usually, they need to be collected manually by a knowledge engineer as, in general, the transformation from relational database cannot be made automatically. However, in our case we took the advantage of semantically annotated data which actually represent the actual knowledge, needed to construct the knowledge base.

```
(deffacts knowledgeBase
  (IS_A_PROJECT Kalimo DevelopmentProject)
  (IS_DONE_BY Kalimo KalimoTeam)
  (REQUIRES Kalimo FishPhilosophy)
  (HAS Luka CompSciBSc)
  (HAS Vili CompSciPhD)
  (SATISFIES CompSciBSc programming)
  (SATISFIES CompSciBSc ISdesign)
  (SATISFIES CompSciBSc ISdevelopment)
  (SATISFIES CompSciMSc FishPhilosophy)
  (MASTERS Luka TeamWork)
  (COVERS TeamWork TeamMotivation)
  (IMPLIES TeamMotivation FishPhilosophy)
)
```

Fig. 6. An excerpt of data, transformed from RDF into CLIPS facts

5   Conclusion

More and more people are realizing that there is a high potential in using SWT for back-office solutions even in closed enterprises. Presented paper proposes a new way of helping large project-oriented enterprises on building project teams.

For building project teams of highly skilled, personally compatible and interested individuals we combined existing knowledge management solutions with semantic web ideas and technologies. For this purpose we have proposed a portal system with the use of SWT such as URI, RDF and OWL in the background. Due to problems with inferring technologies we introduced the use of non-procedural rule-based system as an inferring engine. In this manner, the main ontology for project team members selection together with the rule-based system for reasoning is also presented.

To summarize, the paper proposes an approach to select project team members based on semantically annotated distributed profiles, connected with an intelligent service and ontology in the background. For now, it works for simpler cases. However, in order to make it appropriate for real world everyday use a number of features should be improved. In this manner we plan to improve the inferring capabilities of the system by including an advanced component for collecting personal skills information automatically from the existing data (performed projects, research reports). Similarly, a web mining component for collecting data to infer about similar work areas should improve the overall system. And not the least, the improvement of the presented ontology itself is anticipated as we will proceed with our work.

References

1. Passin, T.B.: Explorers guide to Semantic Web. Manning, Greenwich (2004)
2. Berners-Lee, T.: Business Model for the Semantic Web (2001),
   http://www.w3.org/DesignIssues/Business
3. Manola, F., Miller, E. (eds.): RDF Primer. W3C Consortium recommendation (2004)

4. Lassila, O., Swick, R.R.: Resource Description Framework (RDF) Model and Syntax Specification. W3C Consortium (1999)
5. McGuiness, D.L., Harmelen, F. (eds.): OWL Web Ontology Language Overview. W3C Consortium recommendation (2004)
6. Bechhofer, S., Harmelen, F., Hendler, J., Horrocks, I., McGuinness, D.L., Patel-Schneider, P.F., Stein, L.A.: OWL Web Ontology Language Reference. W3C Consortium (2004)
7. Horrocks, I., Patel-Schneider, P.F., Boley, H., Tabet, S., Grosof, B., Dean, M.: SWRL: A Semantic Web Rule Language Combining OWL and RuleML. W3C Consortium (2004), http://www.w3.org/Submission/SWRL/
8. Gruber, T.R.: Towards Principles for the Design of Ontologies used for Knowledge Sharing. In: Guarino, N., Poli, R. (eds.) Proc. International Workshop on Formal Ontology, Padova, Italy (1993)
9. Francis, D., Young, D.: Improving Work Groups: A Practical Manual for Team Building. University Associates, San Diego (1979)
10. Lau, T., Sure, Y.: Introducing Ontology-based Skills Management at a large Insurance Company. In: Modellierung 2002: Modellierung in der Praxis – Modellierung für die Praxis, pp. 123–134 (2002)
11. Biesalski, E., Abecker, A.: Integrated Processes and Tools for Personnel Development. In: 11th International Conference on Concurrent Enterprising, University BW Munich (2005)
12. Stader, J., Macintosh, A.: Capability Modelling and Knowledge Management. In: Applications and Innovations in Expert Systems VII, ES1999 – 19th Int. Conf. of the BCS Specialist Group on Knowledge-Based Systems and Applied Artificial Intelligence, pp. 33–50. Springer, Berlin (1999)
13. Jarvis, P., Stader, J., Macintosh, A., Moore, J., Chung, P.: What Right Do You Have to Do That? In: Proceedings of the 1st International Conference on Enterprise Information Systems, ICEIS, Portugal (1999)
14. Liao, M., Hinkelmann, K., Abecker, A., Sintek, M.: A Competence Knowledge Base System as Part of the Organizational Memory. In: Puppe, F. (ed.) XPS 1999. LNCS (LNAI), vol. 1570, pp. 125–137. Springer, Heidelberg (1999)
15. Sure, Y., Maedche, A., Staab, S.: Leveraging Corporate Skill Knowledge - From ProPer to OntoProPer. In: Mahling, D., Reimer, U. (eds.) Proceedings of the 3rd International Conference on Practical Aspects of Knowledge Management (2000)
16. Colucci, S., Di Noia, T., Di Sciascio, E., Donini, F.M., Mongiello, M., Mottola, M.: A Formal Approach to Ontology-Based Semantic Match of Skills Descriptions. Journal of Universal Computer Science 9(12), 1437–1454 (2003)
17. Jena – A Semantic Web Framework for Java, http://jena.sourceforge.net/
18. CLIPS – A Tool for Building Expert Systems, http://www.ghg.net/clips/CLIPS.html
19. JClips — CLIPS for Java, http://www.cs.vu.nl/~mrmenken/jclips/

Simulation on Cloud Computing Infrastructures of Parametric Studies of Nonlinear Solids Problems

Elina Pacini[1], Melisa Ribero[1,2], Cristian Mateos[3],
Anibal Mirasso[2], and Carlos García Garino[1,2]

[1] Instituto para las Tecnologías de la Información y las Comunicaciones (ITIC) – UNCuyo,
Mendoza Argentina
{epacini,cgarcia}@itu.uncu.edu.ar
[2] Facultad de Ingeniería, UNCuyo, Mendoza, Argentina
melisaribero@yahoo.com.ar, aemirasso@uncu.edu.ar
[3] ISISTAN - CONICET. Tandil, Buenos Aires, Argentina
cmateos@conicet.gov.ar

Abstract. Scientists and engineers are more and more faced to the need of computational power to satisfy the ever-increasing resource intensive nature of their experiments. Traditionally, they have relied on conventional computing infrastructures such as clusters and Grids. A recent computing paradigm that is gaining momentum is Cloud Computing, which offers a simpler administration mechanism compared to those conventional infrastructures. However, there is a lack of studies in the literature about the viability of using Cloud Computing to execute scientific and engineering applications from a performance standpoint. We present an empirical study on the employment of Cloud infrastructures to run parameter sweep experiments (PSEs), particularly studies of viscoplastic solids together with simulations by using the CloudSim toolkit. In general, we obtained very good speedups, which suggest that disciplinary users could benefit from Cloud Computing for executing resource intensive PSEs.

Keywords: Parameter Sweep, Viscoplastic Solids, Cloud Computing.

1 Introduction

Parameter Sweep Experiments, or PSEs for short, is a very popular way of conducting simulation-based experiments among scientists and engineers through which the same application code is run several times with different input parameters resulting in different outputs [1]. From a software perspective, most PSEs are cluster friendly since individual inputs of an experiment can be handled by independent tasks. Therefore, using a software platform such as Condor [2], which is able to exploit the distributed nature of a computer cluster, allows these tasks to be run in parallel. In this way, not only PSEs execute faster, but also more computing intensive experiments can be computed, and hence more complex simulations can be performed. This idea has been systematically applied to execute PSEs on Grid Computing [3], which are basically infrastructures that connect clusters via wide-area connections to increase computational power.

F.V. Cipolla-Ficarra et al. (Eds.): ADNTIIC 2011, LNCS 7547, pp. 58–70, 2012.
© Springer-Verlag Berlin Heidelberg 2012

A recent distributed computing paradigm that is rapidly gaining momentum is Cloud Computing [4], which bases on the idea of providing an on demand computing infrastructure to end users. Typically, users exploit Clouds by requesting from them one or more machine images, which are virtual machines running a desired operating system on top of several physical machines (e.g. a datacenter). Among the benefits of Cloud Computing is precisely a simplified configuration and deployment model compared to clusters and Grids, which is extremely desirable for disciplinary users.

In this paper, we will show the benefits of Cloud Computing for executing PSEs through a case study. The application domain under study involves PSEs of viscoplastic solids, which explore the sensitivity of solid behavior in terms of changes of certain model parameters (viscosity parameter η, sensitivity coefficient, and so on). In this sense parametric studies previously discussed for imperfections [5] are extended for material parameters case, which were computed on Clouds by using the CloudSim simulation toolkit [6]. Results show that by executing our experiments in our simulated Clouds, depending on the configured computational capabilities and the scheduling policy being used, near-to-ideal speedups can be obtained.

The next Section provides more details on Cloud Computing and the motivation behind considering this distributed computing paradigm for executing PSEs. The Section also explains CloudSim. Section 3 describes our case study. Later, Section 4 presents the results obtained from processing these problems on Cloud Computing. Finally, Section 5 concludes the paper and describes prospective future works.

2   Background

Running Parameter Sweep Experiments (PSE) [1] involves many independent jobs, since the experiments are executed under multiple initial configurations (input parameter values) several times, to locate a particular point in the parameter space that satisfies certain criteria. Interestingly, PSEs find their application in diverse scientific areas like Bioinformatics, Earth Sciences, High-Energy Physics, Molecular Science and even Social Sciences.

When designing PSEs, it is necessary to generate all possible combinations of input parameters, which is a time-consuming task. Besides, it is not straightforward to provide a general solution, since each problem has a different number of parameters and each of them has its own variation interval. Another issue, which is in part a consequence of the first issue, relates to scheduling PSEs on distributed environments, which is a complex activity. Therefore, it is necessary to develop efficient scheduling strategies to appropriately allocate the workload and reduce the computation time.

In recent years Grid Computing [3] and even more recently Cloud Computing technologies [4] have been increasingly used for running such applications. PSEs are well suited for these environments since they are inherently parallel problems with no or little data transfer between nodes during computations. Since many applications require a great need for calculation, these applications have been initially addressed to dedicated High-Throughput Computing (HTC) infrastructures such as clusters or pools of networked machines, managed by some software such as Condor [2]. Then, with the advent of Grid Computing new opportunities were available to scientists, since Grids offered the computational power required to perform large experiments. Despite the widespread use of Grid technologies in scientific computing, some issues still make the access to this technology not easy for disciplinary users. In most cases scientific Grids feature a prepackaged environment in which applications will be executed. Then, specific tools/APIs have to be used, and there could be limitations on the hosting operating systems or the services offered by the runtime environment. On the other hand, although Grid Computing favors dynamic resource discovery and provision of a wide variety of runtime environments for applications, in practice, a limited set of options are available for scientists, which are not in addition elastic enough to cover their needs. In general, applications that run on scientific Grids are implemented as bag of tasks applications, workflows, and MPI (Message Passing Interface) [7] parallel processes. Some scientific experiments could not fit into these models and therefore have to be redesigned to exploit a particular scientific Grid.

2.1   Cloud Computing: Overview

Cloud Computing [4], the current emerging trend in delivering IT services, has been recently proposed to address the aforementioned problems. By means of virtualization technologies, Cloud Computing offers to end users a variety of services covering the entire computing stack, from the hardware to the application level, by charging them on a pay per use basis. This makes the spectrum of options available to scientists, and particularly PSEs users, wide enough to cover any specific need from their research. Another important feature, from which scientists can benefit, is the ability to scale up and down the computing infrastructure according to the application requirements and the budget of users. They can have immediate access to required resources without any capacity planning and they are free to release resources when no longer needed.

Central to Cloud computing is the concept of virtualization, i.e. the capability of a software system of emulating various operating systems. By means of this support, scientists can exploit Clouds by requesting from them machine images, or virtual machines that emulate any operating system on top of several physical machines, which in turn run a host operating system. Usually, Clouds are established using the machines of a datacenter for executing user applications while they are idle.

Interaction with a Cloud environment is performed via Cloud services [4], which define the functional capabilities of a Cloud, i.e. machine image management, access to software/data, security, and so forth. Cloud services are commonly exposed to the outer world via Web Services [8], i.e. software components that can be remotely invoked by any application. By using these services, a user application can allocate machine images, upload input data, execute, and download output (result) data for further analysis. To offer on demand, shared access to their underlying physical resources, Clouds dynamically allocate and deallocate machines images. Besides, and also important, Clouds can co-allocate N machines images on M physical machines, with $N \geq M$, thus concurrent user-wide resource sharing is ensured.

A Cloud gives users the illusion of a single, powerful computer in which complex applications can be run. The software stack of the infrastructure can be fully adapted and configured according to user's needs. This provides excellent opportunities for scientists and engineers to run applications that demand by nature a huge amount of computational power. Precisely, for parametric studies such as the one presented in this paper or scientific applications [9] in general, Cloud Computing has an intrinsic value.

2.2   The CloudSim Toolkit: Simulation of Cloud Computing Environments

CloudSim [6] is an extensible simulation toolkit that enables modeling, simulation and experimentation of Cloud Computing infrastructures and application provisioning environments. CloudSim supports both system and behavior modeling of Cloud system components such as data centers, virtual machines (VMs) and resource provisioning policies. A virtual machine (VM) is a software implementation of a machine (i.e. a computer) that executes programs like a physical machine. The core hardware infrastructure services related to Clouds are modeled by a Datacenter component for handling service requests. A Datacenter is composed by a set of hosts that are responsible for managing VMs during their life cycle. Host is a component that represents a physical computing node in a Cloud, and as such is assigned a pre-configured processing capability, memory, storage, and scheduling policy for allocating processing elements (PEs) to VMs.

CloudSim supports scheduling policies at the host level and at the VM level. At the host level it is possible to specify how much of the overall processing power of each PE in a host will be assigned to each VM. At the VM level, the VMs assign a specific amount of the available processing power to individual task units -called cloudlet by CloudSim- that are hosted within its execution engine. At each level, CloudSim implements the *time-shared* and *space-shared* allocation policies. When employing the space-shared policy only one VM can be running at a given instance of time. This policy takes into account how many PEs will be delegated to each VM. The same happens for provisioning cloudlets within a VM, since each cloudlet demands only one PE. If there are other cloudlets ready to run at the same time, they have to wait in the run queue (because one PE is used exclusively by one cloudlet). Last but not least, with the time-shared policy, the processing power of hosts is concurrently shared by the VMs. Therefore, multiple cloudlets can simultaneously multi-task within the same VM. With this policy, there are no queuing delays associated with cloudlets.

3   Case Study: A PSE for Nonlinear Solids Problems

In order to assess the effectiveness of Cloud Computing environments for executing PSEs, we have processed a real experiment by using different Cloud infrastructures simulated via CloudSim. The case study chosen is the problem proposed in [10], in which a plane strain plate with a central circular hole is studied. The dimensions of the plate are 18 x 10 m, R = 5 m. Material constants considered are E = 2.1 10^5 Mpa;

ν = 0:3; σ$_y$ = 240 Mpa; H = 0. A linear Perzyna viscoplastic model with m = 1 and n = ∞ is considered. The large strain elasto/viscoplastic Finite Element code SOGDE [11] is used in this study. A detailed presentation of viscoplastic theory, numerical implementation and examples can be found in the works [12], [13].

We have previously studied parametric problems where a geometry parameter of imperfection was chosen [5]. In this case a material parameter is selected as a parameter. Different viscosity values of η parameter are considered: 1.10^4, 2.10^4, 3.10^4, 4.10^4, 5.10^4, 7.10^4, 1.10^5, 2.10^5, 3.10^5, 4.10^5, 5.10^5, 7.10^5, 1.10^6, 2.10^6, 3.10^6, 4.10^6, 5.10^6, 7.10^6, 1.10^7, 2.10^7, 3.10^7, 4.10^7, 5.10^7, 7.10^7 and 1.10^8 Mpa. Here, a mesh of 1,152 elements and Q1/P0 elements was used. Imposed displacements (at y=18m) are applied until a final displacement of 2000 mm is reached in 400 equals time steps of 0.05 mm each one. δ = 1 has been set for all the time steps.

4   Experimental Results

This section presents the results obtained from our experimental study, which aims to evaluate the viability of using Cloud Computing to perform PSEs. First, in a single machine we run the PSE of the previous section by varying the elasticity parameter η and measuring the execution time for 25 different experiments (resulting in 25 input files with different input configurations). The PSE were solved using the SOGDE solver. The characteristics of the machine on which the experiments were carried out are shown in Table 1. The machine model is AMD Athlon(tm) 64 X2 3600+, running Ubuntu 11.04 kernel version 2.6.38-8.

The obtained real information (execution times, input/output file sizes) was then used to feed CloudSim. The information regarding processing power was obtained from the benchmarking support of Linux and as such is expressed in bogomips. Bogomips (from bogus and MIPS), is a metric used by Linux operating systems that indicates how fast a computer processor runs. After that, we performed a number of simulations involving executing the PSE on Cloud infrastructures by using CloudSim. The simulations have been carried out by taking into account the bogomips metric. This is, once the execution times have been obtained from the real machine, we calculated for each experiment the number of executed instructions by the following formula: NI_i = bogomipsCPU* T_i, where NI_i is the number of million instructions to be executed by or associated to a task i, bogomipsCPU is the processing power of our real machine measured in bogomips and T_i is the time that took to run a task i on the real machine. Here is an example of how to calculate the number of instructions of a task that took 117 seconds to be executed. The machine where the experiment was executed has a processing power of 4,008.64 bogomips. Then, the resulting number of instructions for this experiment was 469,011 MI (Million Instructions). CloudSim was configured as a data center composed of a single machine –or "host" in CloudSim terminology– with the same characteristics as the real machine where the experiments were performed. The characteristics of the configured host are shown in Table 2.

Table 1. Machine used to execute the PSE	
Feature	Characteristic
CPU power	4,008.64 bogoMIPS
Number of CPUs	2
RAM memory	2 Gbytes
Storage size	400 Gbytes
Bandwidth	100 Mbps

Table 2. Host characteristics	
Host Parameters	Value
Processing Power	4,008
RAM	4,096
Storage	409,600
Bandwidth	100
PE	2

Processing power is expressed in MIPS (Million Instructions Per Second), RAM memory and Storage capacity are in MBytes, bandwidth in Mbps, and finally, PE is the number of processing elements (CPUs/cores) of a host. Once configured, we checked that the execution times obtained by the simulation coincided or were close to real times for each independent task performed on the real machine. The results were successful in the sense that one experiment (i.e. a variation in the value of η) took 117 seconds to be solved in the real machine, while in the simulated machine the elapsed time was 117.02 seconds. Once the execution times have been validated for a single machine on CloudSim, a new simulation scenario was set, which consisted of one datacenter with 10 hosts, each with the same hardware capabilities as the real single machine, and 40 VMs, each with the characteristics specified in Table 3. A summary of this simulation scenario is shown in Table 4.

Table 3. VM characteristics	
VM Parameters	Value
MIPS	4,008
RAM	1,024
Image Size	102,400
Bandwidth	25
PE	1
Vmm	Xen

Table 4. CloudSim configuration	
Parameter	Value
Number of Hosts	10
Number of VMs	40
Number of Cloudlets	from 25 to 250

With this new scenario, we performed several experiments to evaluate the performance of our PSE in a simulated Cloud Computing environment as we increase the number of tasks to be performed, i.e. 25 * i tasks with i = 1, 2, ..., 10. This is, a base subset comprising 25 tasks was obtained by varying the value of η, while the extra tasks were obtained not by further varying this value but cloning the base subset. The reason of this was to stress the various experimental Cloud scenarios.

Each task, called cloudlet by CloudSim, is described by its Length, required PEs, and Input File and Output File sizes. The Length parameter is the number of instructions to be executed by a cloudlet in MI (Million Instructions). PE is the number of processing elements required to perform a task (CPUs). Input File and Output File sizes are expressed in bytes. The values used in the simulation were between 244,127 and 469,011 (Length), 1 (PEs), 93,082 bytes (Input File size) and 2,202,010 bytes (Output File size).

To perform the simulation we have considered, on one hand, that PSE cloudlets have similar processing times. The processing times are similar because both input and output files have the same size. The size of the input files is equal because only one parameter is varied within them. One cloudlet corresponds to execute an instance of a PSE of viscoplastic solid. On the other hand, the goal is to assign tasks to Cloud hosts so that the total completion time, also known as makespan, is minimized. Finally, the order in which cloudlets are processed on a particular host is not relevant, since we assume they are completely independent and do not share data.

In CloudSim, the amount of available hardware resources to each VM is constrained by the total processing power and system bandwidth available within the associated host. Therefore, scheduling policies must be applied in order to assign the VMs to the host and get a maximum use of resources. On the other hand, cloudlets must also be scheduled with some scheduling policy for a maximum resource performance and minimize the makespan. In the next subsections we report the obtained results when executing the 25 experiments of our PSE using the scheduling policies described in subsection 2.2. In addition, we have considered two types of environments, i.e. homogeneous and heterogeneous, which are explained below.

4.1   Without Resource Heterogeneity

In this subsection we analyze how each scheduling policy responds when Cloud hosts and VMs follow the specifications described in Table 2 and 3.

4.1.1   Space-Shared Provisioning
Fig. 1a presents the provisioning scenario where the space-shared policy is applied for both VMs and tasks (cloudlets). Here, the makespan of the whole cloudlets is shown.

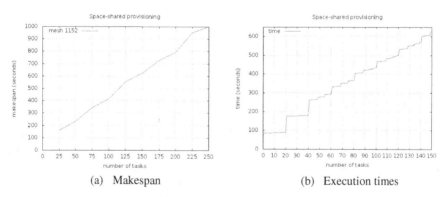

(a) Makespan   (b) Execution times

Fig. 1. Space-shared: Results

The makespan has shown a linear growth with respect to the number of cloudlets. After creating VMs, cloudlets were incrementally sent to VMs in groups of 25 to measure the makespan as we increase the workload on the VMs. The makespan rose from 160.25 to 1,000.86 seconds when the number of cloudlets went from 25 to 250.

As each VM requires one PE for processing (see Table 3), with the space-shared policy only two VMs can actually run in a host at a given instant of time, because each host has two PEs as shown in Table 2. Therefore, given a scenario consisting of a total of 10 hosts and 40 VMs, at a given instant of time may be assigned 20 VMs to the hosts, i.e. one VM by each PE, and the rest of the VMs can be assigned once the former set complete their execution. As the number of PSEs and hence cloudlets in regard to the available amount of resources increases, the estimated start time of each cloudlet depends on the position of the cloudlet in the execution queue, since each PE is used exclusively by one cloudlet under the space-shared policy. Remaining cloudlets are queued when there are not free processing elements to use for execution.

Fig. 1b presents the progress of execution times when we sent to execute a group of 150 cloudlets, i.e. a group of 150 PSEs as described in the previous section. Since, under this policy, each cloudlet had its own dedicated PE, the queue size (cloudlets waiting to be run) did not affect execution time of individual cloudlets. As shown, the execution times were increasing linearly approximately every 20 tasks. This is because as mentioned above, only 20 VMs were created with the space-shared policy, so the cloudlets are sent to the VMs to run in groups of 20 until they finish their execution. When the first submitted group of cloudlets finishes their execution, 20 more are sent, and so on until all cloudlets are executed.

4.1.2   Time-Shared Provisioning

In this scenario a time-shared allocation is applied. Fig. 2a shows the makespan as the number of cloudlets increases from 25 to 250. Here, the processing power within a host is concurrently shared by its associated VMs, and the PEs of each VM are simultaneously divided among its cloudlets. As a consequence, there are no queuing delays associated with cloudlets. CloudSim assumes that all the computing power of PEs is available for VMs and cloudlets, and it is divided equally among them. In this scenario, the makespan rose from 280.94 to 1,328.13 seconds when the number of cloudlets was increased from 25 to 250.

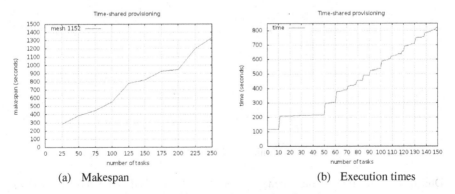

(a)   Makespan   (b)   Execution times

Fig. 2. Time-shared provisioning: Results

Fig. 2b illustrates the progress of execution times when we sent to execute a group of 150 cloudlets, or a group of 150 PSEs. Since using the time-shared policy in the hosts the processing power available is concurrently shared by VMs, here 40 VMs have been created in the 10 available hosts. Here, the execution times were increasing gradually over the first 50 cloudlets. The remaining 100 tasks took considerably longer than the 50 first tasks. This latter effect occurs because the VMs available for processing within hosts begun to be switched between their PEs, which takes time.

4.2   With Resource Heterogeneity

In this subsection we analyze how each scheduling policy responds when using a Cloud with heterogeneous hosts. To analyze the performance of the scheduling algorithms, one characteristic that is of importance in real world scenarios is how the algorithms perform in the presence of resource heterogeneity. In this analysis, we have considered hosts with a random number of PEs between 1 and 6, while the other specifications are the same shown in Tables 2 and 3. Until now, each VM had only one PE. Next, we discuss the same scenarios of the previous section, and perform a comparison of task assignment with respect to homogeneous and heterogeneous infrastructures.

4.3   Space-Shared Provisioning

Fig. 3 presents a scenario where the space-shared policy is applied. After creating VMs with a random number of PEs, cloudlets were incrementally sent to VMs in groups of 25 to measure the makespan as the workload on the VMs increased. The number of cloudlets to be performed ranges from 25 to 250 as in the previous subsection. In the Figure, the allocation of cloudlets to heterogeneous resources is illustrated by the curve in blue. The red curve shows the same scenario that was discussed in subsection 4.1.1 for the case of homogeneous resources.

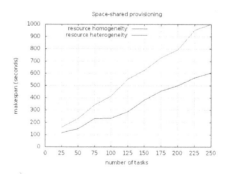

Fig. 3. Space-shared provisioning using resource heterogeneity: Results

Due to the fact that in this scenario the entire Cloud had more number of PEs available to run the experiments (between 1 and 6 per resource), the runtimes were reduced significantly with respect to the homogeneous scenario. The makespan of the first group of 25 cloudlets was very close to the makespan of the homogeneous scenario. This makespan was 160.25 seconds for the homogeneous scenario and 117.12 seconds when using heterogeneous resources. The makespan is close because in the worst case (homogeneous scenario) the number of PEs available to execute the cloudlets is nearby to the number of executed cloudlets (20 VMs to execute 25 cloudlets). Then, each cloudlet is executed in one PEs until the former finishes. For the following groups of cloudlets –between 50 and 250- the makespan was always lower when using heterogeneous resources. The makespan was 117.12, 150.24, 231.38, 235.43, 288.54, 380.74, 454.94, 499, 563.07, and 604.22 seconds.

4.4   Time-Shared Provisioning

In this subsection we present the results for a heterogeneous scenario where the time-shared policy is applied. Fig. 4 illustrates the progress curve in blue of execution times as the number of cloudlets increase from 25 to 250.

In this heterogeneous scenario, the makespan was 146.37 seconds and 677.64 seconds when the number of cloudlets was equal to 25 and 250, respectively. In the figure, we have performed the comparison with the scenario composed of homogeneous resources (curve in red). Overall, we obtained that, with this heterogeneous scenario, the makespan for the entire set of cloudlets was significantly reduced.

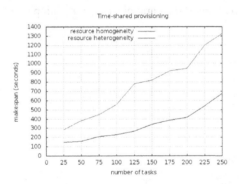

Fig. 4. Time-shared provisioning using resource heterogeneity. Results.

5   Summary and Discussion

In the previous sections we have reported the results obtained from executing our PSE on a simulated Cloud under two different scenarios and also taking into account whether the resources are homogeneous or heterogeneous. When the space-shared policy is used to assign VMs to hosts, the scheduler assigns as many VMs as PEs have available on the hosts (20 VMs in the proposed scenario). Instead, when time-shared policy is used, the PEs share their time slots among all VMs to be created (40 VMs). On the other hand, the cloudlets are sent to be executed something similar happens. When using the space-shared policy each cloudlet is assigned to a VM until it completes its execution. With the time-sharing policy processing power must be shared among several cloudlets, generating a lot of exchanges for completing their execution, which makes each cloudlet to take longer to finish.

The better performance obtained by the space-shared policy is mainly because each VM can allocate and get all the processing power that needs to execute assigned cloudlets from the host where the VM executes. Instead, with the time-shared policy, each VM receives a time slice on each processing element, and then distributes the slices among the PSEs to be executed. Due to the fact that the VMs have less processing power (time slices) the experiments took longer to complete. As a result, the space-shared policy was more appropriate to this type of PSEs.

Then, we performed the analysis of the same scenarios, but in a heterogeneous environment. The behavior of the different combinations of scheduling techniques was exactly the same as the case of homogeneous resources. Although the scheduling criteria to assign VMs to hosts and cloudlets to VMs were the same, the makespan was reduced for all scenarios. This improvement was because in the heterogeneous environment as many PEs as needed to run experiments were available.

Finally, we performed a speedup analysis to measure the performance of each technique (space-shared and time-shared) to execute the PSEs on the Cloud with respect to the sequential execution on a single machine (see Fig. 5).

The speedup is calculated as $S_p = T_1 / T_p$, where p is the number of processing elements, T_1 is the completion time of the sequential execution in a single machine, and T_p is the completion time of the parallel execution with p processing elements.

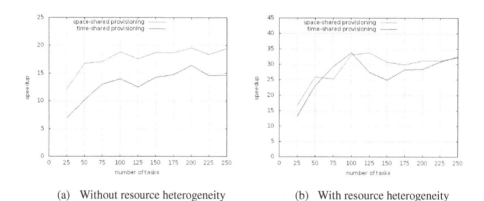

(a)   Without resource heterogeneity   (b)   With resource heterogeneity

Fig. 5. Speedup achieved by space-shared and time-shared policies: Results

We conclude that a scenario in which the space-sharing policy is used for the VMs allocation to hosts enables a better speedup than the time-sharing policy in both scenarios (homogeneous and heterogeneous). While for the experiments we have conducted in this paper a space-share policy for the allocation of VMs to hosts yields better results, due to the fact that the employed cloudlets are sequential –i.e. they have no inner parallelism to exploit–, a time-share policy to assign the VMs to hosts would be more appropriate for other types of applications (not batch or sequential) and also could be good to improve not only the makespan but also the perceptible response time to the user, since incoming tasks could be periodically scheduled and then executed in small groups, thus giving sign of progress.

6 Conclusion

Cloud Computing is a new paradigm that offers the means for building the next generation parallel computing infrastructures. Although the use of Clouds finds its roots in IT environments, the idea is gradually entering scientific and academic ones. Even when Cloud Computing is popular, little research has been done with respect to evaluating the benefits of the paradigm for scheduling and executing resource intensive scientific applications. Through a real case study and simulations, we have reported on the speedups obtained when running PSEs on Clouds. Results are quite encouraging and support the idea of using Clouds in the academia.

We are extending this work in several directions. First, we are conducting studies with other kind of PSEs, such as tension tests in metals [13], to further support our claims. Second, one of the key points to achieve good performance when using Clouds concerns task scheduling. In particular, there is an important amount of work in this respect in the area of Cloud Computing and distributed systems in general that aim at building schedulers by borrowing notions from Swarm Intelligence (SI), a branch of Artificial Intelligence that comprise models that resemble the collective behavior of decentralized, self-organized systems like ants, bees or birds. Moreover, a recent survey of our own [14] shows that there is little work regarding SI-based schedulers for Cloud Computing. Therefore, we aim at designing a new SI-based scheduler that is capable of efficiently run PSEs. We are also planning to embed the resulting scheduler into CloudSim in order to provide empirical evidence of its effectiveness. Eventually, we could implement the scheduler on top of a real (not simulated) Cloud platform, such as Eucalyptus (http://www.eucalyptus.com).

References

1. Youn, C., Kaiser, T.: Management of a parameter sweep for scientific applications on cluster environments. Concurrency and Computation: Practice and Experience 22, 2381–2400 (2010)
2. Thain, D., Tannenbaum, T., Livny, M.: Distributed computing in practice: The Condor experience. Concurrency and Computation: Practice and Experience 17, 323–356 (2005)
3. Foster, I., Kesselman, C.: The Grid: Blueprint for a New Computing Infrastructure. Morgan Kaufmann Inc., San Francisco (2003)
4. Dikaiakos, M.D., Katsaros, D., Mehra, P., Pallis, G., Vakali, A.: Cloud Computing: Distributed Internet Computing for IT and Scientific Research. IEEE Internet Computing 13(5), 10–13 (2009)
5. Careglio, C., Monge, D., Pacini, E., Mateos, C., Mirasso, A., García Garino, C.: Sensibilidad de resultados del ensayo de tracción simple frente a diferentes tamaños y tipos de imperfecciones. Mecánica Computacional XXIX, 4181–4197 (2010)

6. Calheiros, R.N., Ranjan, R., Beloglazov, A., De Rose, C., Buyya, R.: Cloudsim: a toolkit for modeling and simulation of cloud computing environments and evaluation of resource provisioning algorithms. Software - Practice and Experience 41, 23–50 (2011)
7. Gropp, W., Lusk, E., Skjellum, A.: Using MPI: Portable Parallel Programming with the Message Passing Interface. MIT Press (1994)
8. Erickson, J., Siau, K.: Web Service, Service-Oriented Computing, and Service-Oriented Architecture: Separating hype from reality. Journal of Database Management 19, 42–54 (2008)
9. Wang, L., Tao, J., Kunze, M., Castellanos, A.C., Kramer, D., Karl, W.: Scientific cloud computing: Early definition and experience. In: 10th IEEE International Conference on High Performance Computing and Communications, pp. 825–830 (2008)
10. Alfano, G., Angelis, F.D., Rosati, L.: General Solution procedures in elasto-viscoplasticity. Computer Methods in Applied Mechanics and Engineering 190, 5123–5147 (2001)
11. García Garino, C., Oliver, J.: Un modelo constitutivo para el análisis de sólidos elastoplásticos sometidos a grandes deformaciones: Parte I formulación teórica y aplicación a metales. Revista internacional de métodos numéricos para cálculo y diseño en ingeniería 11, 105–122 (1995) (in Spanish)
12. Ponthot, J., García Garino, C., Mirasso, A.: Large strain viscoplastic constitutive model. Theory and numerical scheme. Mecánica Computacional XXIV, 441–454 (2005)
13. García Garino, C., Gabaldón, F., Goicolea, J.M.: Finite element simulation of the simple tension test in metals. Finite Elements in Analysis and Design 42, 1187–1197 (2006)
14. Pacini, E., Mateos, C., García Garino, C.: Planificadores basados en inteligencia colectiva para experimentos de simulación numérica en entornos distribuidos. In: Sexta Edición del Encuentro de Investigadores y Docentes de Ingeniería ENIDI 2011 (2011)

New Technologies of the Information and Communication: Analysis of the Constructors and Destructors of the European Educational System

Francisco V. Cipolla Ficarra[1, 2], Valeria M. Ficarra[2], and Miguel Cipolla Ficarra[2]

HCI Lab. – F&F Multimedia Communic@tions Corp.
[1] ALAIPO: Asociación Latina de Interacción Persona-Ordenador
[2] AINCI: Asociación Internacional de la Comunicación Interactiva

c/ Angel Baixeras, 5 – AP 1638, 08080 Barcelona, Spain
via Tabajani, 1 – S. 15 – CP 7, 24121 Bergamo, Italy
ficarra@alaipo.com, {info,ficarra}@ainci.com

Abstract. In the current work presents a detailed survey of the state of the art of the elements that boost and hinder the study of the latest technologies in communication and information technologies and their derivations in Southern Europe. Also a first parallelism is drawn with the same studies in the economically developed countries and those which are called emerging. Finally, we present a table of dichotomy heuristic evaluation to evaluate the quality of those components that are called builders and destroyers of the college educational system, which has transited and is still transiting in our days, between the old and the new millennium.

Keywords: Education, ICT, Computer Science, New Mass Media, Sociology.

1 Introduction

The notion of constructors and destructors that we use a reference from the C++ language. C++ is a programming language designed in the mid 80s by Bjarne Stroustrup, in the Bell labs [1]. The intention of its creation was to extend the C programming language with mechanisms that allow the manipulation of objects. In that sense, from the point of view of object oriented languages, C++ is a hybrid language. The name C++ was proposed by Rick Maseim in the year 1983, when the language was used for the first time outside the scientific environment. Formerly the name had been used as "C with classes". In C++ the expression "C++" means "increase of C" [2] [3], and it means that C++ is an extension of C. C++ is a multi-platform language, which has influenced languages such as: Java, LPC, Perl, PHP, etc. Some essential notions which we have used in our heuristic evaluation table deriving from C++ are: objects, constructors, destructors, structures, classes, variables, functions, pointers. In the following we will present a short explanation of these essential notions, but the interested reader can go deeper into them in the following bibliography references [1] [4]. In this context, when we create an object of

F.V. Cipolla-Ficarra et al. (Eds.): ADNTIIC 2011, LNCS 7547, pp. 71–84, 2012.

a class, we always follow the same steps to call a set of methods that initialize the data of the object. In C++ a special function, the constructor, is defined, which is called when a new object of the class. This builder may receive parameters, just like any other function. The most important characteristics of a constructor are:

- The constructor has the same name as the class to which it belongs.
- The constructor doesn't return anything.
- Arguments can be transferred to the constructor in the statement of an object.

When an object of a class is created, the constructor is automatically called. In few words, a constructor is a function. The destructor is very similar to the constructor, except that it is called automatically when each object gets out of its validity field. Let's remember that the automatic variables have a limited scope, since they cease to exist when they get out of the block where they have been declared. When an object is automatically released, its destructor, if it exists, is automatically called. A destructor has the same name as the class to which it belongs. Similar to the constructor, a destructor doesn't give back anything.

These structures were already present in C [2]. Some see them as a class, but without methods (they only store data). Let's suppose that we want to make a listing of the grades of our students. We would need an array of chains to store their names, another for their second names and another for their grades or marks. This may make the program look disorderly and hard to follow. And here is where structures come to our help. The pointers to structures must not point just to any place, we must give it a valid direction to point to. We can't for instance create a pointer to a structure and put in the data directly through a pointer, we don't know where the pointer is pointing, and the data would be stored anywhere. Finally, we have the classes. The main goal of a object oriented language is that several objects may be created which contain the data and the methods to manipulate them. Besides, the programmer can decide whether the data and the methods are visible or not to the rest of the programme. In C++ these objects are implemented through classes.

Some of these concepts have been used in the current work to set down the differences between the structure and the system from a social and educational point of view. Culturally speaking, a structure needs longer for its change than a system. Here is one of the reasons why the changes in the educational systems are more frequent than in the structure, especially in the so called emerging countries. Both notions will be explained in detail in section 2.

With regard to the information and communication technologies it is important to stress that there will always be new changes, since we are immersed in a society where the scientific changes from the technological perspective as a rule go ahead of social changes. In this context, it is better to put the adjective "last" before the adjective "new", because since the democratization of the computers in the late 80s and other devices used in the classrooms just like the slides for the physical geography classes, the recorders for the language lessons, the record players for the music classes, etc., technology has helped the work of the professors. Obviously at those times the computers were scheduled for activities in neighbourhood academies, such as the typing courses or the so-called CAE systems (computer aided education).

Then as now the latest in information and communication technologies does not mean the replacement of the teachers in the classrooms in all the disciplines of the sciences.

However, from the point of view of the training of trainers or professors, in Southern Europe and especially in the Mediterranean coasts, CAE has generated a special phenomenon in the process of training of the future trainers or educators. That is, professionals who haven't gone through the college classrooms, but rather through specialization courses of the regional autonomous governments, where the language knowledge of those regions prevailed over the degrees, diplomas, engineering, etc. and even PhD the future educators might have. That is, the priority knowledge was the local language rather than the knowledge of the subjects to be taught by the professors. A Catalan phenomenon in the 90s which took place with the expansion of the European Union and that to a certain extent entailed protecting the local or national education system. This destructive model of the social-educational structure would widen to other regions, as is the case of some autonomous regions from Northern Italy [5]. In the last decade, they also tend to boost the local dialects. The main destructive aspects are analyzed in section 2.

The work that we present here is structured in the following way: state of the art of the changes of symptoms and structure, the genesis of educational antimodels, the exportation and importation of negative models and the social economic consequences in the ICT (Information and Communication Technologies) field, the first table of heuristic evaluation, conclusions and future lines of work. Each one of these sections is accompanied by real life examples.

2   Differences between Systems and Educational Structures

The same as a program written in C++, generating new structures entails a long previous design task, carried out by the analyst, who together with the programmer and the operators must not only generate it, but also put it in motion, make the modifications and the corresponding maintenance tasks over time [6] [7], so that they do not easily outdate. These are tasks that implicitly entail a key word "planning". A word which traditionally is not held in esteem in a great part of the Latin environment [8]. Currently, due to the global economic factors, also in the Anglo-Saxon environment, they start to rule out this term in many projects related to the educational structures for the young, adults and seniors. Therefore, the educational structures tend to not aim at a higher quality of the contents and at the basis of the educational pyramid. In view of the lack of a direction, the dilemma between private education, public education and mixed education comes into play. This last modality is something peculiar, to be found in places where parochialism has a strong presence. This parochialism makes a public structure be managed and/or ruled by church representatives, as it happens in some French, Italian, Spanish, Portuguese, German provinces, etc., where everything turns around the belfry. The reader who is interested in educational parochialism may widen these notions in the following bibliographical references [1] [9].

In contrast, the system may be considered as the functions that the variables must fulfil that make up the structure in the C++. Now a system may work correctly if it belongs to the structure to which it refers. The educational systems of the different societies, for instance, are made in relation to the context where they are immersed. Evidently, it is positive and correct to talk of the current and future curricula inside computer science, such as [6], [7], [10], but to extrapolate them automatically and without making the necessary adjustments to the Latin American or Asian context, just to mention two geographical examples, will never yield the same results, because they work with different variables. In that sense, those who just devote themselves to "copy and paste" of foreign solutions in the emerging countries are only inserting to the local educational structure systems that will never be able to work correctly as in their place of origin. The reason is simple, those systems were designed for different educational structures. This statement is also valid for those who prior to the global financial crisis and from the economically developed countries tend to impose educational models at thousands of kilometres distance from other cultures from overseas. In this case, these salesmen of international educational systems, under the format of classrooms and virtual campuses, should control whether said campuses have worked correctly in their local communities, seeing the high number of unemployed there are, according to the specialized press of the industrial sector as the following example shows (Il Sole 24 ore: www.ilsole24ore.it –10.30.2011):

Fig. 1. Total number (%) of young people who neither work nor study in Italy in 2011

Fig. 2. Spain's unemployment crisis ranges (almost five million out of work). Newspaper "El País" –www.elpais.com, 10.28.2011.

In these Italian and Spanish examples we see that the data come from information sources with a certain credibility value. Currently there are plenty of works related to the ICT, where figures, percentages, totals, etc. are presented without knowing the veracity of the sources [11] [12]. In this sense during the exponential growth of the Internet in the south of the Mediterranean one of the reliable sources was the EITO (European Information Technology Observatory) [13]. However, starting from the new millennium, many of its studies were based on the realities present of the ICT – related fairs, thus losing one of the main aspects of scientific knowledge: neutrality.

A neutrality which is not feasible in view of the dichotomy between structure and/or public and private system, when the talk focuses on quality or excellence in teaching. Even now in the Latin American countries there is the generalized opinion that educational excellence only exists in the private university sector, for instance. These mistakes usually derive from the parochialism on the other side of the Atlantic which extrapolates mirages and dogmatically imposes functions since they lack the structures they originated from. It is a reality that points to the presence of non-secular universities through different geographical points of the planet, mistakenly thinking that the quality existing in New York in the religious private university, for instance, is the same in Barcelona, Bogotá, Brussels or Panama. However, in those private universities as in some mixed ones, which devote themselves to opening courses related to the new audiovisual technologies, multimedia, virtual reality, computer aided design, etc., do it without any planning, and with merely mercantilist goals. In these European contexts we can find heads of labs of these new technologies with garbage contracts. This name was assigned to this kind of contract in Spain in the 90s, because they are renewed every semester or yearly. That is, private and/or mixed institutions which allegedly invest in the latest technology hardware, investing great sums in publicity campaigns, whether it is in the analog media, such as the traditional specialized press (that is, magazines and papers) as digital (that is, television spots, radio, banners on-line, etc). All of this to attract the future "clients", that is, the students, which exponentially increased the academic slavery of the teaching staff in the ICT sector. For instance, in the late 90s in Barcelona the monthly fee of three multimedia engineering students was tantamount to the salary of the head of a lab, whereas with a monthly fee of a student of those centers two months of the salary of the assistant of the head of the lab were paid. Evidently, study centres are based in all the continents of the planet, but if we take two realities to analyze, New York and Barcelona, the human and social factors inside the ICT sector, the results that are attained in Barcelona are the antimodels of the university educational sector [5] [14] [15] [16].

Obviously, the antimodels in Southern Europe are not an exclusivity of the private sector, they also exist in the public sector, as it will be analyzed in the audiovisual example in the next section. However, all those antimodels of the educational, public, private and mixed sector are destroyers of the systems and structures of the local and global education.

3   Educational Antimodels and Their Exportation through the Latest Technologies

A successful educational model requires variables where all have access to qualitative education, with low costs and if possible, with costs equal to zero for the students, as it happens in many countries of the world. Not for nothing education and healthcare are the two main cornerstones of the communities that are known as developed. However, there is the generalized belief that it is in the private sector where the excellence of the educational models is located. Besides, the equation is applied that the higher the monthly cost of the expenses in studies, the greater the quality in teaching. A way to disguise these costs and justify them in the eyes of those who pay them every month is through the latest information technologies, that is, giving access to their students to the new emerging models of social communication, virtual tutors, etc. However, with the greed to increase the educational structure, widen the educational offer, in many communities of Southern Europe many universities have been opened, such as during the decade of the 90s in Spain. Universities that have not had the time nor the qualified professionals to generate their own model. However, they have counted with financial resources from the European social funds, which have allowed them to temporarily hire professors from other regions of the world for the generation of the curricula, subjects related to the latest technological inventions, problem solving with heterogeneous groups of students in classrooms, etc. under the equation of costs (salaries) and times to solve problems (garbage contracts) which were very low. A first example are the multimedia courses in the Lombardy mixed universities, where the students of literature and foreign languages were mixed with students registered at the dole and who hadn't finished their studies. However, both groups shared the same classroom (name/s and surname/s of the mentor/s of this educational abnormality and/or educational antimodel were hidden with the green color of Lombardy flag):

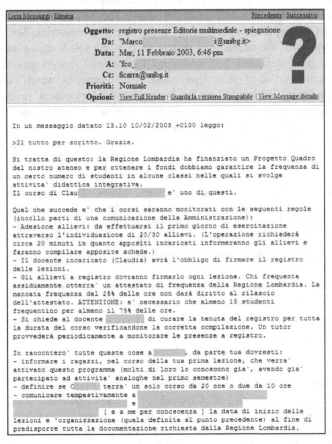

Fig. 3. Mixed of the students (juniors graduated, adults with primary or secondary level, etc.) in a multimedia classroom of Lombardian university (2003), without permission or authorization of the titular professor

A second example is putting the students of the first term of the degree in audiovisual, without previous knowledge in computer science and English, to carry out practically in an autonomous way computer tridimensional animations, with handbooks in English and in less than two months. This was the reality in some mixed or public universities aimed at R&D, ICTs, transfer of technologies, etc. [17] which worked with the subventions of the regional or autonomous government in the 90s, and which still persist in our days [16].

Now the exportation of educational systems in the last two decades has taken place on the basis of the novelty of the technological aspect, instead of the pedagogical aspects. Here it can be seen how the factual sciences take a second place in relation to the formal sciences. For instance, exporting an educational model related to a totally virtual university, for instance, Universitat Oberta de Catalunya (www.uoc.edu), has a greater commercial or marketing value than doing it on virtual classrooms or virtual courses, where even the minimal aspects have been studied and evaluated, both from the theoretical and the practical point of view. The target of these educational antimodels are the populations belonging to the emerging countries. Sometimes part of the components of the educational system such as the self-learning multimedia e-courses, have been designed and developed by analysts, programmers, computer science engineers and/or systems from those same countries which currently call themselves emerging. However, at the moment of development products and/or services are generated for the local users. The opening of those virtual universities towards the emerging countries has taken place at the end of the first decade of the century. The reasons are in the financial crisis that prevents the public universities from getting financial subsidies from Brussels, for instance. In this exportation of models or antimodels there is no real intention of transferring cutting edge knowledge and/or technologies to the target communities, which sometimes share the same language, but which referentially may compete in the educational field, not only at local level, but in the international arena. In few words, sometimes the antimodels that are exported in the educational context are in order to destroy the formation of "future thinking generations", that is, potential competitors in the most varied fields of the sciences.

The diffusion or importation of educational models and antimodels is backed by the social communication media and/or non governative organization: www.alzado.org, www.cadius.org, etc. Realities have a common denominator among the populations and the cultures of the European Mediterranean. Still in Barcelona, there are some antimodels of scientific communication stemming from the Catalan context which join the Italians, since from the public universities a control of the social communication media is exerted. An example of this will be found in a program of social research of Channel 3 "Pressa Diretta" from the RAI (Radiotelevisione Italiana) with the date 02.10.2011 where a journalist is invited to explain the alleged wonders of the current ICT sector in Catalonia through the Italians who have migrated to Catalonia to work [18], when in fact Spain has the highest rate of unemployment in the EU in 2011 (see figure 2) The interested readers may look up on-line the whole program in Italian. In those audiovisual narratives we have Italians who are allegedly responsable of the "Barcelona Super Computing Center" whose supercomputer (so-called "Mare Nostrum") is installed in a church chapel of the Tower Girona (Barcelona Computer Faculty of the Universitat Politécnica de Catalunya –UPC). In the decade of the 90s in that computing faculty the European students couldn't finish their PhDs because after passing the doctorate courses, they had difficulties overcoming the research proficiency issues related with multimedia, since they were declared lacking in interest in the computer science department. Besides, in that faculty the locals got a PhD in computing in the record time of three years, whereas the Latin Americans came back home without the degree. The few fortunate took a decade in receiving the PhD. Besides, in that special program of the RAI it could be seen how the Catalan printed press also contributed to spread working mirages of the ICT through another Italian journalist who is a steady staffer of the newspaper "La Vanguardia" (www.lavanguardia.com) . When in reality in Catalonia in the 90s there was no trade union section of the press that represented the thousands of journalists who worked as collaborators, directly without working contracts. Another sector that is also approached in that special television program is the editorial sector,. In short, there are some information systems that constantly distort the reality of ICT, from the university environment (public, private and mixed) and which involve both traditional communication media and the emerging communication media in the network.

Fig. 4. A scientific "mirage" from job sector in Barcelona Computer Faculty of the Universitat Politécnica de Catalunya –UPC, http://www.rai.tv/dl/RaiTV/programmi/media/ContentItem-f6aa9f48-95fe-483b-a263-f6207f3b98a3.html#p=0 –access 11.11.2011

Leaving aside those examples of antimodels, we find original research works coming from the other side of the European borders. Those works draw the models to be followed in the immediate future in the sector of the new technologies, including the software sector, for instance [19-21]. In that research there are reflections on the practices of the future students, the transfer of bidirectional technology among colleges, and the productive sector of goods and services, the syllabus, the academic curricula of the professors, the insertion of other environments of the formal and factual sciences in keeping with the evolution of the societies and the labour market, etc. The keyword of these research works is originality. An originality that sometimes is not to be found in a myriad similar works in Southern Europe because the more financial subsidies they get from the EU, the more they resort to copy and paste, lessening the creativity present in the educational centres, inside and outside the classrooms. There are research and academic modi operandi which are different at both sides of the Atlantic Ocean. That is, there are those professionals of the ICT and its derivations which work in agreement with the epistemological principles of the sciences. They counterbalance those who are only interested in the political aspect exercised through those new technologies. This political aspect which can be measured in the amount of international agreements signed among different universities, for instance.

In short, scientific realities which play the role of constructors and destructors of the diffusion of the knowledge among the population and which need to be measured periodically to introduce the necessary structural and systemic changes, tending to increase the quality of living of the population.

4   Table of Heuristic Evaluation of Constructors and Destroyers

The table below is the result of the direct observation carried out during decades in American and European universities. In our case we will focus on the main aspects related to the systems and educational structures of Southern Europe. In some specific cases, parallels will be drawn to the systems and structures of other continents. The table is made up by an attribute and an example. These attributes stand for quality. They have a positive sign if they are constructors, and a negative if they are destructors. In the cases where there are both signs, it means that they depend on the human factor rather than on the technological factor. Besides, a communicability expert may turn these attributes into quality metrics and attain heuristically quantifiable results of the systems and educational structures where the study is made. Next the listing of the components, following the alphabetic order:

- Adaptability of the university contents to the social evolution (+). It is important that there is a constant interrelation among the formal and the factual sciences in the context where these develop. That is, that the requirements of society towards the future professionals that will join it once they finish their studies are taken into account. For instance, if in the 90s a many similar universities from the structural point of view were opened, from Perpignan (France) to Cadiz (Spain), in the face of the global crisis, the merger among them or their temporary closure would be in order.
- Clearness of the systems and the structure (+). The main variables and functions that constitute the educational structures and systems are not presented through the new technologies and ometimes use simple plagiarisms or rehashes from other universities. For instance, the complete programmes, with their matching bibliographies and professors, related to the masters, specialization courses, continuous training, etc., are not published integrally in the portals of the Southern Europe colleges. This opacity in the education system is a common practice in the following universities: UAB (Universitat Autònoma of Barcelona), UdL (Universitat of Lleida), UdG (Universitat of Girona), UIB (Universitat de les Illes Balears), UPF (Pompeu Fabra University), etc. In contrast, the transparency in

Australia or New Zeland universities is a common denominator in this kind of educational offer.

- Continuity in the research lines (+). The constitution of research teams and the allocation of financial resources entails a logical direction of the research in the short, mid and long term. Often, once the financial resources to finance projects in local, provincial, regional funds are attained, those projects are given up in the short or mid term. However, the heads of the projects and their collaborators constantly resort to the local mass media for self-promotion as scientists, but then they disappear when those projects are parked or abandoned.

- Creativity in the transformation of technologies and the results of the university research in the community (+). This transformation does not happen mechanically or automatically, it needs innovation in order to generate new products and/or services in a fast, economic and competitive way. For instance, there are centennial Lombardy textile industries with a turnover of nine digit number amounts in euros, but they haven't invested in R&D labs in their premises. The local industrial model allows them to use the college labs for their own profits, at a zero cost. Besides, the transfer "sui generis" of the industry towards the local university consists in influencing the curriculum of masters programs of the textile sector or the participation of employees as instructors who present themselves as great expert in new information technologies and communication, although their knowledge in ICT is equal to zero.

- Equality between formal and factual sciences (+). The interrelations between both sciences should tend towards a balance of human and economic resources. For instance, in some mixed or private universities exists a trend to open ICT labs without technological resources available for all the participants in the courses. This action of opening courses without resources is a result of the prevalence of the mercantilist factor over the scientific factor.

- Originality of the educational offer (+). The diversification of the disciplines in the college classrooms, where the scientific premises that boost innovation in the training of professionals are followed. That is, professionals who may approach varied problems from a 360° vision. In this sense it is necessary to point out that the universality of knowledge must serve to widen the specialization fields making always a difference between transdisciplinarity, multidisciplinarity and interdisciplinarity. For instance, universality is not synonymous with humanism, as many experts claim in Southern Europe. Universality inside the ICTs entails an intersection of knowledge of the formal and factual sciences.

- Plurality of nations in the university structure (+). The wealth of the different cultures boosts the adaptability of the future professionals towards the global work market. For example the linguistic barriers posed by dialects or regional languages in Europe prevent the training of professionals for globalization in the new millennium.

- Purpose of the educational activities (+/-). Sometimes the task of training the future generations is secondary in college politics. For instance, the diffusion of educational antimodels in the American continent is due to the agreements signed among the universities, allegedly because there is an interchange of students from theoretical towards practical environments with last generation technologies.

However, in those technological environments there is a lack of the theoretical basis of their models or original software.

- Width of the educational coverage and influences (+/-). The educational coverage refers to the geographic aspect which covers the teaching of a university, whether it is through the classrooms and e-learning through the new technologies. The influences also refer to the geographic aspects, but related to the social or geopolitical factors that expand the covering. For instance, a Lombardy nuclear professional may have an influence in many R&D projects related to the latest communication and information technologies, not only   across the Italian peninsula, but also for example in Switzerland, or the south and north of the Mediterranean Sea.
- Working stability of the educational staff (+). The hiring of the professor is temporary or stable (undetermined time). For instance, the lack of working stability of the professionals with experience and high academic training denotes the presence of what we could call "personality duplicators", through the cloning of the academic curricula [22]. That is, to hire temporarily professionals in order to later generate their clones and be able to use for decades the knowledge of the temporarily hired staff.

The enumerated attributes are the main cornerstones of the educational structure which sometimes were strengthened by the constructors and weakened by the destructors. Evidently, this represents a first set and can be complemented in future research.

5   Learned Lessons and Future Works

The quality attributes which are enumerated in the table are the starting point of work that will evolve over time, through the generation of quality metrics, analysis of each of the attributes in its components or primitives which may be quantifiable. It is a task that a communicability expert can perfectly develop, which doesn't require special labs, nor great sums of money to conduct research which in the end will serve to increase the quality of education.

Defining systems and educational structures in the ICTs sector is not an easy task, because they require great financial resourcesto be in the technological avant-garde as well as to have highly qualified staff available. The solution planned in the emerging countries is relying on international agreements among universities and the interchange of experts. Contesting the validity of those agreements for being mistaken from the point of view of the balance in the knowledge and/or experience exchange, is technically impossible once they are signed. Sometimes the educational model of the emerging populations is superior compared to those that are theoretically developed. For instance, the recently founded universities in Southern Europe, even if they possess the latest technologies and sufficient financial resources, are still learning from the universities with several centuries of history inside and outside the European borders. The reason of that learning is simple: they lack and educational model of their own. Working it out requires time, and vast human and financial resources.

Evidently, many centennial universities have had excellent educational models, which have been exported all along the national geography and even cloned abroad.

Now from a technological perspective and due to the digital gap in the population, in the public centennial universities, located in Latin America, as a rule their students have no access to the latest software commercial applications, or the new hardware models. A factor that may level those technological shortcomings are the curricula. Public universities whose curricula enable their students from the early courses of computer and/or systems engineering to acquire knowledge, skills, and abilities to set up a personal computer starting from the basic components. Once they have installed those computers, they know how to program C++ applications, for instance. Obviously, this educational reality outside the EU is not so favourable to the marketing or international publicity image as it can be done with some courses in Southern Europe, related to computer aided design, multimedia, virtual reality, microcomputing, multimedia mobile phones, videogames, etc., where the students are mere users of cutting edge commercial applications or consumers of microcomputing hardware or multimedia mobile phones. Sometimes the destructors of the ICT originate from the marketing policies of the three kinds of universities that we have mentioned in the current work and which turn the national or international educational system into a simple consumer product. Now the equation to a greater educational cost, greater educational quality is totally false, because the destroyers also exist in the private and mixed environments of education.

6   Conclusion

Resorting to statistic data of ICT without knowing the veracity of the sources is a fashion which may seriously harm the efforts that are made by scientists in the daily search of the intersections between the formal and the factual sciences. Besides, a non-statistic language may be positive in the tasks of systems building and solid structures in the current and future education. In this sense we need to aim at an objective language and avoid the mercantilism which is made of education in the private or mixed university institutions, for instance. In that direction, a programming language has a set of rules which have to be fulfilled so that the applications work in a correct way. The use of constructors and destructors of C++ has allowed to classify a first set of quality attributes aimed at university teaching which should be kept along time. Evidently, the contextual and human factor influences sometimes in a positive way and many other times in a negative way. In the current work onlysome of them have been presented in the table, but this could be subject of deeper analysis applying notions from social psychology, sociology, the cultural systems and pedagogy, just to mention a few examples.

Acknowledgments. A special thanks to Maria Ficarra (ALAIPO & AINCI), Pamela Fulton (ALAIPO & AINCI), Mary Brie (Blue Herons Editions), and Carlos for their helps.

References

1. Stroustrup, B.: The C++ Programming Language. Pearson, Indianapolis (2000)
2. Kernighan, B., Ritchie, D.: C Programming Language. Pretince Hall, Uppler Saddle River (1988)

3. Cipolla-Ficarra, F.: C, el lenguaje de las virtudes. Autocad Magazine 23(2), 28–31 (1993) (in Spanish)
4. Schildt, H.: C++ the Complete Reference. McGraw-Hill/Osborne Media, Berkeley (2002)
5. Cipolla-Ficarra, et al.: Quality and Communicability for Interactive Hypermedia Systems: Concepts and Practices for Design. IGI Global, Hershey (2010)
6. Petrenko, M., et al.: Teaching Software Evolution in Open Source. IEEE Computer 40(11), 25–31 (2007)
7. Frezza, S., Tang, M., Brinkman, B.: Creating an Accreditable Software Engineering Bachelor's Program. IEEE Software 23(6), 27–35 (2006)
8. Cipolla Ficarra, F.V., Ficarra, V.M.: Software Managment Applications, Textile CAD and Human Factors: A Dreadful Industrial Example for Information and Communication Technology. In: Cipolla Ficarra, F.V., de Castro Lozano, C., Pérez Jiménez, M., Nicol, E., Kratky, A., Cipolla-Ficarra, M. (eds.) ADNTIIC 2010. LNCS, vol. 6616, pp. 121–131. Springer, Heidelberg (2011)
9. Cipolla-Ficarra, F.: Persuasion On-Line and Communicability: The Destruction of Credibility in the Virtual Community and Cognitive Models. Nova Publishers, New York (2010)
10. Vliet, H.: Reflections on Software Engineering Education. IEEE Software 23(3), 55–61
11. Balsamo, A.: Designing Culture: The Technological Imagination at Work. Duke University Press, Dirham (2011)
12. Scolari, C.: Hipermediaciones. Elementos para una Teoría de la Comunicación Digital Interactiva. Gedisa, Barcelona (2008) (in Spanish)
13. Lamborghini, B.: European Information Technology Observatory. EITO-EEIG, Frankfurt (2001)
14. Cipolla-Ficarra, et al.: Advances in Dynamic and Static Media for Interactive Systems: Communicability, Computer Science and Design. Blue Herons Editions, Barcelona (2011)
15. Cipolla-Ficarra, et al.: Computational Informatics, Social Factors and New Information Technologies: Hypermedia Perspectives and Avant-Garde Experiences in the Era of Communicability Expansion. Blue Herons Editions, Bergamo (2011)
16. Cipolla-Ficarra, F., Kratky, A.: Computer Graphics for Students of the Factual Sciences. In: Proc. First International Symposium Communicability, Computer Graphics and Innovative Design for Interactive Systems, CCGIDIS 2011. Springer, Berlin (2011) (in press)
17. Cipolla-Ficarra, F., Nicol, E., Cipolla-Ficarra, M.: Vademecum for Innovation through Knowledge Transfer: Continuous Training in Universities, Enterprises and Industries. In: Innovation through Knowledge, Transfer 2010, pp. 139–149. Springer, Berlin (2011)
18. Cucchiarato, C.: Vivo altrove. Mondadori, Milano (2010) (in Italian)
19. Roble, D., Zafar, N.: Don't Trust Your Eyes: Cutting-Edge Visual Effects. IEEE Computer 42(7), 33–41 (2009)
20. Cantrill, S.: Computers in Patient Care: The Promise and the Challenge. Communications of the ACM 53(9), 42–47 (2010)
21. McFarland, D., Wolpaw, J.: Brain-Computer Interfaces for Communication and Control. Communications of the ACM 54(5), 60–66 (2011)
22. Cipolla-Ficarra, F.V., Cipolla-Ficarra, M., Ficarra, V.M.: Copyright for Interactive Systems: Stratagems for Tourism and Cultural Heritage Promotion. In: Cipolla Ficarra, F.V., de Castro Lozano, C., Nicol, E., Kratky, A., Cipolla-Ficarra, M. (eds.) HCITOCH 2010. LNCS, vol. 6529, pp. 136–147. Springer, Heidelberg (2011)

A Multi-agent Model That Promotes Team-Role Balance in Computer Supported Collaborative Learning

Rubén Fares and Rosanna Costaguta

Departamento de Informática, Facultad de Ciencias Exactas y Tecnologías (FCEyT)
Universidad Nacional de Santiago del Estero (UNSE)
Avda. Belgrano (S) 1912, Santiago del Estero, 4200, Argentina
estebanfares@hotmail.com, rosanna@unse.edu.ar

Abstract. Organizing students in groups does not guarantee their learning. The behaviors that student show while solving a task in a computer-supported collaborative environment, that is, the roles they play, are vital to reach teaching and learning goals successfully. In this context, we present a multi-agent model that monitors students' participation in a group, recognizes their team roles as they work collaboratively, automatically builds their profiles, diagnoses the state of the collaboration considering balance of team roles as an ideal situation, and proposes corrective actions when the group behavior is far from this ideal. The proposed model will be developed in the context of an e-learning environment and will be validated using real groups of students working collaboratively.

Keywords: Computer Supported Collaborative Learning, Team Roles, Team Role Balance, Intelligent Agents, Collaboration Profiles.

1 Introduction

Collaborative learning (CL) describes a situation in which certain types of interactions among people that promote their learning are expected, although not guaranteed [12]. The use of computational tools in the collaborative learning area originated new teaching and learning scenarios and research opportunities in Computer-Supported Collaborative Learning (CSCL), with the goal of facilitating collaboration and communication with new technologies. CSCL was soon adopted by the e-learning community because students become independent of the time and space variables. Thus, in a CSCL system, students can work collaboratively while situated in distant locations and even contributing in different times.

In CSCL the concept of group is fundamental. A group is a dynamic set of students that work together, discussing some topic, to eventually achieve some predefined goal [6], where each student is responsible for his/her actions, but they work together on the same problem or exercise accepting the abilities and contributions of the other members. On the other hand, forming groups and encouraging their members to work collaboratively is not enough to guarantee neither collaborative learning nor carrying out the tasks in a coordinate and efficient manner.

F.V. Cipolla-Ficarra et al. (Eds.): ADNTIIC 2011, LNCS 7547, pp. 85–91, 2012.

In a learning group it is essential that members perform different functions or roles that allow for a coordinated and collaborative learning and achieve success. A role is defined as a tendency to behave, contribute and interrelate with others in a particular way [2]. While the behaviors or roles of an individual in a team can be infinite, the range of useful behaviors that make a real contribution to the team is finite [3]. There are nine different roles to be manifested by the members of a group that affect the effectiveness of the work. These roles are: Plant, Implementer, Team Worker, Finisher, Coordinator, Shaper, Resource Investigator, Monitor Evaluator, and Specialist [2]. As a result of her investigations, Belbin [2] proposes a classification based on nine team roles, which has been widely used. Belbin also argues [3] that only when an adequate balance of roles is achieved within a group, this group will carry out task in a coordinate fashion. This balance appears when we can find most of the roles present in a group, and these roles are not repeated among team members.

The success or failure of the learning experience depends, among other things, on the roles that each team member is capable of playing. However, when a team can balance the appearance of these roles, the successful achievement of a coordinated work is guaranteed [3]. Thus, it emerges a need to identify the roles that effectively each of the members of a group shows, and diagnosing the current state of collaboration in order to intervene at the right time, promoting a balance of roles and successful collaborative learning.

Many systems record users' behavioral characteristics when they interact with others. One of the most widely used approaches to do this is using intelligent agent technology [7, 16, 17]. The intelligent agent paradigm aims at designing and developing entities that can act in an autonomous and rational way [11, 13]. There are several types of agents. We will concentrate on interface agents, which capture users' interests in a non intrusive way and record this information by building a user model or user profile [13].

In the context mentioned before, this research seeks to answer the following question: Is it possible to create a multi-agent model in the field of CSCL, able both to recognize the roles that students show while working in a group, as to intervene with corrective action when roles do not manifest properly? Consequently, we propose the creation of a multi-agent model capable of analyzing the interactions among students in a CSCL system, diagnosing the state of collaboration evaluating the roles played by group members, and proposing corrective actions to achieve a team role balance.

This article is organized as follows. Section 2 describes our proposed approach. Section 3 discusses some related works. Finally, section 4 shows our conclusions and future work.

2   Proposed Approach

The multi-agent approach presented in this paper aims to monitor, evaluate and improve the collaborative process of the students as they develop a computer mediated activity in a collaborative way. Our approach considers the existence of a shared workspace where students submit their contributions while working in groups.

For each group of students there are two kinds of artificial agents: a group agent that recognizes the balance of roles, and several personal agents, one for each student who makes up the computer (Figure 1).

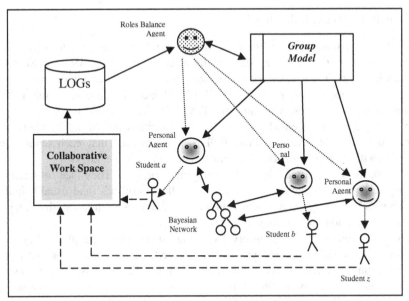

Fig. 1. Proposed Multi-agent Approach

The structure chosen to model the dialogue between the students in each discussion group will be discussion trees, where the original exercise or task proposed by the teacher will be the root node of the tree, from which new branches will be incorporated as students propose new ideas or discuss different alternatives or solutions. The participation of students will be carried out using opening sentences, i.e. they will select from the interface the phrase with which they want to start their contribution to the dialogue and then continue writing free text [18]. With the help of a Psychologist we will identify communication patterns most frequently used by students to determine each of the roles proposed by Belbin [2]. This will define the set of opening sentences to implement at the interface. During experimentation all the student interactions originated during their group work will be stored. A group agent, the Roles Balance Agent, will review these interactions to update the group model. This agent will diagnose the state of collaboration and determine whether any intervention is needed to balance the roles expressed by group members. When this occurs, the Roles Balance Agent will notify the Personal Agent of each student in the group. These Personal agents, considering the information contained in the group model and in a Bayesian network designed specifically, will recognize the corrective actions to be implemented to promote team role balance in the group. This Bayesian network and the corrective actions will be defined with the advice of a Psychologist. This proposal corresponding to the highest category presented in [9], is this, the CSCL systems that perform recommendations.

In the following sections we describe two of the main characteristics of our approach: the team role model we will use and the main concepts related to Bayesian networks.

2.1 Belbin's Team Role Model

In the Belbin's team role model there are nine roles: *Plant, Implementer, Team Worker, Finisher, Coordinator, Shaper, Resource Investigator, Monitor Evaluator,* and *Specialist* [2]. These roles are categorized in three kinds: action oriented, people oriented, and thought oriented [2, 3]. While Shaper, Implementer, and Finisher are action oriented roles, Coordinator, Team Worker and Resource Investigator are considered people oriented roles, and Plant, Specialist and Monitor Evaluator are defined like thought oriented roles. Belbin also affirmed that each team role is expressed with typical behavioral, presenting characteristic weaknesses.

The *Shapers* are dynamic and extroverted people. They see obstacles as challenges, enjoy stimulating others, consider all possibilities, and usually find the best approaches to problems. Their potential weaknesses may be that they are argumentative, and that they may offend people's feelings.

The *Implementers* are conservative and disciplined people. They work systematically, efficiently and very well organized, performing actions and plans. Their potential weaknesses may be that they are inflexible and resistant to change.

The *Finishers* are perfectionist people. They dislike errors or omissions, pay attention to details; and they are very concerned with deadlines. Their potential weaknesses may be that they not delegate job and they worry unnecessarily.

The *Coordinators* are traditionally team-leaders people. They guide the team, they are able to recognize the value of each team member; they are calm, good listeners, and also able delegate tasks very effectively. Their potential weaknesses may be that they tend to be manipulative and they delegate away too much personal responsibility.

The *Team Workers* are negotiators. They provide support and make sure that the team is working together. They are flexible, diplomatic, perceptive, and popular. Their potential weaknesses may be that they are indecisive and usually maintain uncommitted positions during discussions.

The *Resource Investigators* are innovative and curious people. They are enthusiastic, outgoing, extroverted, receptive to ideas, and are able to identify and work with external stakeholders, explore available options, develop contacts, and negotiate for resources. Their potential weaknesses may be that they lose enthusiasm quickly and are also overly optimistic.

The *Plants* are creative and innovator people. They are introverted, prefer to work alone, and dislike the criticism. Their potential weaknesses may be that they are poor communicators and can tend to ignore given parameters and constraints.

The *Monitor Evaluators* are critical thinkers perceived as unemotional people. They are best to analyze and evaluate ideas of other people, are very strategic in their approaches, carefully weigh the pros and cons of all the options before coming to a decision. Their potential weaknesses may be that they are poor motivators.

The *Specialists* are people with specialized knowledge. They work to maintain their professional status, within the team are be considered experts. Their potential weaknesses may be that limit their contribution and tend to think in technicalities.

The Belbin's Team Roles Model can be used in several ways, to analyze the group, as a guide to develop team's strengths, and to manage its weaknesses in several ways. In this work we will use it to reach team balance.

2.2 Bayesian Networks

Bayesian networks, also known as causal networks, are one of the techniques from Artificial Intelligence commonly used to model uncertain domains. A Bayesian network consists of a set of nodes that represent variables of interest, and directed arcs connecting these nodes represent the causal relationships between variables [8]. Each node in a Bayesian network can take different states, depending on the values that the variable representing that node can take. The basic concept in the treatment of uncertainty in Bayesian networks are the conditional probabilities. For each child node the model specifies the probability of each of its states based on the possible combination of states of their parent nodes. There are different ways to obtain the values for these probabilities: they can be specified by an expert in the domain considered, they can be obtained from statistical information, or they can be calculated from a dataset using a machine learning algorithm. Also, each independent node has an associated probability, called evidence or marginal likelihood, which corresponds to a simple or unconditional probability.

Inference mechanisms in Bayesian networks are based on Bayes' Theorem, which allows us to infer the state of a given variable depending on the status of any combination of other variables in the network [8]. In this paper, a Bayesian network created specifically for the balance of roles agent, will define what intervention strategy to implement in order for the group to reach the desired balance of roles.

3   Related Works

We will mention four CSCL systems that could be linked to this proposal, as they give advise based on the analysis of interactions recorded: COLER [4]; aLFanet [14] DEGREE [1] and SAVER [5]. However, none of them considers the roles played by students. On the other hand, there are few research-oriented studies of team roles in CSCL. In [19] the authors discuss two experiments carried out to determine the roles that appear in CSCL, distinguishing between functional and nonfunctional roles. The authors conclude that there is a better performance in groups that highlight the functional roles. In [15] the authors discussed the influence of student characteristics, and group tasks, on the knowledge acquired by groups in CSCL. The authors demonstrate there is a greater influence on the characteristics of the tasks, with the roles as one of the characteristics considered. In [10] researchers apply data mining techniques (clustering) to analyze the interactions recorded in CSCL sessions and discover key roles. In the literature we studied, no records were found associated with the use of Artificial Intelligence techniques applied to promote the balance of roles in groups of CSCL.

4   Conclusion

This article proposes the creation of a multi-agent model that promotes team roles balance in groups in order to achieve successful learning. Note that the originality of this proposal lies both in the use of interface agents to diagnose the state of the collaboration in the group considering the roles expressed by the members, as well as the use of other agents capable of intervening in time for the group to reach role balance.

At the time of writing the research is still under development. The proposed model will be implemented on a distance learning environment. To validate its functionality, we will carry out experiments with real students who will use the system in collaborative work sessions planned by teachers in the Department of Information Technology (FCEyT - UNSE).

References

1. Barros, B., Verdejo, M.: Analysing student interaction processes in order to improve collaboration. The DEGREE approach. International Journal of Artificial Intelligence in Education 11 (2000)
2. Belbin, M.: Team Roles at Work, 2nd edn. Butterworth-Heinemann, Oxford (1996)
3. Belbin, M.: Managing without Power. Butterworth-Heinemann, Oxford (2001)
4. Constantino Gonzalez, M., Suthers, D., Escamilla de los Santos, J.: Coaching Web-based Collaborative Learning based on Problem Solution Differences and Participation. International Journal of Artificial Intelligence in Education 13 (2003)
5. Costaguta, R., Amandi, A.: Training Collaboration Skills to Improve Group Dynamics. In: ACM Proc. Euro American Conference on Telematics and Information Systems, Brasil (2008)
6. Delgado, A., Olguín, C., Ricarte, I.: Monitoring Learners Activities in a Collaborative Environment. In: Proc. 7th IEEE International Workshop on Groupware, Germany (2001)
7. Godoy, D., Schiaffino, S., Amandi, A.: Interface agents personalizing Web-based tasks. Special Issue on Intelligent Agents and Data Mining for Cognitive Systems, Cognitive Systems Research Journal 5(3), 207–222 (2004)
8. Jensen, F.: An introduction to Bayesian Networks. UCL Press, London (1998)
9. Jermann, P., Soller, A., Mühlenbrock, M.: From Mirroring to Guiding: A Review of State of Art Technology for Supporting Collaborative Learning. In: Proc. 1st European Conference on Computer Supported Collaborative Learning, pp. 324–331 (2001)
10. Liao, J., Li, Y., Chen, P., Huang, R.: Using Data Mining as Strategy for Discovering User Roles in CSCL. In: IEEE Proc. 8th Int. Conference on Advanced Learning Technologies, Spain (2008)
11. Maes, P.: Agents that reduce work and information overload. Communication of the ACM 37(7) (2004)
12. Maisonneuve, J.: La dinámica de los grupos. Nueva Visión, Buenos Aires (1998) (in Spanish)
13. Nwana, H.: Software Agents: An Overview. Knowledge Engineering Review 11(3) (1996)
14. Santos, O., Barrera, C., Gaudioso, E., Boticario, J.: ALFANET: An adaptive e-learning platform. In: Proc. 2nd International Meeting on Multimedia and Information and Communication Technologies in Education, pp. 1938–1942 (2003)

15. Schellens, T., Van Keer, H., Valcke, M., De Wever, B.: The Impact of role Assignment as Scripting Tool on Knowledge Construction in Asynchronous Discussion Groups. In: ACM Proc. 2005 Conference on Computer Support for Collaborative Learning, Taiwan (2005)
16. Schiaffino, S., Garcia, P., Amandi, A.: eTeacher: Providing personalized assistance to e-learning students. Computers and Education 51(4), 1744–1754 (2008)
17. Schiaffino, S., Amandi, A.: Building an expert travel agent as a software agent. Expert Systems with Applications 36(2), 1291–1299 (2009)
18. Soller, A.: Supporting Social Interaction in an Intelligent Collaborative Learning System. International Journal of Artificial Intelligence in Education 12, 40–62 (2001)
19. Strijbos, J., de Laat, M., Martens, R., Jochems, W.: Functional versus Spontaneous Roles during CSCL. In: ACM Proc. 2005 Conference on Computer Support for Collaborative Learning, Taiwan (2005)

A Memetic Algorithm for Collaborative Learning Team Formation in the Context of Software Engineering Courses

Virginia Yannibelli[1,2] and Analía Amandi[1,2]

[1] ISISTAN Research Institute, UNCPBA, Tandil, Buenos Aires, Argentina
[2] CONICET, Consejo Nacional de Investigaciones Científicas y Técnicas, Argentina
{vyannibe,amandi}@exa.unicen.edu.ar

Abstract. In this paper, we propose a memetic algorithm with the aim of assisting professors when forming collaborative learning teams in the context of software engineering courses. This algorithm designs different alternatives to divide a given number of students into teams and evaluates each alternative as regards one of the grouping criteria most analyzed and appropriate in the context of software engineering courses. This criterion is based on taking into account the team roles of the students and on forming well-balanced teams according to the team roles of their members. To analyze the performance of the proposed algorithm, we report the computational experiments developed on eight different data sets. In this respect, the algorithm has obtained high-quality solutions for each one of the utilized data sets.

Keywords: Collaborative Learning, Learning Team Formation, Team Roles, Memetic Algorithms.

1   Introduction

Professors of software engineering courses generally divide students into collaborative learning teams to perform different collaborative learning tasks. This kind of tasks requires students to work together to solve problems, discover information, and complete software projects. In this context, the grouping criterion (i.e., the criterion to form learning teams) is relevant since the way in which a team is made up affects the learning level and the social behavior of the students belonging to the team as well as the performance of the team [3, 4, 5, 6, 2].

In the literature, one of the most analyzed grouping criteria in the context of software engineering courses is the grouping criterion recommended by the Belbin's team role model [10, 11]. This criterion is based on taking into account the team roles of the students and on forming well-balanced teams according to the team roles of their members. A team role is the way in which a person tends to behave, contribute and interrelate with others throughout a collaborative task. The Belbin's model [10, 11] defines nine team roles and balance conditions. Different works that employed the Belbin's model [10, 11] to study teams of students tasking software engineering group

F.V. Cipolla-Ficarra et al. (Eds.): ADNTIIC 2011, LNCS 7547, pp. 92–103, 2012.
© Springer-Verlag Berlin Heidelberg 2012

projects showed that considering the Belbin's roles [10, 11] can impact positively on the performance of the teams and on the learning level and the social behavior of the students [9, 7], and can provide a prediction of the performance of the teams based on the composition of the roles within the teams [8]. Besides, the grouping criterion recommended by the Belbin's model [10, 11] has been widely used in training activities by many organizations, consulting firms and executive education programs [12, 13, 14, 15, 16, 17, 18].

However, the formation of well-balanced collaborative learning teams according to the team roles of their members is a task requiring a considerable amount of time, effort and knowledge of the team roles of the students and the formation of well-balanced teams. Therefore, it is valuable to assist professors when forming collaborative learning teams. In this line of thought, the aim of automatically forming learning teams is to build teams efficiently (i.e., the time required by automation is shorter than the time required by professors) and effectively (i.e., wrong decisions are minimized when all the available knowledge of the team roles of the students and the formation of well-balanced teams is considered). Through automation it is thus possible to considerably reduce the workload of professors and optimize the formation of collaborative learning teams.

In this paper, we address the problem of forming collaborative learning teams automatically in the context of software engineering courses. As part of the problem, we consider that teams must be made up in such a way that the balance among the team roles of their members is maximized. This grouping criterion is defined on the basis of the model proposed by Belbin [10, 11] and the balance conditions established by this author. To the best of our knowledge, the criterion considered in this paper has not been considered in previous works that address the problem of forming collaborative learning teams automatically.

To solve the problem, we propose a memetic algorithm. The memetic algorithms are a kind of hybrid evolutionary algorithms where evolutionary-based search is augmented by the addition of one or more phases of local search [20].

We have decided to propose a memetic algorithm because the problem addressed in this paper is an NP-Hard optimization problem and the memetic algorithms have been proved to be effective and efficient when resolving a wide variety of NP-Hard optimization problems [19, 20].

The rest of the paper is organized as follows. Section 2 presents a description of the problem addressed. Section 3 describes the memetic algorithm designed to solve the problem. Section 4 presents the computational experiments carried out to evaluate the memetic algorithm and an analysis of the results obtained. Section 5 presents related works. Finally, Section 6 presents the conclusions of this work.

2   Problem Description

A class S is made up of n students, $S = \{s_1, s_2, ..., s_n\}$. The professor must divide the n students into g teams, $G = \{G_1, G_2, ..., G_g\}$. Each G_i team is made up of a z_i number of member students, and each student can only belong to one team. As regards team size, students must be divided in such a way that the g teams have a similar number of students each. Specifically, the difference between the size of a team and the size of the other teams must not exceed one. The values of the terms S, n and g are known.

As regards the students, they naturally assume or play different roles when taking part in a collaborative task. A role is the way in which a person tends to behave, contribute and interrelate with others throughout a collaborative task. In relation to the roles that can be played by the students, the nine roles defined in Belbin's model [10, 11] are taken into account in this work. Table 1 shows the nine roles and a brief description of the features of each. Belbin [10, 11] considers that each person has a preference level for each role, and in this sense, defines four preference levels: low, average, high and very high. The preference level indicates how naturally a person can play a given role. Then, Belbin [10, 11] considers that if a person has a high or very high preference level for a given role, that person is capable of playing that role naturally. Furthermore, Belbin [10, 11] points out that a person can play one or several roles naturally.

Table 1. Belbin's role characteristics

Role	Characteristics
Plant (PL)	Creative, imaginative, unorthodox. Solves difficult problems.
Resource Investigator (RI)	Extrovert, enthusiastic, communicative. Explore opportunities. Develops contacts.
Co-ordinator (CO)	Mature, confident, a good chairperson. Clarifies goals, promotes decision-making, delegates well.
Shaper (SH)	Challenging, dynamic, thrives on pressure. Has the drive and courage to overcome obstacles.
Monitor Evaluator (ME)	Sober, strategic and discerning. Sees all options. Judges accurately.
Teamworker (TW)	Co-operative, mild, perceptive and diplomatic. Listens, builds, averts friction.
Implementer (IM)	Disciplined, reliable, conservative and efficient. Turns ideas into practical actions.
Completer/Finisher (CF)	Painstaking, conscientious, anxious. Searches out errors and omissions. Polishes and perfects.
Specialist (SP)	Single-minded, self-starting, dedicated. Provides knowledge and skills in key areas.

According to Belbin's model [10, 11], each student naturally plays one or several of the nine roles described in Table 1. In this respect, the roles naturally played by each student are known data. These roles are obtained through the Belbin Team-Role Self-Perception Inventory (BTRSPI) developed by Belbin [10, 11]. The BTRSPI determines the preferred team roles of the persons by giving them self-evaluation tests [10, 11].

As part of the problem, teams must be made up in such a way that the balance among the roles of their members is maximized. This grouping criterion requires analyzing the balance level in the formed teams. In order to analyze the balance level, the balance conditions established by Belbin are considered [10, 11]. These conditions are presented below.

Belbin [10, 11] states that a team is balanced if each role specified in his model is played naturally by at least one team member. In other words, in a balanced team, all team roles are naturally played. Further, Belbin states that each role should be naturally played by only one team member [10]. Belbin states that a team is unbalanced if some roles are not played naturally or if several of its members play the same role naturally (i.e., duplicate role) [10, 11].

Formulas (1) and (2) have been designed in order to formally express the balance conditions established by Belbin [10, 11]. Formula (1) analyzes the way in which a given r role is played within a given G_i team and gives a score accordingly. If r is naturally played by only one member of G_i team, then 1 point is awarded to G_i. Conversely, if r is not naturally played by any member of G_i, or otherwise r is naturally played by several members of G_i, then 2 points and p points are taken off respectively.

Formula (2) sets the balance level in a given G_i team. This balance level is established based on the scores obtained by G_i, through Formula (1), in relation to the nine roles. In this way, the greater the number of non-duplicate roles (i.e., roles played naturally by only one member of G_i), the greater the balance level assigned to G_i. Conversely, the fewer the number of roles played naturally, or the more duplicate roles, the lower the balance level assigned to G_i. The balance conditions established by Belbin [10, 11] can be seen in Formula (2). Using this formula, a perfectly balanced team will obtain a level equal to 9.

Formula (3) has been designed in order to formally express the grouping criterion considered as part of the problem. This formula maximizes the average balance level of g teams defined from the n students in the class. In other words, the objective of this formula is to find a solution (i.e., set of g teams) that maximizes the average balance level of g teams. This is the optimal solution to the problem addressed. In Formula (3), set C contains all the sets of g teams that may be defined from the n students in the class. The term G represents a set of g teams belonging to C. The term $b(G)$ represents the average balance level of the g teams belonging to set G. Then, Formula (3) uses Formula (2) to establish the balance level of each G_i team belonging to the G set. Note that in the case of a G set of perfectly balanced g teams, the value of the term $b(G)$ is equal to 9.

$$nr(G_i, r) = \begin{cases} 1 & \text{if } r \text{ is naturally played by only one member of } G_i \\ -2 & \text{if } r \text{ is not naturally played in } G_i \\ -p & \text{if } r \text{ is naturally played by } p \text{ members of } G_i \end{cases} \tag{1}$$

$$nb(G_i) = \sum_{r=1}^{9} nr(G_i, r) \tag{2}$$

$$\max_{\forall G \in C} \left(b(G) = \frac{\sum_{i=1}^{g} nb(G_i)}{g} \right) \tag{3}$$

3   Memetic Algorithm

The general behavior of the memetic algorithm proposed here is as follows. Considering a class of n students who shall be divided into g teams, the algorithm starts the evolution from an initial population of feasible solutions. Each of these solutions codifies a feasible set of g teams which may be defined when the n students are divided. Then, each solution of the population is decoded (i.e., the set of g teams inherent to the solution is built) and evaluated by a fitness function. This function evaluates each solution in relation to the optimization objective of the problem. As explained earlier, the objective here is to maximize the balance level of the g teams formed from n students. Therefore, taking into consideration a given solution, the function evaluates the balance level of the g teams represented by the solution. In order to perform that evaluation, the function is based on knowledge of the students' roles.

Once the solutions are evaluated, a selection process is applied to the current population. Some solutions of the population are selected and then paired. In general, the solutions with the greatest fitness values have more chances of being selected. Then a crossover process is applied to each pair of solutions to generate new feasible ones. A mutation process is later applied to the generated solutions by the crossover. This mutation process is aimed at introducing genetic diversity in solutions. Then a local search improvement process [20] is applied to the generated solutions by the mutation. This local search process is aimed at fine-tuning solutions. Finally, a strategy known as deterministic crowding [19, 20] is used to create a new population from the solutions in the current population and the new generated solutions.

This process is repeated until a predetermined number of iterations is reached.

3.1   Representation of the Solutions

Each solution is encoded as a list with a length equal to n (i.e., a list with as many positions as students in the class). Specifically, each position j ($j = 1,\ldots, n$) on this list contains a different student (i.e., repeated students are not admitted). Besides, each student s_k ($k = 1,\ldots, n$) may be in any position on the list. In short, the list is a permutation of the n students.

To decode the G set of g teams from the list, we use a decoding process specially designed. In this process, the g teams are built taking into account the two restrictions considered as part of the problem. The first restriction is that each student may belong to only one team. While the second restriction holds that the difference between the size of a team and the size of the rest of the teams must not exceed one. The decoding process is as follows.

In this process, the size of the teams is considered to depend on the relationship between the values n and g. Therefore, the process starts by calculating the value of the term $z = (n/g)$. If z is an integer, then the list is divided into g equal segments, each of which has a size equal to z and represents to a different team. Thus, g teams having the same size are built.

In case z is not an integer (i.e., z is a real number), g teams having the same size cannot possibly be built. Furthermore, the process must consider that the difference between the sizes of any two teams must not exceed one. Thus, the process builds g teams which do not have the same size, but which respect the restriction mentioned above. Specifically, the process divides the list into g segments: the first g_1 segments have a size equal to ((integer part of z) + 1) and the remaining segments have a size equal to (integer part of z), considering $g_1 = (n - ((\text{integer part of } z) \times g))$. Each segment represents to a different team. Thus, the process builds g_1 teams with a size equal to ((integer part of z) + 1) and $(g - g_1)$ teams with a size equal to (integer part of z).

3.2   Initial Population

A random method has been designed so as to generate each of the solutions of this population. This kind of methods guarantees a good level of genetic diversity in the initial population, and therefore, helps prevent the premature convergence of the algorithm [19, 20].

The method begins as follows: an empty list of length n is built. Then, n iterations are developed so as to define the content of the positions on the list. In each iteration m ($m = 1,\ldots, n$), a student from the L_m set is randomly selected and positioned at m on the list. The L_m set is made up of those students in the class who, up to the m iteration, have not been included on the list. A permutation of the n students in the class is therefore generated.

3.3   Fitness Function

Considering a given encoded solution, the fitness function decodes the G set of g teams represented by the solution. The decoding is carried out by applying the process described in Section 3.1. Then, the function calculates the value of the term $b(G)$ (Formulas (3), (2), and (1)). This value represents the average balance level of the g teams composing the G set, and thus, determines the fitness level of the encoded solution.

In order to calculate the value of the term $b(G)$, the function needs to know the roles inherent to each of the n students in the class. As was mentioned in Section 2, the roles of the students are known.

3.4   Selection of Parents, Crossover and Mutation

In relation to the selection process, we applied the 2-tournament selection scheme, one of the most applied in the literature [19, 20].

The crossover and mutation operators were defined on the basis of the representation proposed for the solutions. In this case, each solution consists of a permutation of n elements and, therefore, we have considered feasible operators for permutations of n elements.

In relation to the crossover operator, we have considered an operator known as order crossover. This operator is described in [20]. The crossover operator is applied with a probability of P_c.

In relation to the mutation operator, we have considered an operator known as swap mutation. This operator is described in [20]. The mutation operator is applied with a probability of P_m.

The above-mentioned crossover and mutation operators are two of the most applied for permutations in the literature [20].

4   Computational Experiments

In order to develop the experiments, we designed 8 data sets. The main characteristics of each data set are shown in Table 2. Each data set contains a list of n students. For each data set, we established a g number of teams to be built from n students. It should be noted that the size of the g teams is equal to 6 members. In the literature, this size is considered one of the optimal sizes for collaborative learning teams [1, 2].

Moreover, we defined specific roles for each student of each of the 8 data sets. These roles belong to the Belbin's model [10, 11] containing 9 roles (i.e., IM, CO, SH, PL, RI, ME, TW, CF y SP) as described in Table 1. Specifically, in each data set, g students have the role IM, g students have the role CO and the role SH, g students have the role PL and the role RI, g students have the role ME and the role TW, g students have the role CF, and g students have the role SP.

Thus, in each data set, each of the 9 roles is represented by g students of the data set, and each student of the data set represents one or two roles. In this way, from the n students of the data set, it is possible to build at least a set of perfectly balanced g teams. In other words, it is possible to build at least a set of g teams in which each of the nine roles is represented by only one team member. According to the fitness function defined in Section 3.3, a set of perfectly balanced g teams has a fitness level (i.e., the average balance level of the g teams) that is equal to 9. This fitness level is the maximal possible fitness level.

Based on the above-mentioned, it may be stated that there is at least one solution with a maximal fitness level for each of the data sets. Then, considering that a solution with a maximal fitness level outperforms all other possible solutions, this solution may be considered an optimal solution. Thus, it is possible to state that for each of the 8 designed data sets, there is at least one optimal solution with a fitness level equal to 9.

The memetic algorithm was run 20 times on each of the 8 data sets. To perform these runs, the algorithm parameters were set with the values shown in Table 3. The parameters were fixed thanks to preliminary experiments that showed that these values led to the best and most stable results.

Table 4 presents the results obtained by the algorithm on each data set. The first column provides the name of each data set; the second columns indicates the average fitness value of the achieved solutions for each data set; and the third column shows the average computation time of the runs performed on each data set.

Table 2. Description of each data set

Data set	Number of participating students (n)	Number of teams (g)
1	18	3
2	24	4
3	60	10
4	120	20
5	360	60
6	600	100
7	1200	200
8	1800	300

Table 3. Parameter values of the memetic algorithm

Parameter	Value
Crossover probability P_c	0.8
Mutation Probability P_m	0.05
Population size	80
Number of generations	200
Parameters of the local search process	
Depth (stop condition for the outer loop)	Local optimality
Pivot rule (stop condition for the inner loop)	Stop as soon as an improvement is found
Move operator	Insert mutation [20]

Table 4. Results obtained by the memetic algorithm

Data set	fitness value	time (seconds)
1	9	0.42
2	9	1.03
3	9	8.30
4	9	13.20
5	8.92	30.65
6	8.86	41.82
7	8.78	147.75
8	8.68	271.52

Considering that each of the 8 data sets has at least one optimal solution with a fitness level equal to 9, we analyzed the results presented in Table 4. For each of the first four data sets, the algorithm has achieved an optimal solution in each of the runs. For each of the four remaining data sets, the algorithm has achieved an average fitness value that is higher than 8.6. This means that, for the last four data sets, the algorithm has achieved solutions that are very near the optimal solutions. The composition of the obtained solutions for the last four data sets has been analyzed. On the basis of this analysis, it is possible to say that each of these solutions contains a high percentage of perfectly balanced teams.

Regarding the average computation time required by the algorithm, the following points may be mentioned. For each of the first six data sets, the average time required by the algorithm was lower than 60 seconds. Then, for each of the two remaining data sets, the average time required by algorithm was higher than 100 seconds and lower than 300 seconds. Taking into consideration the complexity of the addressed problems, particularly the complexity of the problems inherent in the last two data sets, the average computation times required by the algorithm on the 8 data sets are considered acceptable.

On the basis of these results, it may be said that for each of the 8 data sets, the algorithm has achieved high-quality solutions in an acceptable period of time.

In addition, we compared the performance of the memetic algorithm with that of another search method known as exhaustive method. Unlike the memetic algorithm, the exhaustive method exhaustively enumerates all possible solutions to a given problem, which guarantees that the optimal solution will be found in each run. Therefore, the exhaustive method was run only once on each of the 8 data sets. Table 5 shows the results obtained by the exhaustive method.

Table 5. Results obtained by the exhaustive method

Data set	fitness value	time (seconds)
1	9	59.46
2	9	189.27
3	9	1072.59
4	*N/A*	*N/A*
5	*N/A*	*N/A*
6	*N/A*	*N/A*
7	*N/A*	*N/A*
8	*N/A*	*N/A*

The results show that the exhaustive method was only able to solve the problems inherent in the first three data sets in a reasonable period of time. The reason for this is that the team-formation problem is an NP-Hard problem, so the computation time required by the exhaustive method increases exponentially as the problem size increases. Unlike the exhaustive method, the memetic algorithm has found optimal solutions for the first four data sets and near-optimal solutions for the remaining four data sets. The solutions for all 8 data sets have been found in an acceptable period of time. Furthermore, even though the computation time of the memetic algorithm also increased as the problem size increased, this increase is smaller than the one in the exhaustive method. Therefore, the memetic algorithm may be considered to obtain high-quality solutions efficiently.

5   Related Works

In the literature, different grouping criteria have been considered in order to form collaborative learning teams automatically. Generally, these criteria take into account factors related to the learning state of the students, their learning style, thinking style and personality. However, to the best of our knowledge, the team roles of the students according to the Belbin's model [10, 11] and the balance conditions established by this author have not been considered in previous works that address the problem of forming collaborative learning teams automatically.

Christodoulopoulos and Papanikolaou [21] consider the learning styles of the students according to the Felder & Silverman learning styles model and the Honey & Mumford model. Then, the authors consider two grouping criteria. One of these criteria is based on forming heterogeneous teams in relation to the Sequential/Global axis of the Felder & Silverman model and the Reflective/Active axis of the Honey & Mumford model.

Wang et al. [22] consider the thinking styles of the students collected from questionnaires. Then, the grouping criterion is based on forming heterogeneous learning teams in relation to the thinking styles.

Cavanaugh et al. [23] consider some characteristics of the students such as gender, skills, and students' schedules. Then, the grouping criterion is based on forming teams homogeneous in relation to some characteristics and heterogeneous in relation to other characteristics.

Graf et al. [24] consider a grouping criterion that is based on forming heterogeneous teams in relation to the students' personality traits (interest for the subject, achievement motivation, self confidence, and shyness), their level of performance in the subject, and fluency in the language of instruction.

Lin et al. [25] consider the understanding level and interest of the students in relation to different topics of the course. Then, the grouping criterion is based on forming heterogeneous teams in relation to the understanding level and interest.

6   Conclusion

In this paper, we addressed the problem of forming collaborative learning teams in the context of university software engineering courses automatically. As part of the problem, we considered one of the most analyzed grouping criteria in the context of software engineering courses. This criterion is based on taking into account the team roles of the students according to the Belbin's model [10, 11] and on forming well-balanced teams in respect of the team roles of their members. To the best of our knowledge, the criterion considered in this paper has not been considered in previous works that address the problem of forming collaborative learning teams automatically.

To solve the addressed problem, we proposed a memetic algorithm. Taking into account a given students' class that must be divided into a given number of teams, the algorithm designs different alternatives to divide the students into learning teams and evaluates each alternative with respect to the grouping criterion considered as part of the problem. This evaluation is conducted based on knowledge of the team roles of the students.

We presented the computational experiments developed for evaluating the memetic algorithm's performance. These experiments involved solving team formation problems inherent in eight data sets with different levels of complexity.

Based on the results obtained by the memetic algorithm on the eight data sets, we may state that this algorithm has been able to achieve high-quality solutions in an acceptable computation time for each of the data sets used. Therefore, we consider that the algorithm could be used in order to form well-balanced collaborative learning teams according to the team roles of their members.

In future works, we will analyze the usefulness of other grouping criteria in the context of software engineering courses. In case that there are other useful criteria, we will include these criteria into the addressed problem and we will adapt the fitness function of the memetic algorithm. On the other hand, in future works, we will propose new feasible crossover and mutation processes for the defined representation of solutions.

References

1. Barkley, E.F., Cross, K.P., Howell Major, C.: Collaborative learning techniques. John Wiley, New York (2005)
2. Michaelsen, L.K., Knight, A.B., Fink, L.D.: Team-based learning: A transformative use of small groups in college teaching. Stylus Publishing, Sterling (2004)
3. Beane, W.E., Lemke, E.A.: Group variables influencing the transfer of conceptual behavior. Journal of Educational Psychology 62(3), 215–218 (1971)
4. Dalton, D.W., Hannafin, M.J., Hooper, S.: Effects of individual and cooperative computer-assisted instruction on student performance and attitudes. Educational Technology Research and Development 37(2), 15–24 (1989)
5. Hooper, S., Hannafin, M.J.: Cooperative CBI: the effects of heterogeneous versus homogeneous group on the learning of progressively complex concepts. Journal of Educational Computing Research 4(4), 413–424 (1988)
6. Webb, N.M.: Student Interaction and learning in small groups. Review of Educational Research 52(3), 421–455 (1982)
7. Winter, M.: Developing a group model for student software engineering teams. Master's thesis. University of Saskatchewan (2004)
8. Johansen, T.: Predicting a Team's Behaviour by Using Belbin's Team Role Self Perception Inventory. PhD thesis. University of Stirling (2003)
9. Stevens, K.: The Effects of Roles and Personality Characteristics on Software Development Team Effectiveness. PhD thesis. Faculty of Virginia Polytechnic Institute and State University (1998)
10. Belbin, R.M.: Management Teams: Why They Succeed or Fail. Butterworth-Heinemann, Oxford (1981)
11. Belbin, R.M.: Team Roles at Work. Butterworth-Heinemann, Oxford (1993)
12. Jeffries, P., Grodzinsky, F., Griffin, J.: Advantages and Problems in Using Information Communication Technologies to Support the Teaching of a Multi-institutional Computer Ethics Course. Journal of Educational Media 28(2-3), 191–202 (2003)
13. Jeffries, P., Grodzinsky, F., Griffin, J.: Building successful on-line learning communities across international boundaries: a Case Study. In: Proc. ETHICOMP 2004 (The Seventh ETHICOMP International Conference on the Social and Ethical Impacts of Information and Communication Technologies). University of the Aegean, Syros (2004)
14. McFadzean, E.: Supporting virtual learning groups. Part 2: an integrated approach. Team Performance Management: An International Journal 7(5-6), 77–92 (2001)
15. Prichard, J.S., Stanton, N.A.: Testing Belbin's team role theory of effective groups. The Journal of Management Development 18(8), 652–660 (1999)
16. Sommerville, J., Dalziel, S.: Project teambuilding – the applicability of Belbin's team-role self-perception inventory. International Journal of Project Management 16(3), 165–171 (1998)

17. Park, W., Bang, H.: Team role balance and team performance. In: Belbin Biennial Conference "Changing Role of Management in the 21st Century". Clare College, Cambridge (2002)
18. Cameron, S.: Business Student's Handbook: Learning Skills for Study and Employment. Prentice Hall, Harlow (2002)
19. Goldberg, D.E.: Genetic Algorithms in Search, Optimization, and Machine Learning. Addison-Wesley, New York (2007)
20. Eiben, A.E., Smith, J.E.: Introduction to Evolutionary Computing. Springer, Berlin (2007)
21. Christodoulopoulos, C.E., Papanikolaou, K.A.: A Group Formation Tool in an E-Learning Context. In: 19th IEEE ICTAI 2007, pp. 117–123. IEEE Press, New York (2007)
22. Wang, D.Y., Lin, S.S.J., Sun, C.T.: DIANA: A computer-supported heterogeneous grouping system for teachers to conduct successful small learning groups. Computers in Human Behaviors 23(4), 1997–2010 (2007)
23. Cavanaugh, R., Ellis, M., Layton, R., Ardis, M.: Automating the Process of Assigning Students to Cooperative-Learning Teams. In: 2004 American Society for Engineering Education Annual Conference & Exposition, American Society for Engineering Education, Salt Lake (2004)
24. Graf, S., Bekele, R.: Forming Heterogeneous Groups for Intelligent Collaborative Learning Systems with Ant Colony Optimization. In: Ikeda, M., Ashley, K.D., Chan, T.-W. (eds.) ITS 2006. LNCS, vol. 4053, pp. 217–226. Springer, Heidelberg (2006)
25. Lin, Y.T., Huang, Y.M., Cheng, S.C.: An automatic group composition system for composing collaborative learning groups using enhanced particle swarm optimization. Computers & Education 55, 1483–1493 (2010)

Empirically Derived Guidelines
for Audio-Visual E-mail Browsing

Saad Alharbi

Faculty of Computer Science and Engineering
Taibah University, Madinah, Saudi Arabia
Salharbi20@gmail.com

Abstract. This paper presents a set of design guidelines for the use of information visualization techniques and non-speech sounds such as auditory icons and earcons in email browsing. These guidelines were derived based on a previous experimental work consisted of three experimental phases, each phase aimed at investigating different aspects of email browsing. Several key points were covered in these guidelines such as the presentation of email information, finding email information and using audio metaphors for communicating email information.

Keywords: Design, Guidelines, Information Visualization, Icons.

1 Introduction

The use of email has dramatically changed from since it was first invented. Venolia, et al defined a conceptual model of users' activities in email [1]. A large body of research focuses on the first four activities (i.e. flow, triage, tasks management and archive) where less attention was given to the retrieval activity. Finding archived email messages using the typical ways such as sorting, filtering and searching can become a tedious task especially with the large volume of email information exchanged currently. Furthermore, previous research highlighted different limitations of using automatic filtering and rules for retrieving email data [2,3,4]. Therefore, this paper presents an experimental study that investigates the use of various information visualization techniques to improve the usability of retrieving email data (this process from now and forth with will be called browsing email data).

The paper begins with a brief review of the experimental study carried out in previous work and the results obtained from these experiments. This experimental work was carried out evolutionary into three phases. The paper, then, describes a set of guidelines were derived from the results of the experimental study which can be used for designing email clients that facilitate the browsing of email data are described.

1.1 First Experimental Phase

An initial experiment was carried out, first, to investigate the effect of incorporating various visualization techniques on the usability of browsing email messages and to

F.V. Cipolla-Ficarra et al. (Eds.): ADNTIIC 2011, LNCS 7547, pp. 104–113, 2012.
© Springer-Verlag Berlin Heidelberg 2012

find out the most appropriate visualization techniques for presenting email information. In order to conduct the experiment, two email visualization approaches, called LinearVis and MatrixVis, that presented email messages in multi coordinated views were developed. The two approaches consisted of a dateline, main view and temporal view, and presented email messages as squares. The status of email messages was communicated by colors in the two approaches, too. However, the main aspect that differentiates LinearVis from MatrixVis is the way of classifying messages. LinearVis presented email messages in the main view classified by senders whereas MatrixVis presented email messages in the main view classified by time were messages received on.

Thirty users (n=30) were recruited in this experimental phase and were required to perform ten experimental tasks in the two experimental email approaches and a typical email client (same tasks in each condition). These experimental tasks were designed to be in three complexity levels: easy, medium and difficult. The results obtained were analyzed into effectiveness, efficiency and users' satisfaction. They were also required to fill 1 to 6 Likert rating scale questionnaire after performing the tasks in each condition to identify their satisfaction level as well as they were asked to select the most preferred email condition. Table 1 shows a quantitative review of the results obtained in this experimental phase.

Table 1. Overall Results of First Experimental Phase

Usability Metrics	Dependent Variables	LinearVis	Matrix Vis	Control Condition
Effectiveness	Tasks completed	80%	60%	30%
Efficiency	completion time	29.2	52.9	61.4
	Actions carried out	2.9	10.1	6.6
Users' Satisfaction	Ease of use	5.1	3.9	4.5
	Ease of learning	5	3.6	4.6
	Usefulness	4.7	3.5	4.4
	Overall satisfaction	43.3	32.8	41.5
	Preference (users)	73.3%	6.7%	20%

The results demonstrated that visualizing email messages in multi coordinated views based on a dateline together with senders can significantly improve the usability of email browsing. Moreover, information hiding was not found to be an effective way for reducing the graphical complexity in the inbox. The overall usability of browsing email messages in LinearVis was significantly increased when compared to the typical email client. The overall usability of MatrixVis, on the other hand, was significantly degraded when compared to the typical email client. More details about this experimental phase and the results can be found in [2].

Table 2. Overall Results of Second Experimental Phase

Usability Metrics	Dependent Variables	Linear Vis II	Control Condition
Effectiveness	Tasks completed	83%	25%
Efficiency	completion time	40.3	71.5
	Errors occurred	0.7	1.1
	Actions carried out	2.9	6.6
Users' Satisfaction	Overall satisfaction	2.2	2.6

1.2   Second Experimental Phase

In the second experimental phase, an experimental email visualization, called LinearVis II, was developed based on the findings of the previous experimental phase. In a similar way of LinearVis, it presented email messages using multi coordinated views based on a dateline with senders' names or addresses (see [3] for more details about the experimental platform). However, various aspects differentiated LinearVis II from LinearVis. First, email messages were presented in LinearVis II textually in a list view as the results of the initial experiment demonstrated that list view is the most appropriate way for presenting email messages. On the other hand, messages were presented as square icons in LinearVis. Second, the length of dateline in LinearVis II was reduced to be composed of months instead of day as in LinearVis. Third, senders were displayed alphabetically in LinearVis where they were displayed based on their activities in LinearVis II. Fourth, dynamic filters were implemented in LinearVis II as users can dynamically use the dateline together with the senders' list. Such features were not implemented in LinearVis. Fifth, an instant subject search and attachment panel were added in LinearVis II.

In order to investigate the usefulness of these enhancements in the usability of browsing email messages, a comparative usability evaluation was conducted between the new experimental email approach and a typical email client. Thirty users (n=30) were required to perform twelve experimental tasks, six in each condition. Tasks' accomplishment time, errors carried out whilst performing tasks and actions required to accomplish each task were considered to measure the efficiency of each condition. Users' satisfaction was measured through 1 to 5 Likret rating scale post-experimental questionnaires. Table 2 shows a quantitative review of the results obtained in this experimental phase. The results of the initial experiment were confirmed in this experiment since multi coordinated views were also found to be an effective way for presenting email information. The results also demonstrated that the enhancements applied on the dateline and senders' list helped in the reduction of tasks' accomplishment time, errors and actions carried out to perform tasks when compared with the typical ways used for browsing messages. In overall, LinearVis II was found significantly more usable in terms of effectiveness, efficiency and users' satisfaction than the typical email client. The results of the experimental phase are well documented in [3].

Table 3. Overall Results of Third Experimental Phase

Usability Metrics	Dependent Variables	Textual	Graphical	Multimodal
Effectiveness	Tasks completed	12.5%	38%	63%
	Recognition	2.34	2.16	2.98
Efficiency	Tasks' completion time	69.31	49.47	44.15
	Errors occurred	1.48	1.22	0.96

1.3   Third Experimental Phase

The first two experimental investigated the usability of browsing email messages by the basic email properties such as date, subject and senders. The third experimental phase, on the other hand, was aimed at investigating the usability of browsing email messages by other email data, particularly email threads. The main assumption in this stage was that in order to facilitate the browsing of email data using email threads, contextual information about messages in the thread should be provided to users. Therefore, an experiment that aimed at investigating the most appropriate way of communicating such information was carried out. In order to conduct the experiment, three email threads approaches were implemented and embedded into LinearVis II. The first approach called the textual threads approach where related email messages were presented textually in the main view with contextual information presented in the typical way. The graphical and multimodal email threads approaches presented related messages graphically as nodes connected with arches in the temporal view. However, the graphical approach communicated contextual information graphically while the multimodal approach communicated some contextual information using non-speech sound (i.e. earcons and auditory icons).

These approaches were tested independently by three groups of users, each group consisting of fifteen users (n=45). Each user was required to perform eight experimental tasks in one experimental approach. In these tasks, users were required to find the required email threads with the provided relevant information. Moreover, they were asked to answer a set of questions about the required thread after completing each task. The usability of the three approaches was measured based on effectiveness (i.e. tasks completion rate and identification of threads information) and efficiency (i.e. tasks accomplishment time and errors rate). Table 3 shows a quantitative review of the results obtained in this experimental phase. These results showed that presenting email threads in the main view can significantly reduce the usability of email clients in contrast with the temporal view [4]. Temporal views, on the other hand, were found to be the most useful way for presenting email threads as in the graphical and multimodal approaches. Furthermore, the results demonstrated that users were able to identify contextual information presented by colors in the graphical approach. The results also indicated that auditory metaphors used in the multimodal approach helped users perform the majority of the experimental tasks with an overall usability in comparison with the textual and graphical approaches. In contrast to the graphical representations, these improvements became more explicit when a large volume of information was communicated. Thus, the multimodal email threads approach was found to be the most usable threads approach amongst the three experimental approaches.

2   Empirical Guidelines

The results and findings from the experimental study described above were interpreted into a set of guidelines that can be used for designing email clients that facilitate the browsing of email messages. These guidelines were derived by discussing the results obtained based on the following key points:

2.1   Presenting Email Information Using Multiple View Visualization

Dividing the interface that is used for presenting email data into multiple views was found to be an effective way for improving the accessibility of email information. For instance, the results of the first experimental phase demonstrated that users could accomplish most of the experimental tasks in LinearVis with improved effectiveness, efficiency and satisfaction when compared to the standard email client. These results were also confirmed in the second experimental phase where LinearVis II produced an overall improvement in the usability when compared to the typical email client. However, this may not necessarily always be the case. For example, the results also indicated that users accomplished the majority of the experimental tasks in MatrixVis with significantly reduced effectiveness, efficiency and satisfaction when compared to the standard email client.

One of the crucial factors for the success of using multiple views is that presenting email information based on the appropriate email properties. Furthermore, one of the powerful features that must be considered when presenting email data in a multiple view interface is the coordination between views. This feature allows the presentation of different types of information with one action (e.g. mouse click) and, therefore, helps in retrieving email information with less effort in comparison with typical approaches. In LinearVis II, for example, users were able to browse the email messages and the attachments of a particular sender at the same time by clicking on its name from the senders' list. However, existing guidelines in the design of multiple views visualizations such as [5] must be taken into consideration with the issues mentioned above when presenting email data in a multiple views visualization.

2.2   Reducing the Graphical Complexity in the Inbox

Previous research showed that crowding the user interface with a large volume of graphical information may lead to serious usability problems [6-9]. These problems can be avoided by hiding some information that is thought to be less important. However, hiding message information such as subject and priority was not found to be an appropriate approach for reducing the graphical complexity in the inbox as such information might be critical for users. For example, the overall usability of

MatrixVis was significantly degraded in terms of effectiveness, efficiency and users' satisfaction when compared to the typical email client due to the large scale of hidden information. In contrast, reducing the number of email messages presented in the inbox was found to be a better approach for reducing the graphical complexity of the inbox than hiding message information. As the older email messages get, the less likely they will be looked for [1]. LinearVis II presented email messages that were received within the past month in the main view.

2.3   Using Colors for Presenting Email Information

Colors were found a useful way for communicating various types of email information. However, various design issues must be taken into account when using colors for presenting email information graphically. First, colors must not be used excessively for presenting email information in order to avoid the visual overload. For example, the results of the third experiment showed that users' identification of threads information in the graphical approach was considerably reduced in the last three experimental tasks, where large volume of graphical information was presented. Second, colors should not be used for presenting message information in the main view. Using such approach may enforce the designer to hide some important information such as the subject which breaks the guidelines previous guideline (E). Third, the size of the area dedicated to present email information graphically plays an important role in the identification of such information.

2.4   Using Dynamic Filters for Retrieving Email Information

One of the powerful features that can be implemented in this type of filters is the ability of selecting multiple properties dynamically (i.e. according to users objectives) at the same time. For example, messages with attachment and high priority can be presented in the main view by clicking on the attachment icon then the high priority icon from the main view. Moreover, such filters should also allow users to deselect un-required email properties. Using filters with such features likely can significantly reduce the actions, such as the navigation through menus to find the search command and typing the required email proprieties manually in the search fields, required by users for retrieving messages. However, existing guidelines of the use of dynamic queries for exploring information in the user interface such as [10-12] must also be taken into account together with these key points when employing such approach in email browsing. In fact, using dynamic filters for filtering email messages has two superiorities over the use of rules. First, programming skills is not required for using dynamic filters whereas they are essential for using rules. Second, automatic rules might become obsolete as users' email activities change over the time. Dynamic filters, on the other hand, were designed for this purpose.

2.5   Using Non-speech Sounds for Communicating Email Information

Previous research such as [7, 13-20] showed that non-speech sound can significantly contribute to the usability of user interfaces in different domains. This paper investigated how non-speech sound can be utilized in email clients to assist the browsing of email data. Similarly, the results indicated that it can be used fruitfully for enhancing the browsing of email information. In spite of the fact that non-speech sound was found an effective contributor to browsing email messages, various key points should be considered when it is implemented in email clients. First, it should not be used for conveying information about messages in the main view as textual list was found the best way for presenting such information. In contrast, it can be used effectively for providing users with an overview of the inbox. This can help in lessening the efforts required to find an email message. In fact, rising pitch notes were found to be effective means for communicating countable data in the inbox (i.e. number of unread messages). Therefore, similar types of information such as the number of attachments in an email message and the number of recipients can more likely be successfully communicated with rising pitch. Second, non-speech sounds (i.e. earcons and auditory icons) can also be used for communicating email information that can hardly be presented graphically due to the restriction of presentation area. The results demonstrated that users had difficulties identifying priority of email messages and attachments in the graphical email threads because of the small areas used for presenting this type of information (see Section 4). On the contrary, the identification of the same information was dramatically increased when it is communicated aurally in the multimodal email threads approach. Third, the synergic use of non-speech sounds (i.e. earcons and auditory icons) and graphical representations were found an effective way for communicating information of email threads. The benefits of using such an approach are likely become more explicit when a large scale of information would need to be presented. The results, for example, showed that users' performance in terms of time, errors and identification was remarkably degraded when performing the last three experimental tasks, where a large volume of information was presented, in the graphical email threads approach. In fact, the synergy of non-speech sound and visualization in the multimodal approach helped users in performing this type of tasks with considerably improved performance. Similar results were also found in different problem domains such as the web search results [21, 22]. Furthermore, the guidelines described above showed only how and when to utilize non-speech sound in email retrieval. Therefore, several existing guidelines such as [23-25] should be taken into account to produce effective auditory messages.

2.6   Using Email Threads for Retrieving

Previous studies showed that email threads can be used successfully to enhance the efficiency of email in terms of various aspects [26-34]. This paper, however, investigated whether email threads can be used to improve the browsing of email messages. The results demonstrated that they can significantly improve the usability of browsing messages. One of the powerful features of email threads that they facilitate the accessibility to messages that can hardly be found by common email data such the date and sender. However, several design issues must be taken into account when utilizing threads for retrieving messages. One of the essential information that must be provided in email threads to facilitate the retrieving process is the contextual information about messages within the threads such as the existence of attachment and the status of messages. The existence of such information can significantly reduce the efforts required to retrieve email data. For example, to find an email message with attachment in a thread, email messages with attachment will only be visited if such information was provided; otherwise all messages in the thread would need to be opened. Additional information, such as relationships and chronology, about email threads can also be provided to enhance the usability of browsing messages using threads.

The main view of the email inbox should not be used for presenting email threads as such approach can visually overload users with messages and, consequently, increase usability problems. However, temporal views should be used instead. The experimental results indicated that the method used for presenting the contextual information affects the usability of email threads presented in the temporal view. For instance, the graphical email threads approach, where threads presented in the temporal view and contextual information presented graphically, failed to become more effective than the textual approach due to the large scale of graphically presented information. In contrast, presenting contextual information in a multimodal way (i.e. the multimodal email threads approach) helped users perform experimental tasks with improved effectiveness and efficiency. Thus, the most appropriate way for presenting such information is the multimodal approach.

3   Conclusion

This paper presented the results of previous work that aimed at investigating various visualization techniques and non-speech sounds for enhancing the usability of email clients in terms of message retrieval. The overall interpretation of the experimental results demonstrated that there is a high potential for using such metaphors, in their own or combined together, for improving email browsing. Based on these results, a set of guidelines was derived which is believed to be used together with existing guidelines in visualizations techniques and multimodal interaction for enhancing the usability of browsing email information in email clients. These guidelines contribute to the existing literature in using information visualizations techniques for improving the usability of email clients. Nevertheless, further investigations would need to be undertaken to provide email clients that facilitate the browsing of email data and also to provide additional guidelines in the use of multimodal metaphors for enhancing email browsing.

References

1. Venolia, G.D., et al.: Supporting Email Workflow. Microsoft Research, 2001–2088 (2001)
2. Rigas, D., Alharbi, S.: Graphical Browsing of Email Data: A Usability Based Comparative Study. Journal of Computer Science 5(10), 690–703 (2009)

3. Alharbi, S., Rigas, D.: LinearVis II: Towards More Usable Email Browsing. IAENG International Journal of Computer Science, 36 (2009)
4. Alharbi, S., Rigas, D.: Email Threads: A Comparative Evaluation of Textual, Graphical and Multimodal Approaches (2009)
5. Michelle, Q.W.B., Allison, W., Allan, K.: Guidelines for using multiple views in information visualization. In: Proceedings of the Working Conference on Advanced Visual Interfaces. ACM Press, New York (2000)
6. Alsuraihi, M.M., Rigas, D.I.: Speech Displaces the Graphical Crowd. Journal of Computers 3(6), 47 (2008)
7. Brewster, S.A.: Using Non-Speech Sound to Overcome Information Overload. Displays 17(3), 179–189 (1997)
8. Brewster, S.A., et al.: The sonic enhancement of graphical buttons. In: Human-Computer Interaction, Interact 1995, pp. 43–48 (1995)
9. Rigas, D., Alsuraihi, M.: A Toolkit for Multimodal Interface Design: An Empirical Investigation. In: Jacko, J.A. (ed.) HCI 2007. LNCS, vol. 4552, pp. 196–205. Springer, Heidelberg (2007)
10. Ahlberg, C., Williamson, C., Shneiderman, B.: Dynamic queries for information exploration: an implementation and evaluation. In: Proceedings of the SIGCHI Conference on Human Factors in Computing Systems. ACM Press, New York (1992)
11. Burigat, S., Chittaro, L.: Interactive visual analysis of geographic data on mobile devices based on dynamic queries. Journal of Visual Languages & Computing 19(1), 99–122 (2008)
12. Shneiderman, B.: Dynamic queries for visual information seeking. In: The Craft of Information Visualization: Readings and Reflections, p. 14 (2003)
13. Brewster, S.: Nonspeech auditory output. In: Sears, A., Jacko, J.A. (eds.) The Human Computer Interaction Handbook: Fundamentals, Evolving Technologies and Emerging Applications, pp. 220–239. CRC Press (2003)
14. Brewster, S., Leplâtre, G., Crease, M.: Using Non-Speech Sounds in Mobile Computing Devices. In: First Workshop on Human Computer Interaction with Mobile Devices, Glasgow, pp. 26–29 (1998)
15. Brewster, S.A.: Providing a Structured Method for Integrating Non-speech Audio Into Human-computer Interfaces. PhD dissertation, University of York (1994)
16. Brewster, S.A.: Sonically-enhanced drag and drop. In: Proceedings of International Conference on Auditory Display (ICAD), University of Glasgow, pp. 1–4 (1998)
17. Ciffreda, A., Rigas, D.: A Usability Study of Multimodal Interfaces for the Presentation of Internet Search Results. International Journal of Computers, NAUN 2(2), 120–125 (2008)
18. Rigas, D., Memery, D., Yu, H.: Experiments in using structured musical sound, synthesised speech and environmental stimuli to communicate information: Is there a case for integration and synergy. In: Proceedings of 2001 International Symposium on Intelligent Multimedia Video and Speech Processing, Kowloon Shangri-La, Hong Kong, pp. 465–468 (2001)
19. Rigas, D.I., Alty, J.L., Long, F.W.: Can music support interfaces to complex databases. In: Proceedings of the 23rd EUROMICRO Conference: NewFrontiers of Information Technology, Budapest, pp. 78–84 (1997)
20. Rigas, D.I., Hopwood, D., Memery, D.: Communicating spatial information via a multimedia-auditory interface. In: Proceedings of the 25th EUROMICRO Conference, vol. 2, pp. 398–405 (1999)

21. Rigas, D., Ciuffireda, A.: Multi-Modal Web-Browsing An empirical Approach To Improve the Browsing Process of Internet Retrieved Results. In: International Conference on Signal Processing and Multimedia Applications, pp. 269–276 (2006)
22. Rigas, D., Ciuffreda, A.: An empirical investigation of multimodal interfaces for browsing internet search results. In: Proceedings of the 7th WSEAS International Conference on Applied Informatics and Communications, World Scientific and Engineering Academy and Society (WSEAS), Vouliagmeni (2007)
23. Brewster, S.A., Wright, P.C., Edwards, A.D.N.: Experimentally derived guidelines for the creation of earcons. In: Adjunct Proceedings of HCI, pp. 155–159 (1995)
24. Brown, L.M., et al.: Design guidelines for audio presentation of graphs and tables. In: Proc. International Conference on Auditory Display, Boston (2003)
25. Rigas, D.I.: Guidelines for auditory interface design: an empirical investigation. PhD dissertation, Loughborough University of Technology (1996)
26. Douglas, E.C., Larry, L.P.: Conversation-based mail. ACM Transactions on Computer Systems 4(4), 299–319 (1986)
27. Kerr, B.: Thread Arcs: an email thread visualization. In: IEEE Symposium on Information Visualization, INFOVIS, Seattle, pp. 211–218 (2003)
28. Kerr, B., Wilcox, E.: Designing remail: reinventing the email client through innovation and integration. In: Conference on Human Factors in Computing Systems, pp. 837–852 (2004)
29. Rohall, S., et al.: Email Visualizations to Aid Communications. In: IEEE Symposium on Information Visualization, InfoVis, San Diego (2001)
30. Rohall, S.L.: Redesigning Email for the 21 stCentury Workshop Position Paper. CSCW 2002 Workshop: Redesigning Email for the 21st Century, New Orleans (2002)
31. Rohall, S.L., et al.: ReMail: a reinvented email prototype. In: Conference on Human Factors in Computing Systems, pp. 791–792 (2004)
32. Samiei, M., Dill, J., Kirkpatrick, A.: EzMail: using information visualization techniques to help manage email. In: Proceedings of the Eighth International Conference on Information Visualisation, pp. 477–482. IEEE Computer Society, New York (2004)
33. Whittaker, S., Bellotti, V., Moody, P.: Revisiting and Reinventing Email. Special Issue of Human-Computer Interaction 20(1) (2005)
34. Whittaker, S., Sidner, C.: Email Overload: Exploring Personal Information Management of Email. In: Proceedings of the SIGCHI Conference on Human Factors in Computing Systems: Common Ground, Vancouver, pp. 276–283 (1996)

Intelligent Analysis of User Interactions in a Collaborative Software Engineering Context

Alejandro Corbellini[1,2], Silvia Schiaffino[1,2], and Daniela Godoy[1,2]

[1] ISISTAN Research Institute, UNICEN University,
Tandil, Buenos Aires, Argentina
[2] CONICET, National Council for Scientific and Technical Research, Argentina
{alejandro.corbellini,silvia.schiaffino,
daniela.godoy}@isistan.unicen.edu.ar

Abstract. Software engineering is inherently a collaborative and social activity. Collaborative software engineering is a research area that aims at providing computer-based support to developers in the form of tools for coordination, communication and management. In this context, we present Paynal, an application that provides a set of collaboration facilities integrated into a development environment. Most important, Paynal provides managers and project leaders tools based on social network analysis to discover knowledge about team members and their relationships. We describe a case study in which Paynal has been successfully evaluated.

Keywords: Collaborative Software Engineering, Social Networks, Text Processing.

1 Introduction

Almost all modern software engineering methodologies involve several distinct groups of people working on many artifacts with different types of tools to produce multiple versions of software products. Software engineering is unavoidably collaborative [3]: for example, developer teams work together to design a system, to solve problems that may arise and to produce quality software. It is known that 85% of the time taken to develop a software system is consumed in team or group activities. Thus, social activity is crucial in the daily work of a software engineer and has to be considered if we want such as engineer to succeed in his/her work [6].

Collaborative Software Engineering (CSE) looks at ways of providing computer-based support for programmers and tools for communication, management of artifacts, and coordination of tasks. Particularly, Collaborative Development Environments (CDE) are development tools that provide developers a virtual space to meet and solve design and implementation problems, even when these developers are geographically and temporally separated. The goal of CDEs is supporting the development process during all the process life cycle. While traditional environments focus on the efficiency of an individual developer, collaborative environments aim at improving the efficiency of a team as a whole [1].

F.V. Cipolla-Ficarra et al. (Eds.): ADNTIIC 2011, LNCS 7547, pp. 114–123, 2012.

Software engineers have adopted a wide range of communication and collaboration technologies to support group or team coordination in a project. Examples of these technologies are phones, email, discussion lists, teleconferencing, the Web, instant messaging, VoIP and videoconferencing. However, most of the software engineering tools, such as editors, compilers and debuggers do not provide direct support for collaboration. Collaboration is delegated to control version tools such as CVS (concurrent versioning systems) and SVN (Apache Subversion). Although control versioning systems are effective to archive multiple versions of software, the software engineering processes require engineers to be aware of the tasks carried out by others in order to avoid possible conflicts. Communication and notification of events for coordination are crucial for a successful collaboration in software engineering.

In this context, we present Paynal, a collaborative application that assists developers by enabling them to interact with their team-mates through instant messaging, chat, and participation in discussion forums, among other facilities. In addition, Paynal assists project leaders and managers with tools based on social network analysis that enable them to acquire knowledge about developers and the relationships among them. These tools can help managers to analyze the information flow between team members, discover potential leaders, among others.

The rest of the article is organized as follows. In section 2 we describe the main functionality of Paynal, focusing on the analysis of interactions among users. In section 3 we present a case study in which we evaluated the different tools provided by Paynal in a real setting. Then, in section 4 we briefly discuss some related works. Finally, in section 5 we present our conclusions and future work.

2   Overview of Our Proposal

In this work, we present a CSE application named Paynal, which extends the Eclipse IDE[1] by adding groupware tools. This collaborative application assists programmers by enabling them interact with their team-mates through direct conversations, instant messaging, participation in discussion forum, and exchange of files, among other features. As seen in Fig. 1, users' interactions are stored in a repository; then, they are processed and visually/graphically presented to the user. Paynal also enables the extraction of knowledge about the main topics of interest and skills of each user. The information collected about users' relationships is used to build a social network. Conceptually, a social network is a structure composed of one or more graphs whose nodes represent actors or discrete social units, and edges represent relationships between them [7]. Social network analysis in the context of software development helps us identify, for example, the most active developers, which are the core of a project. In order to perform this analysis, Paynal uses different metrics that enable the study of the social network and determine, for example, the participation of each actor in the structure.

---

[1] http://www.eclipse.org/

The tools provided by Paynal can be useful to different users, such as managers or project leaders, to know the members of a team or of a project. Among the conclusions they can obtain from the knowledge discovered we can mention: group leader detection, identification of possible replacements for developers that leave the company, topics of interest of a set of users, users' skills, among others. In the following sections we will describe the metrics we use as part of the social network analysis (Section 2.1), how Paynal determines the topics discussed by users in conversations (Section 2.2), and the representation we have chosen to visualize these topics (Section 2.3).

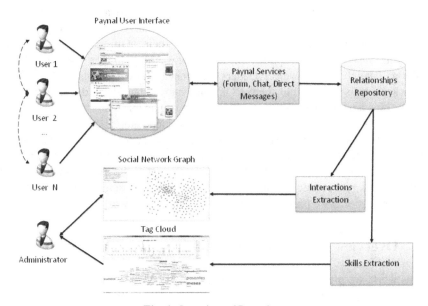

Fig. 1. Overview of Paynal

2.1   Social Networks Analysis

Social network analysis enables us to obtain information about the relationships among individuals [9]. Networks or graphs have become the most important tools to represent a social network in an illustrative way. Paynal enables users to visualize the social network obtained when processing the information extracted from chat conversations, instant messaging, and discussion forum. Nodes or actors represent Paynal users, such as developers and project leaders. Edges or arcs represent the interactions between them. The thickness of the edge is related to the amount of interactions between two users.

There are different approaches to measure the structure of social networks: the analysis of the general structure of the network, and the place each actor takes in the network. To analyze the general structure of the social network, several algorithms have been developed that provide information about this structure, such as components, density, and centrality, among others. On the other hand, to study the position of each actor in the network, the algorithms developed provide information about the individuals' centrality, such as betweenness degree or closeness degreee.

In social network analysis there are certain centrality metrics that determine the relative importance of a node in a network. Centrality measures indicate the contribution of a certain node to the position it occupies in the network. Some measures implemented in Paynal are described below.

– Centrality: it is the number of actors to whom the user is directly related. The bigger this number is, the more important the node is.
– Betweenness: it is the frequency of appearance of an actor in the shortest paths that connect all the pair of nodes in the network.
– Closeness: it is the capacity of a node to reach all the actors in the network. It is calculated by adding the shortest distances to go from an actor to the rest of the actors. High closeness values indicate a better positioning in the network to distribute and access to information.

Another important measure is structural equivalence. Two nodes are structurally equivalent when their relationships with the other nodes are identical. Thus, it is possible to replace one of them by the other without altering the network properties.

Also, Paynal provides different views of the graph where the user can highlight nodes that are very active as regards sent and received messages, nodes with high number of connections, nodes with high betweenness values, and nodes with high closeness values. In turn, when choosing a user, the tool displays a table containing the most similar users regarding structural equivalence.

2.2   Text Processing

In our approach, the text contained in each user-user interaction is analyzed in order to extract the most relevant terms and, in this way, enable users to determine topics in which the other participants are interested in, or skills they have. To carry out this analysis we used different Text Mining techniques, which sequentially filter the text until the most relevant terms are discovered. First, we pre-process text in order to eliminate those words that do not provide useful information. In the case of direct messages the pre-processing involves different steps: signature elimination, URL elimination, HTML elimination, and elimination of common salutation phrases.

A signature is the portion of text that is usually added at the end of an email to provide information about the sender. Frequently, in an email conversation composed of several emails, the same signature appears more than once. Thus the words involved will have a high appearance frequency. Thus, signatures should be eliminated not to affect the relevance of the words in the text. URLs are eliminated because words such as www or http cannot be part of the analysis. Similarly, we extract the text contained between HTML tags because it can refer to images, for example, and can affect negatively the text analysis. Finally, we eliminate the most widely used phrases that appear at the beginning and at the end of an email (e.g. Hi).

Once the pre-processing step is ready, the text is sent to the modules in charge of assigning a grammatical role to each word. The sentence splitter looks for punctuation marks such as "?", ":", "." and "!". The tokenizer determines tokens in each sentence; tokens can be words, numbers and symbols. Then the POST (Part-of-Speech) tagger labels each token according to its grammatical category. We used the GATE (General Architecture for Text Engineering) framework[2] to develop these three processes [4].

We cannot ignore the fact that some words add no meaning to the analysis of interactions and relationships; these words are known as stop words (articles, prepositions) and are easily identified. In our approach, we cannot eliminate stop words before text processing because the POST tagger needs them to recognize the context of words. Thus, we filter out stop words after the POST tagging process. Then we used a stemming algorithm to reduce words to their stems. Fig. 2 shows the pipeline used by Paynal to extract relevant terms from direct messages.

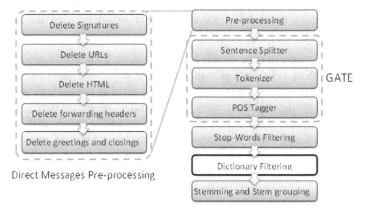

Fig. 2. Text processing in Paynal

2.3   Tag Clouds

The final term list is showed to the user as a tag cloud. A tag cloud is a visual representation composed of a set of words, known as tags, in which the size of the font, the color or any other formatting feature indicate different characteristics of the tags. For example, the frequency of appearance of a word in a text message determines the size of the word in the cloud.

Tag clouds appeared with the advent of different Internet services that provided social tagging, that is, these services enable users to add an arbitrary number of tags to resources contained in a given site so that other users could find those resources. Examples of these services are Flickr[3] and YouTube[4], where users add tags to images and videos respectively. In Paynal the concept of tag cloud is used in a similar way.

---

[2] http://gate.ac.uk/

[3] http://www.flickr.com

[4] http://www.youtube.com

However, tags are not added by users but automatically added by Paynal from the text extracted from the interactions between users. Fig. 3 shows an example of tag cloud representing topics of conversation between two users.

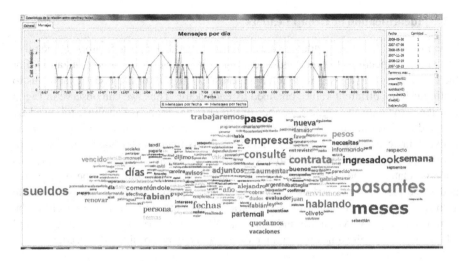

Fig. 3. Example of tag cloud in Paynal

3   Case Study

In this section we describe the experiments carried out to evaluate the usefulness of the tools provided by Paynal to analyze different contexts within an organization. In section 3.1 we describe the dataset used. Then, in section 3.2 we show an example of group leader identification. In section 3.3 we depict how we can analyze the flow of information in the network. Finally, in section 3.4 we show how the information provided can be used to find potential replacements for an actor.

3.1   Dataset Description

To evaluate Paynal we used a set of data composed of the emails sent and received by a group of employees of a software development company. The data contained 833 users and 9827 messages. We focused on the following information:

- The sender of the email (from).
- The recipient of the email (to).
- To whom the email is carbon copied (cc).
- The text part of the email.

From the addresses found, Paynal creates users automatically and adds the connections corresponding to direct messages. We decided to study only the most interesting part of the network, and thus we discarded 847 interactions corresponding to only one message sent. We adopted a parameter value of N in order to discard those interactions associated to less than N messages. We experimentally set this value in 10.

3.2   Identification of Group Leaders

When looking for group leaders, we can consider two different indicators: a node that has many connections to other nodes and that it is also active in the organization. For the first indicator, we use the centrality measure. The size of the nodes enables us to distinguish the different values obtained by each actor. Thus, we can observe in Fig. 4 that the actor with the highest number of direct connections is Carolina, followed by Alejandro. Carolina strongly contributes to the social network, and she is vital for the network interconnection. We can conclude that this node might manage the group of people that are connected to it. However, we have to consider also how strongly this node is related to the other users. Paynal enables the visualization of the most active nodes and provides a mixed indicator about centrality and activity in the graph. Table 1 shows the values obtained for the centrality and activity measures, as well as the mixed indicator for Alejandro and Carolina. We can observe that both Carolina and Alejandro have high values for both measures, and can be considered as leaders.

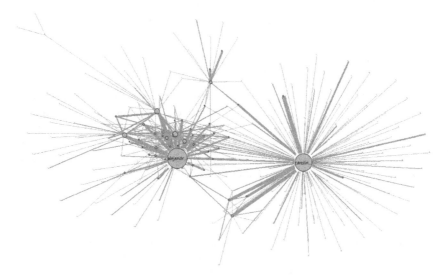

Fig. 4. Centrality and activity measures in a graph

Table 1. Values for centrality, activity, and mixed indicator for Alejandro and Carolina

Node	Centrality	Activity	Centrality and Activity
Alejandro	0.2909	0.3467	0.4704
Carolina	0.6500	0.2861	0.5935

3.3   Studying iInformation Flow in the Network

To analyze the information flow in the social network, we can find those nodes through which most of the information flows. The metric we use is the betweenness degree. In Fig. 5 we can observe that Carolina is the node with the highest value in this feature. The nodes Federico, Vanesa, Juan, Alejandro and Germán follow her with similar measure values. Thus, we can further analyze these nodes in order to determine the flow to and from the network. These nodes have a privilege position to connect different parts of the network; however, the higher the betweenness value, the higher the risk of disconnection of the network is. Consider for example, a node that acts as a bridge between two networks. The elimination of such a node can leave the two networks completely separated. An example of this type of node is Germán, who connects a sub-graph composed of three nodes with the other nodes in the network. Table 2 shows the betweenness degree values for different users.

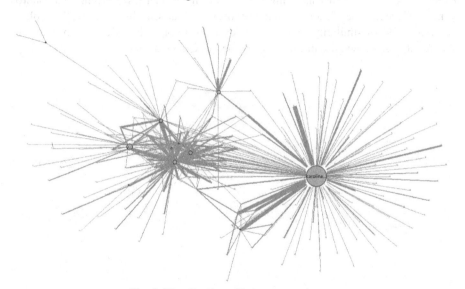

Fig. 5. Visualization of betweenness degree

Table 2. Betweeness and centrality degrees for different users

Node	Betweenness	Closeness
Carolina	0.0839	0.001600
Alejandro	0.0570	0.001300
Federico	0.0078	0.001250
Vanesa	0.0122	0.001190
Germán	0.0036	0.001180
Luis	0.0015	0.001152
Mariano	0.0017	0.001146
Fernando	3.32E-4	0.001131
Analía	4.15E-5	0.001116
Adrián	4.15E-5	0.001111
Sandra	8.30E-5	0.001108
Juan	0.0034	0.001106

3.4   Identification of Replacements

When a node in the network is deleted because, for example, the corresponding user leaves the organization, we might want to keep the connectivity that such user had in the network. We can do this by finding a node that connects the same nodes that the one to be replaced, that is, a node having the same structural equivalence. Fig. 6 shows the selection of the node named Germán and his associated structural similarity table. We can observe that the node Alejandro is the best replacement. The nodes Vanesa and Federico have not too distat values. The tool gives us a hint to find a potential replacement, but we still have to analyze other factors, such as the users' skills or the tag clouds generated, which can give information about the topics of interests of the users involved. Fig. 6 shows the nodes having highest values in the structural equivalence metrics for each of the most relevant actors in the networks. These users are those that have high values in all the metrics: Carolina, Alejandro, Vanesa, Germán and Federico. We can observe that Carolina can easily replace Federico (65% of similarity); however, Federico cannot replace Carolina because he only has access to the 20% of the nodes related to Carolina.

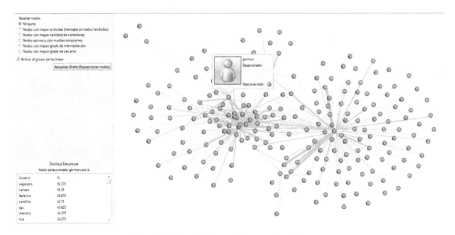

Fig. 6. Visualization of centrality degrees

4   Related Works

We can find some collaborative development environments in the literature. For example, IBM Jazz integrates programming, communication and project management[5]. CAISE [3] is an environment developed to explore the potential of combining CSCW (computer supported collaborative work) features with software engineering. It keeps information about the artifacts in the project with the goal of providing knowledge about relationships among users that edit code concurrently. Some examples of pioneering systems are IRIS and FLECSE. IRIS [2] is a

---

[5] http://www-01.ibm.com/software/rational/jazz/

collaborative editor based on structured documents. It was one of the pioneering works that integrated sincronization tools, concurrent editing and changes notification in a software development environment. Similarly, FLECSE [5] provided a collection for multi-user tools such as editors, code repositories and debuggers. Some more recent works can be found in [8].

However, none of the tools described before and the ones we found in the literature use social network analysis to assist managers and project leaders by providing information about team members and the relationships among them.

5   Conclusion and Future Works

In this article we have presented Paynal, an application for collaborative software development that provides tools to analyze the interactions between users and discover useful knowledge about them, such as their topics of interest. Paynal applies Text Mining techniques and Social Network Analysis to process the information contained in users' interactions. We presented a case study in which Paynal tools enabled the detection of potential group leaders, possible replacements for users leaving the organization, and an analysis of information flow.

Acknowledgments. This work has been partially funded by CONICET through project PIP No. 114-200901-00381.

References

1. Ahmadi, N., et al.: A survey of social software engineering. In: 23rd IEEE/ACM International Conference on Automated Software Engineering Workshops, pp. 1–12 (2008)
2. Booch, G., Brown, A.: Collaborative development environments. Advances in Computers 59, 1–27 (2003)
3. Borghoff, U.M., Teege, G.: Application of collaborative editing to software-engineering projects. In: ACM SIGSOFT, vol. 18, pp. 56–64 (1993)
4. Carrington, P., Scott, J., Wasserman, S.: Models and Methods in Social Network Analysis. Cambridge University Press, London (2005)
5. Cook, C.: Collaborative software engineering: An annotated bibliography. Technical Report TR-COSC 02/04, Department of Computer Science and Software Engineering, University of Canterbury (2004)
6. Cunningham, H., et al.: Text Processing with GATE (2011)
7. Dewan, P., Riedl, J.: Toward computer-supported concurrent software engineering. IEEE Computer 26(1), 17–27 (1993)
8. Mistrík, I., et al.: Collaborative Software Engineering. Springer, Berlin (2010)
9. Scott, J.: Social Network Analysis: A handbook. Sage Publications, London (2000)

Motivation for Next Generation of Users versus Parochialism in Software Engineering

Francisco V. Cipolla Ficarra[1,2], and Valeria M. Ficarra[2]

HCI Lab. – F&F Multimedia Communic@tions Corp.
[1] ALAIPO: Asociación Latina de Interacción Persona-Ordenador
[2] AINCI: Asociación Internacional de la Comunicación Interactiva

c/ Angel Baixeras, 5 – AP 1638, 08080 Barcelona, Spain
via Tabajani, 1 – S. 15 – CP 7, 24121 Bergamo, Italy
ficarra@alaipo.com, info@ainci.com

Abstract. We present a heuristic technique called DISITA (Diachronic and Synchronic Interactive Technologies Assessment) based on the social sciences and with the main purpose of picking up data on the motivation in the human-computer interaction. In the current work we aim at the young users of the emerging interactive technologies such as computers as well as on-line and off-line multimedia systems for school homework and entertainment in Southern Europe in the last two decades. We also present the main social and human factors stemming from university software engineering which discourage the training of professionals in the field of computer science.

Keywords: Software, Human Factors, Design, Communicability, Evaluation, Multimedia, Human-Computer Interaction, Education, Motivation.

1 Introduction

The technologies in the classrooms have been an issue approached by psychologists, computer science experts, mathematicians, etc. since the 80s. Some of the pioneers in this context have been Jean Piaget [1], Nicholas Negroponte [2], Bill Gates [3], Steve Jobs, [4] etc. They backed and explained in detail in their publications the positive aspects of introducing technologies in the classrooms to motivate the students. The novelty factor of the latest breakthroughs in the information and communication technologies has always been positively received by the students, the parents, the professors, and the authorities of the educational system. Those were times in which those still undeveloped societies faced real crossroads, since they wanted to acquire those technologies for didactic use, regardless of the fact whether they were used in public, private or hybrid institutions.

In this sense the communication and the very notion of multimedia also evolved with the technologies. For instance, Nicholas Negroponte [2] in the late 80s and early 90s declares the convergence of television, print and computing towards

F.V. Cipolla-Ficarra et al. (Eds.): Adntiic 2011, LNCS 7547, pp. 124–133, 2012.
© Springer-Verlag Berlin Heidelberg 2012

"a multimedia technology based on the computer". However, there are several multimedia technologies related to linked to the computer which have to be differentiated in order to avoid linguistic ambiguities. In relation to the degree of cohesion with computing of the different interaction techniques, we can make the following classification, bearing in mind commercial technology between 1980 and 1995:

- Sequential multimedia: is the classical multimedia technology stemming from the print and television which is characterized by the lack of computer science. For instance, when in a class on cartography several didactic tools are used at the same time: slides, with background music and the voice of the professor who explains what is seen.
- "Partially" interactive multimedia: It is the case of the emulations of manual operations controlled from the computer, such as the forward or rewind of a song in a CD. The structuring of the information admits a partial interactivity.
- "Totally" interactive multimedia. Each source of information is in digital format and allows a high degree of user-computer interaction. In the example of figure 1, the user activates the different multimedia nodes (1, 2, 3) in different sequential moments, which is depicted by the vertical line. As it can be seen in the figure, the different elements of the nodes (animation, audio and text) do not have the same length, which damages the quality of the system by losing the synchronization between the different media. This was a very common usability mistake of the early off-line systems of commercial multimedia in the 90s. The products made by Microsoft, Musical Instruments, Art Gallery, Beethoven, Encarta, etc. [6] were not free from such quality mistakes. Graphically some of these mistakes can be seen in the figure 1. In the first node, the user sees text, listens to the associated sound, but does not see the animation yet; in the second node all the components start at the same time, although the end of sequentiality will be disparate among them. And in the third, while the animation and the text still continue, the audio has finished. Besides, the current access speed to the different nodes in the off-line multimedia systems (interaction with a CD-ROM in a personal computer or a single user work station) can be superior when examining on-line multimedia applications [7] [8]. When we talk of the speed of access on-line it is always important to take the historic development of the technological structure into account [9], because the current speed of the Internet, thanks to the optical fiber (for instance, 100 Mb per second) or microprocessors [10] [11] is different than what existed earlier with the standard landlines and modems (modulator-demodulator) used since the 60s [7]. In the 90s the external commercial models of modems, for instance the V32 bis with a transmission at 14.400 bit/s (1991), or the V34 bis modem built under the standard V14, with a bidirectional data transfer of 33,6 kbit/s, were using the same modulation in PSK –Please Shift Keying (standard approved in 1998).

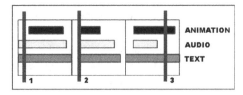

Fig. 1. Classical graphic representation of the fruition of several multimedia nodes (each node is linked to a frame)

This constant bipolar exercise between diachronic and synchronic vision is what has allowed to develop the DISITA technique, regarding the resources of the past as very important to understand the current situation. A conjuncture in which not only the digital gap exists in the emerging countries because of economic reasons, but currently it entails severe motivational consequences for the future generations, affecting directly and indirectly the ICT (Information and Communication Technologies) context. Even inside the same societies that for decades have been regarded as industrial avant-gardes in the world context of personal computer. Today that reality is a mere mirage of the past and always requires a diachronic analysis to understand it. Starting from this diachronic-synchronic analysis the necessary measures can be taken for the negative conjecture of those communities such as depicted in the following digital communication media, i.e., il Sole 24 ore – www.ilsole24ore.com, November 7, 2011 or unemplyment in Spain (see Annex #1).

Fig. 2. "Neet" Italian generation (NEET –Not in Education, Employment or Training), whose ages range between the 15-29 years of age, they neither study nor work. They make up 2.2 million of the population in Italy. That is, one out of every four youth makes up the "Neet" set.

Our universe of study focuses on these ages, but starting from the 90s down to the year 2010, thus encompassing students from computer institutes, professional training aimed at computer science, college students of subjects related to computer science and systems, multimedia engineering, degrees in audiovisual, etc. in two provinces that belong to two regions that are part of the so-called economic and/or industrial engines of Europe: Catalonia and the Lombardy. In our case we have split the users of interactive systems and emerging technologies in relation to their ages in the following way: child (4-11), junior (12-17), adult (18-64), senior (65+). The study is focused the current study among juniors and adults and structured in the following way: techniques and methodologies of the social sciences with purposes of heuristic assessment, human factors in software engineering, learned lessons and future lines of research.

2   The Genesis of DISITA

The intersection of the formal and factual sciences is the origin of the DISITA technique, which is based mainly on questionnaires from classrooms of computer science, multimedia, computer animations, etc. over the years. Besides, direct observation has been used to generate data for the study. The main theoretical bases are in the social sciences which were adapted to the computer context. This is a normal flow in the transfer of scientific knowledge, but this flow does not in the opposite direction, from the applied sciences such as usability engineering [12]. That is, from the formal sciences the issues of the factual sciences are approached, but not as intersections, but as unions of small subsets of methods and techniques to the general set of the heuristic evaluation [12].

The questionnaires in the social sciences have a great spread and acceptance and they are a known tool that is easily accepted by a great part of the computer users. However, for the creation of such questionnaires specialists are required, since it is necessary to follow accurate rules or norms. Although a questionnaire is a tool for data compilation, rigorously standardized, the translation of certain problems which are the object of research, such as −in our case− the time spent in front of computers to play or learn the use of certain educational applications, can be a difficult challenge. This metamorphosis in a set of applications takes place through the written formulation of a set of questions. Questions that allow to study hypothesis or factsthat have been posed at the start of the research. According to Ander-egg [13], two of the main prerequisites or methodological demands that must met by such surveys are reliability and validity. The former refers to the fact that the questionnaire, as a tool to collect data, is tested by its capacity to obtain equal or similar results applying the same questions about the same phenomena. Whereas validity consists in grasping the object of research in an accurate and satisfactory way. Obviously in this adaptation there is also an implicit transformation, that is, that the questionnaire must adapt to the object of research and the validity of the indicators of the questions. In other words, a questionnaire is valid if the data that are obtained adjust to reality without a distortion of the facts. Now other implicit or secondary requisites are the possibility of comparing the answers among the members of the set, to ease tabulation and the analysis of the picked data.

With the goal of increasing the reliability of the surveys as a tool of data obtainment in the making of our technique, we have resorted to the cross-checking of questions by following methods: contrasting them between the written and the real behaviour of the respondents (in this case we resort to the direct observation technique), random probe (use of questions to clear answers and determine the degree of understanding of the respondents), and the combination of the same questions in an open modality (text writing), dychotomies or binaries (yes or no, true or false, etc.), closed (with multiple options). In our case we have used the following order at the moment of inserting the questions of the questionnaire: binary at the beginning, then the closed ones and then the open questions. This order could be repeated several times inside the questionnaire. The questionnaire was always written on the board at the start of the first class.

Structurally, the questionnaires were made up by five big areas. In the first a few personal data (the first and second names were always excluded in order to keep the anonymity of the respondents) were gathered with a wide margin to collect the tastes and preferences of the interactive systems in use, the computers and peripherals, the level of experience in the use of computers, etc. In the second section we asked questions aimed at the technical aspects of computer science (software and hardware), operating systems, commercial applications related to office automation (Word, Excel, Power Point, etc.), eventual programming of systems, etc. In the third section stress was laid on the time the users spent in front of the computer, and the purpose of the interaction with it, that is, study, search and/or looking up information, pastime (videogames), etc. In this section it was also important to determine the time they spent inside and outside the home (for instance, in the public libraries, cybercafés, etc.). The fourth area of the questionnaire focused on the aspects the respondent liked best and those he/she liked less in the interaction with the computers, bearing in mind the design of the interfaces, the organization of the contents, the structure for navigation, the hardware, etc. Finally, the fifth section contained questions about what users wanted in the future of computer science, and also about the course they were about to take. Each one of these sections had one of the modalities of questions that were previously mentioned, but there was a pyramid-shaped structure for the closed and binary answers at the start, whereas at the end they were open in 99% of cases.

The compilation of the questionnaire made the students have a high motivation because in this way they covered the three temporal stages of their knowledge and expectations in the personal computer environment: the past, the present and the future. Besides, it was useful to the teacher to constitute efficient working groups that had to reach the academic goals in a record time and in very peculiar situations, like those that took place in some Catalan colleges, in the 90s. The interested reader can find more information about.it in the following reference [14]. This study presents the strategy followed to turn the anonymous questionnaires into nominal questionnaires, for instance. Now the data compiled in the questionnaires were verified through direct observation. That is, when a student wrote that he was an expert in generating relational data bases for Microsoft Access but in practice and in an individual way he didn't know how to organize the registers that make it up. It was in this way that each one of the 5745 questionnaires that make up our universe of study related to the human-computer interaction were verified. Consequently, our technique DISITA has been developed in the computer, multimedia classrooms etc. with real users and resorting to the questionnaires and direct observation for the verification of the stored data. Some of the global results (%) that motivate the young and adult users at the moment of interacting with on-line and off-line multimedia systems through computers can be seen in the following graphics:

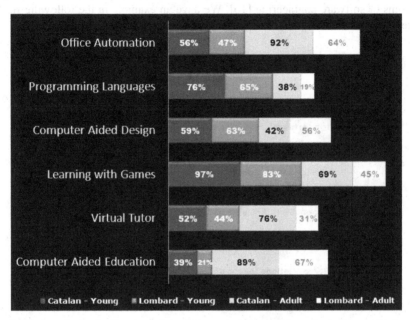

Fig. 3. Diachronic motivational results of the young and adult users in some Catalan and Lombardian provinces when they interact with multimedia systems

The chart presents main indicators showing how the combination of 2D and 3D animations in the computer, the increase of realism in the videogames, the simplicity of the interfaces, the speed in the access to the databases, the scarce navigation errors, the wealth of contents in the off-line commercial multimedia systems, etc. have prompted the young users to be future computer science professionals, in the field of education, entertainment, trade, etc. However, this motivation practically disappears in the adult age because of the contextual and human factors (i.e., parochialism) existing in software engineering (S.E.), just to mention a discipline inside the computer science environment.

3   Software Engineering and the Loss of Motivation of the Future Generations in Southern Europe

The videogame industry has been essential for the ICT sector in the late 90s and early 2000s in Europe, due to the stagnation of R&D in the new technologies [15]. The predictions made from software engineering in the 90s haven't hit the mark at all or far from it in Europe [16]. Evidently, we must take into account that we are talking of one of the most dynamic sectors of the society of information, nevertheless, Students who are very motivated to go into this sector, are very quickly discouraged by the university professors. Even those students who have got excellent qualifications in the stage prior to coming into college are totally discouraged in less than a term in the university. This is due to factors like parochialism, the fritter-funnel, and the phantoms of software engineering [16]. We have an example in the following figure. Those interested in the details of this phenomenon may look up [16] [17] [18].

Ghosts or Phantoms in Software Engineering

Open Source Artificial Intelligence Humanism Neuronal Networks Lasser

Musical Instruments (Piano, Saxophone, Trombone, etc.) **Free Software**

Algorithms Education Robotics LINUX Prolog Cognitive Models Java

Friends or Relatives (Priest, Bishop, Monsignor, etc.) Technology **Ethics**

Oracle Nacionalism Virtual Reality Physics Multimedia Anthropology

Arts Religious Schools (elementary, secondary, universitary, etc.) **Models**

Experts Systems Usability Social Web Quality Commerce Podcasting

Nonprofit Associations (Labor Union, Italian Onlus, etc.) Internet **List**

Databases Meta Models Information Systems Seismic Evaluation

Computer Architecture Automation **Levees Safety**

Political Affiliation and/or Lobbyists

... and a long etcetera

Making Educational Anti-Models and Castes Systems in Software Engineering

Fig. 4. Indispensable requisites and phantom knowledge of the alleged experts in software engineering in Lombardian and Catalan parochialism (1990 - 2011)

4   Learned Lessons

The social sciences have a wealth of techniques and methods that have been improved over the course of the 20th century, especially with the momentum of the massive or social communication media. One of them has been the statistics through the compilation of questionnaires, interviews, etc. Some of these techniques like a simple questionnaire and direct observation may serve the communicability (21st century) or usability experts (20th century) to elaborate a global technique tending to analyze the components that boost or inhibit the motivation in the future generations and in the adults in the context of software engineering. A software engineering which sometimes may have a credibility equal to zero as to short and middle term predictions of the future. Currently the statistic data in the USA, Europe, etc., are used as mere publicity banners even in the very same scientific context. That is, statistics whose data are used without being confirmed, in a myriad of examples in the formal and factual sciences (the millions of iPod users, the sales volume of the on-line virtual shops etc.) In other words, the veracity of the sources of information is equal to zero. In our case we have worked with real cases, generating our own data bases. These data bases are constantly being updated. Our next goal is to generate a quality system to increase the motivation of the computer sciences students and/or its derivations. That is, a system where the data of the past and the present interact. Our secondary goal is to elaborate trends for the future generations, based on the predictions and successful experiences of the past, for instance. The observations made over time in two European regions make apparent a great interest of the young towards the emerging technologies, human-computer interaction, videogames programming, etc. However, one has to consider the variables that may exclude the potential professionals in the context of the hardware and software of the new millennium, such as the lack of a theoretical basis or the presence of phantom professionals in S.E. In this sense, it is necessary to avoid the import of foreign models in university education, especially in the disciplines related to the new information and communication technologies.

5   Conclusion

A heuristic technique like DISITA makes apparent that no big sums of money are necessary to generate techniques, models or methods oriented at increasing the quality of the science professionals to-be. Given the financial resources wasted by the Lombardian and Catalan parochialism in our field of study, in order to generate tools to improve the quality of services and computer products nationally and/or internationally, a methodology is needed). With DISITA you only need perseverance and professionals who are the intersection of the formal and factual sciences. Currently there are many funnels and a great parochialism, phantoms of software engineering which may be nefarious for the educative evolution of those colleges which enjoy an excellent educational quality, even if they don't have the latest breakthroughs or technological fashions at their disposal. Educational mercantilism leaves in the background the scientific aspects. The factual sciences still take a second place in relation to the formal sciences, especially in the communities that theoretically called themselves "developed", financially or economically speaking. In this context in the last two decades educational antimodels have been generated, which should not be imported by the countries currently known as emerging.

Acknowledgments. A special thanks to Maria Ficarra, Sonia Flores, Pamela Fulton, Doris Edison, and Carlos for their collaboration.

References

1. Piaget, J.: The Children Machine. Basic Books, New York (1993)
2. Negroponte, N.: Being Digital. Knopf, New York (1995)
3. Glatin, J.: Bill Gates –The path to the future. Avon, New York (1999)
4. Elliot, J., Simon, W.: The Steve Jobs Way: iLeadership for a New Generation. Vanguard Press, New York (2011)
5. Reisman, S.: Developing Multimedia Applications. IEEE Computer Graphics & Applications 11(4), 52–57 (1991)
6. Cipolla Ficarra, F.V.: Synchronism and Diachronism into Evolution of the Interfaces for Quality Communication in Multimedia Systems. In: CD Proc. HCI International 2005, Las Vegas (2005)
7. Meleis, H.: Toward the Information Network. IEEE Computer 29(10), 69–78 (1996)
8. Muller, N.: Multimedia over the Network. Byte, 73–83 (1996)
9. Mikkonen, T., Taivalsaari, A.: Reports of the Web's Death Are Greatly Exaggerated. IEEE Computer 44(5), 30–36 (2011)
10. Borkar, S., Chien, A.: The Future of Microprocessors. Communications of the ACM 54(5), 67–77 (2011)
11. Bourianoff, G., et al.: Boolean Logic and Alternative Information Pocessing Devices. IEEE Computer 41(5), 38–46 (2008)
12. Nielsen, J., Mack, R.: Usability Inspection Methods. Willey, New York (1994)
13. Ander-egg, E.: Techniques of Social Investigation, 21th edn. Hvmanitas, Buenos Aires (1986)
14. Cipolla Ficarra, F.V., et al.: Advances in Dynamic and Static Media for Interactive Systems: Communicability, Computer Science and Design. Blue Herons Editions, Barcelona (2011)
15. Frej Edvardsen, F., Kulle, H.: Educational Games: Design, Learning and Applications. Nova Publishers, New York (2011)
16. Cipolla-Ficarra, et al.: Computational Informatics, Social Factors and New Information Technologies: Hypermedia Perspectives and Avant-Garde Experiences in the Era of Communicability Expansion. Blue Herons Editions, Bergamo (2011)
17. Cipolla Ficarra, F.V., Nicol, E., Ficarra, V.M.: Research and Development: Business into Transfer Information and Communication Technology. In: Cipolla Ficarra, F.V., de Castro Lozano, C., Pérez Jiménez, M., Nicol, E., Kratky, A., Cipolla-Ficarra, M. (eds.) ADNTIIC 2010. LNCS, vol. 6616, pp. 44–61. Springer, Heidelberg (2011)
18. Cipolla Ficarra, F.V., Nicol, E., Cipolla Ficarra, M.: Vademecum for Innovation through Knowledge Transfer: Continuous Training in Universities, Enterprises and Industries. In: Howlett, R.J. (ed.) Innovation through Knowledge Transfer 2010. Smart Innovation, Systems and Technologies, vol. 9, pp. 139–149. Springer, Heidelberg (2011)

Annex #1

Fig. 5. Unemployment in Spain (five million). Digital newspaper: El País –www.elpais.com, October 28, 2011.

Group and Students Profiles to Support Collaborative Learning in a Multiagent Model

Rosanna Costaguta and Elena Durán

Departamento de Informática, Facultad de Ciencias Exactas y Tecnologías (FCEyT)
Universidad Nacional de Santiago del Estero (UNSE)
Avda. Belgrano (S) 1912, Santiago del Estero, 4200, Argentina
{rosanna,eduran}@unse.edu.ar

Abstract. Computer Supported Collaborative Learning (CSCL) systems have recognized advantages. However, using these systems does not guarantee an effective collaborative learning. Success or failure of the learning experience depends on the collaborative skills the students show in the group. This work presents a multiagent model applied to CSCL environment, which aims both at recognizing conflicts occurring in group dynamics and also at providing personalized training of collaborative skills demonstrated by group members. Conflicts are recognized with the aid of information stored in a group model and by applying the Interaction Process Analysis method. Personalization is achieved through Bayesian networks that consider students' collaborative characteristics, stored in a collaborative student model, to elucidate the most suitable training strategy.

Keywords: Collaborative Learning, Personalization, Multiagent Model, Student Model, Group Model, Collaborative Skills.

1   Introduction

Students learn effectively in group when they ask questions, explain and justify their opinions, articulate their reasoning, and produce and ponder their own knowledge. Nevertheless, the benefits of collaborative learning are fully reaped only by means of well articulated learning groups. At present, the effect of Collaborative Learning (CL) depends on the quality of interactions that take place among group members. These interactions depend on the different collaborative skills students have, which are often conditioned by the collaborative context in which the students are participating.

Personalized assistance to students in collaborative learning environments has been recognized in recent years [15, 18]. Consequently, it is important that this kind of assistance is made effective for the users to accept it. To meet this goal, it is crucial to record data about students' personal characteristics, knowledge and collaborative skills for the construction of a student model.

Numerous student models for CSCL environment have been provided [5, 13, 14, 15, 18]. All these models are composed of only two kinds of profiles: student profile with personal characteristics and group profile with group characteristics. The

F.V. Cipolla-Ficarra et al. (Eds.): ADNTIIC 2011, LNCS 7547, pp. 134–139, 2012.
© Springer-Verlag Berlin Heidelberg 2012

collaborative skills that a given student possesses have not been recorded in student profiles. In a previous work [8] we proposed a collaborative student model with three different profiles: Personal, Collaborative and Group Profiles.

On the other hand, there is less research studies related to the training of collaborative skills. According to Prichard et al. [16], this fact could be attributed to an extended belief that every student already has developed these collaborative skills, or because it is generally accepted that the student acquired them by the mere practice of doing collaborative work. Recent research on this CL area proves that the group achievement and the process of learning of each individual in the group are enhanced with the aid of training [16]. Since there is a close relation between CL and CSCL, it is reasonable to suppose that these findings in the area of the CL can be successfully transferred to the CSCL environment.

Research can also be found about this subject, in which, taking into account the analysis of registered interactions, such recommendations to the users were generated [9, 10, 11, 12, 18].

In this paper we propose a multiagent system with a group model to recognize conflicts occurring in group dynamics and also a collaborative student model to provide personalized training of collaborative skills demonstrated by group members. This article is organized as follows. Section 2 presents the group and student models. Section 3 describes our proposed multiagent system. Finally, section 4 shows our conclusions and future work.

2   Group and Student Models

Based on a previous work [8] we propose to use a student model in the multiagent system with two components: individual profile and collaborative profile, and a group model; each one recording a different category of data:

Individual Profile: It contains three data categories: demographic data (user identification, first name, last name, date of birth, sex and nationality), knowledge domain data (level of knowledge that the student possesses about a domain); and data about individual personality traits (learning style).

Collaborative Profile: A student's collaborative profile consists of a set of inputs, each one represented by a collaborative skill and a context in which it appears. The collaborative skills considered in this work are those included in Collaborative Learning Conversation Skill Taxonomy [17] (Table 1), which has been designed to facilitate the recognition of dialogue during active learning. Soller's taxonomy breaks down each type of learning dialogue skill (active learning, conversation, and creative conflict) into sub skills (for instance: request, inform, acknowledge), and attributes (e.g., suggest, rephrase). The content of collaborative profile is given for each one of these subskills that a student reveals in a given collaborative context. The context was defined using three sets of variables [6]: characterization of collaborative situation, the group and the task.

Group Model: with the following data: code, which identifies the group, students that compose the group; type of group, which indicates if the group is composed only of peers or of peers and a tutor; behavior (Bales's classification is followed [1]; value, which expresses how many times the behavior is manifested; and percentage, which expresses the percentage of times that such behavior appears in relation to all possible behaviors.

Table 1. Collaborative Learning Conversational Skills Taxonomy

SKILL	SUBSKILL	ATTRIBUTE
Creative	Mediate	Teacher Mediation
Conflict	Argue	Conciliate, Agree, Disagree, Offer Alternative, Infer, Suppose, Propose exception, Doubt
Active	Motivate	Encourage, Reinforce
Learning	Inform	Rephrase, Lead, Suggest, Elaborate, Explain/Clarify, Justify, Assert,
	Request	Information, Elaboration, Clarification, Justification, Opinion, Illustration
Conversatior	Acknowledge	Accept/Confirm, Reject,
	Maintenance	Request Attention, Suggest Action, Request Confirmation, Listening, Apologize,
	Task	Coordinate Group Process, Request Focus Change, Summarize Information, End Participation

3   Multiagent System to Support Assistance in CSCL

The designed multiagent model is created to monitor, evaluate and improve the process that students perform during a collaborative task. There is in the model a space for shared work where the students deposit their contributions, which are stored in a logs base, for further analysis. For each group of students working in the CSCL environment, there are three classes of artificial agents: a Conflict Recognizer Agent, responsible for maintaining the Group Model and detecting group problems; a Student Model Agent, responsible for maintaining the two profiles Student Model (individual and collaborative); and several Personal Agents, one for each student comprising the group, responsible for training the student in those collaborative skills that are needed to avoid group conflict generation (Figure 1).

The Student Model Agent and the Conflict Recognizer Agent periodically process the logs base. The aim of the first one is to update the Collaborative Profile, and to this purpose a method based on Web Usage Mining is applied, which, using Association Rules, allows the model to recognize the student collaborative skills. This method is explained in [7]. The second agent calculates the indicators to evaluate the group behavior and to recognize the disturbances in the work dynamics. It applies for this purpose the Interaction Process Analysis (IPA) method [1], which allows the group behaviors to be sorted into twelve specific categories. IPA, by means of these categories, sorting them in pairs and considering certain limit values for each one of them, is able to recognize six types of conflicts (communication, evaluation, control, decision, stress reduction and integration conflicts) through which a group can flow during their dynamics cycle. In order to pave the way for applying the IPA method, a mapping was designed [2] between the collaboration attributes (Table 1) and the various group behaviors which are associated to the conflicts. As soon as a conflict is detected, the Conflict Recognizer Agent communicates the situation to the Personal Agents in order to have the corrective actions performed.

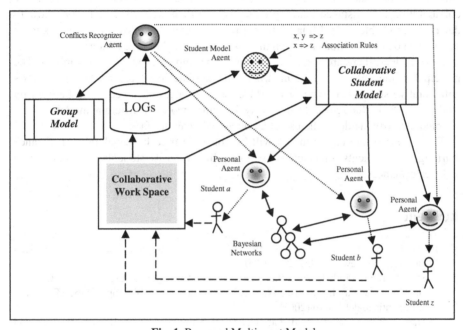

Fig. 1. Proposed Multiagent Model

When receiving the attention call of the Conflict Recognizer Agent, each Personal Agent determines in which skills the student should be trained in order to have the group stepping forward in the collaboration process, using for this purpose the specially created Bayesian nets. A correction action involves a box that pops up where the Personal Agent suggest the student to perform the interaction that the net has learned, which is necessarily connected to the student training needs. The design of the six Bayesian nets, tailored for each one of the six types of IPA conflicts, is documented in [3].

For the model validation, in a first stage a validation of the generation and maintenance of the Collaborative Student Model was separately made, and the result was documented in [6]; besides, the validation of the Conflicts Recognizer Agent and Personal Agents have also been validated and documented [4]. In a second stage it is planned to perform the complete validation of the multiagent model as a whole. For this purpose a development of the multiagent model will be made and implemented in distance education with MOODLE platform. Then the model will be tested with distance education courses implemented in this platform.

4   Conclusion

Main advantage of the proposal of a multiagent model is the possibility to improve collaborative learning environments with the following two models approach: a student model, that allows the detection of personal skills for a more effective collaboration in a distance learning environment; then a group model, that allow to detect group problem. And finally three kinds of agents that allow these models to be maintained detect conflicts and train the students in collaborative actions.

Nevertheless, there are some limitations in the implementation of this model. The principal is the need to use semi-structured dialogue interfaces to detect student's collaborative skills. This type of interface lacks the flexibility needed to be used by students in their dialogues. That is why in future works a different model will be adopted, one which allows the use of an open dialogue interface.

The proposed multiagent model will be apt to be used by developers of distance learning environments, enhancing the possibility to assist students in collaborative task performances.

References

1. Bales, R.: A set of categories for the analysis of small group interaction. American Sociological Review 151, 257–263 (1950)
2. Costaguta, R.: Habilidades de Colaboración Manifestadas por los Estudiantes de Ciencias de la Computación. In: Revista Nuevas Propuestas, vol. 43-44, pp. 55–69. Ediciones UCSE, Santiago del Estero (2008)
3. Costaguta, R.: Entrenamiento de habilidades colaborativas. In Tesis Doctoral, Universidad Nacional del Centro de la Provincia de Buenos Aires, Tandil (2008) (in Spanish)
4. Costaguta, R., Amandi, A.: Training collaboration skills to improve group dynamics. In: ACM-DL Proceedings of the 2008 Euro American Conference on Telematics and Information Systems, EATIS 2008. ACM Press, New York (2008)
5. De Andrade, A., et al.: A Computational Model of Distance Learning Based on Vygotsky's Socio-Cultural Approach. In: Proceedings of the MABLE Workshop, X International Conference on Artificial Intelligence on Education, San Antonio, Texas (2001)
6. Durán, E., Amandi, A.: Collaborative Student Profile to Support Assistance in CSCL Environment. In: ACM-DL Proceedings of the 2008 Euro American Conference on Telematics and Information Systems, EATIS 2008. ACM Press, New York (2008)
7. Durán, E., Amandi, A.: WUM approach to detect student's collaborative skills. Journal of Web Engineering 8(2), 93–112 (2009)
8. Durán, E., Amandi, A.: Personalised collaborative skills for student models. In: Psotka, J., Wheeler, S. (eds.) Interactive Learning Environment, vol. 19(2), pp. 143–162. Taylor & Francis Group, Routledge (2011)
9. Israel, J., Aiken, R.: Supporting Collaborative Learning With An Intelligent Web-Based System. International Journal of Artificial Intelligence in Education 17, 3–40 (2007)

10. Kumar, R., et al.: VMT-Basilica: an environment for rapid prototyping of collaborative learning environments with dynamic support. In: Proceedings of the 9th International Conference on Computer Supported Collaborative Learning, vol. 2 (2009)
11. Loll, F., Pinkwart, N., Scheuer, O., McLaren, B.: An Architecture for Intelligent CSCL Argumentation Systems. In: Proceedings of the 9th International Conference on Computer Supported Collaborative Learning, vol. 2 (2009)
12. Moreno Cadavid, J., Ovalle, D., Arias, F.: Integration Model of E-Learning based on Pedagogical Software Agents and Collaborative Learning Environments. In: Proceedings of the 9th World Conference on Computers in Education (2009)
13. Noguez, J., Espinoza, E., Hernandez, Y.: Work in progress: Afective Models for Collaborative Learning. In: Proceedings of 36th ASEE/IEEE Frontiers in Education Conference (TIH-15), San Diego (2006)
14. Paiva, A.: Lerner Modelling for Collaborative Learning Environments. In: du Boulay, B., Mizoguchi, R. (eds.) Proceedings of Artificial Intelligence in Education, pp. 215–230. IOS Press, Kobe (1997)
15. Peña, A.: Collaborative Student Modeling by Cognitive Maps. In: Proc. of the First International Conference on Distributed Frameworks for Multimedia Applications (DFMA 2005). IEEE Press, New York (2005)
16. Prichard, J., Bizo, L., Stratford, R.: The educational impact of team-skills training: Preparing students to work in groups. British Journal of Educational Psychology 76, 119–140 (2006)
17. Soller, A.: Supporting Social Interaction in an Intelligent Collaborative Learning System. International Journal of Artificial Intelligence in Education 12, 40–62 (2001)
18. Vizcaíno, A.: A Simulated Student Can Improve Collaborative Learning. International Journal of Artificial Intelligence in Education 15, 3–40 (2005)

Teaching Scrum to Software Engineering Students with Virtual Reality Support

Guillermo Rodríguez[1,2], Alvaro Soria[1], and Marcelo Campo[1,2]

[1] ISISTAN, Research Institute – UNICEN, Argentina
[2] Consejo Nacional de Investigaciones Científicas y Técnicas (CONICET)
{grodri,asoria,mcampo}@exa.unicen.edu.ar

Abstract. Scrum has received significant academic attention because of its widespread application in software development industries. Teaching agile software development can be illustrated by teaching with lecture-based classes. However, involving students in a real software environment is a trendy alternative which fosters their engagement. Software engineering graduates are not appropriately prepared for applying their skills in a real software project. Thus, we focus on teaching and integrating teamwork-oriented skills in a real software development environment based on Scrum. In this work, we present *Virtual Scrum (VS)*, a virtual reality environment that assists students with the running of a software project following the Scrum framework. *VS* supports artifacts needed for carrying out Scrum meetings and media-based tools to achieve permanent communication among Scrum members. A survey of students, who used the tool in a Software Engineering (SE) course, showed that *VS* is helpful to exercise Scrum practices.

Keywords: Virtual Reality, Software Engineering, Scrum.

1 Introduction

The increasing use of Agile Methods (AM) for software development has reoriented the education of future computer and information science engineers. AMs emerge as a feasible alternative to teach software engineering practices in order to prepare students to face problems associated to current software development. Teaching AM offers students opportunities to put theoretical concepts into practice [2].

Out of the various agile software development approaches, Scrum and Extreme Programming are commonly selected to be taught in software engineering courses. Particularly, Scrum has gained wide acceptance because it concentrates on managing software projects and includes monitoring and feedback activities [3]. These features allow students to acquire skills beyond technical and scientific scenarios, such as teamwork-related abilities. Thus, these aspects are welcome for SE teachers because they enable students to get acquainted with agile methods and, at the same time, provide mechanisms for evaluating individual agile concepts. Several works [5, 6, 7] have aimed to teach a few practices of software engineering like programming, testing, estimating and planning techniques. However, they have not considered the implementation of a teaching environment. Other approaches have stated Scrum covers

F.V. Cipolla-Ficarra et al. (Eds.): ADNTIIC 2011, LNCS 7547, pp. 140–150, 2012.
© Springer-Verlag Berlin Heidelberg 2012

a big number of good software engineering practices [8, 9]. For this reason, Scrum seems to be the most suitable alternative of AM to obtain a high level of coverage of software engineering practices. So far, there is not much evidence about teaching Scrum. Mahnic (2010) taught Scrum through a capstone project and described the course details, student perceptions and teacher observations after the course [2]. However, there is a lack of approaches to teach Scrum involving students in real software development. Scrum provides good software engineering practices.

To effectively learn how to work with Scrum, students have to setup a Scrum-based Team Room. This way, students are introduced to the use of tools and techniques for supporting different Scrum roles within a capstone project. However, setting up a Team Room for each group of students in a Software Engineering course is not always possible due to the cost of the required didactic material and, more important yet, the availability of university facilities.

In this context, we find virtual worlds highly suitable for helping students to feel familiar with development contexts by viewing software artifacts which are naturally intangible. These 3D environments provide a physical topology of the structure of information in a software project, which would allow accessing the project information [4]. For instance, one objective is to have the information readily available, visualize the traceability of requirements, and be aware of team progress. In this context, the artifacts are always shared in an integrated development environment. As a consequence, virtual worlds have to be as close to real life as possible by exploiting the 3D metaphor.

In this work, we present *Virtual Scrum*, a virtual world that provides students with a platform in which they can experience several aspects of the Scrum framework to prepare them for their future software development jobs and consequent exposures to the software process. To evaluate how much *Virtual Scrum* helps students in different aspects of the Scrum framework, we conducted a case study with students of a Software Engineering course at UNICEN University of Argentine. To record the perception of students of this study, we designed a questionnaire to collect students' opinions with respect to tool performance and usability. The results showed that there are some positive and some negative effects by introducing *Virtual Scrum*. The most notably positive effect is that students are clearly motivated to use the tool. However, there are some issues to improve which affect the tool performance, such as avatar movement controls, little friendly graphic user interface and tool deployment. Those issues were considered by students in the questionnaire because they affected tool usability.

The remainder of the paper is organized as follows. Section 2 reports background on collaborative work in software development. Section 3 gives an overview of *Virtual Scrum*. Section 4 describes experimental results. Finally, Section 5 concludes this research and identifies directions for future work.

2   Background

Scrum is a methodology that organizes projects into small, self-organized and cross functional teams, called Scrum Teams. Work is organized and prioritized according to

Product Backlogs. The backlog items are called *user stories*. These user stories are grouped into a serie of short iterations called Sprints. During the Sprint, a management representative, called Scrum Master, enforces Scrum practices and helps the team to make decisions or acquire resources as needed. A brief meeting held daily communicates to the team the work that has been accomplished, what work needs to be done, and asks for input concerning impediments that the team sees in reaching the goal. A planning session is held that defines backlog items to be grouped into a Sprint. Sprint Retrospectives in which team members discuss issues, accomplishments, and lessons learned about the previous Sprint are held [3]. Customer input is highly sought, and customers may become part of the team. The customers must be able to provide the time and energy required to produce a good product. Working, intermediate products are verified by customer or verified internally in increments; that is, as pieces or parts of the entire final product. These intermediate products are delivered in whole at the end of the entire development cycle. Each delivery builds more and more functionality into the product. It should be noted that this incremental development approach relies on brevity, i.e. brief meetings, brief planning sessions, and brief customer commitment time periods. It also relies on frequency, i.e. frequent meetings, frequent planning and re-planning, and frequent customer interaction [18].

In order to support Scrum practices, tools for planning, meetings, information visualization and requirement management are needed. There are some 2D tools for collaborative development in agile methods like CollabNet TeamForge[1] and ScrumWall[2] which allow developers to visualize and develop software artifacts in a distributed environment. However, those tools permit neither virtual interaction nor meetings among developers.

The advent of better Internet connections and more powerful computers have encouraged the creation of Virtual Worlds in which people get together and interact. Massive multiplayer online games (MMOG), like Second Life[3] and Wonderland[4], illustrate this trend.

In the light of the above, a 3D virtual environment allows developers to know about tasks performed by their peers, and even hold meetings regardless their physical location. Also, a 3D environment can be used to provide a physical topology of information structure in a software project, which allows a faster access to information [15]. Thus, these platforms are profitable to setup meetings and interact since people do not have to go one place to another.

In addition, several tools exploit collaborative integration features to provide group awareness and communication. For example, one aim is to have the information always available through a configuration management platform. In that context, artifacts are always shared in an integrated development environment [10]. In short, a 3D environment helps developers get familiar with the development context by visualizing software artifacts which are naturally intangible [16].

---

[1] http://www.collab.net
[2] http://www.scrumwall.com
[3] http://www.secondlife.com
[4] http://java.net/projects/wonderland

As a consequence, 3D virtual environments arise as viable solution to hold meetings. Nowadays, the best known virtual world is Second Life from Linden. Second Life is not a game, but a general purpose virtual world. It provides a Software Development Kit (SDK) in which people are able to create elements inside the world and design avatars to interact with those elements. Nevertheless, so far, this virtual world does not provide support for holding software meetings.

On the other hand, Wonderland, because of being Open Source, provides a toolkit that allows users to adapt the world to what they need. Wonderland project is totally developed in Java and freed under GPL license to create 3D collaborative virtual worlds. Once users connect to environment, they are capable of communicating through high fidelity audio, sharing desktop applications and documents, and holding real business.

In 2009, Wonderland presented a virtual world oriented to software development [14]. However, this tool is mostly focused on teaching agile methods rather than supporting software development and team member interaction.

Also, [12, 13] have worked on using virtual worlds to hold meetings but not software meetings. Thus, those environments were built without considering software artifacts related to a methodology. Furthermore, exploiting 3D metaphors for incorporating software artifacts to support meetings along the Scrum life cycle seems to be a limitation in existing virtual worlds.

3   Virtual Scrum

In order to introduce Scrum into a teaching context, teachers need to provide planning cards, whiteboards, and other artifacts so as to support the practices proposed by Scrum. So, we have developed *Virtual Scrum*, a groupware that provides support to the running of a software project following Scrum. Fig. 1 shows the artifacts of *Virtual Scrum* into the Scrum framework. The process starts with the load and prioritization of the Product Backlog, which is represented by *Virtual Product Backlog* artifact. This artifact allows students, who play the role of Scrum Team, to load user stories and also supports the prioritization process between the team and the Product Owner, who is the professor. At the beginning of each Sprint, students select the user stories to be developed during the iteration. These user stories are loaded into the Sprint Backlog represented by *Virtual Sprint Backlog* artifact which shows user stories of the current Sprint.

For the preparation of the Sprint, students estimate the user stories by using the *Virtual Planning Poker* artifact as shown in Fig. 2 (b). This artifact provides a mechanism for voting based on Planning Poker technique [1]. At the end of the activity, the team visualize the results through a shared board provided by the artifact.

During the Sprint, students use the *Virtual Spring Backlog* to set a color to each user story so as to keep track of its progress status. Red indicates a user story is not started (TO DO). Yellow denotes the user story is being performed (DOING). Green shows that the user story is completed (DONE).

At the different stages of the Scrum life cycle, the tool supports virtual meetings. The meetings play an important role in the communication among Scrum members in order to identify and plan corrective actions to possible issues or impediments to the development process. Also, the artifacts used in the meetings are very important to visualize and remember what has been discussed and analyzed. For example, it is helpful to use post-it notes on a board, sketches on flip charts, and writings on the whiteboard to support discussion and argumentation.

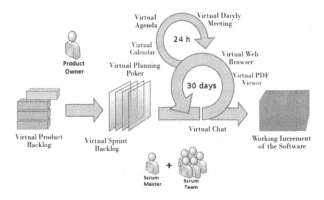

Fig. 1. Virtual *Scrum* in the Scrum life cycle

However, when a meeting is held among members physically distributed, those tools become obsolete. Thus, high fidelity tools able to support collaborative and distributed work are required. As a consequence, *Virtual Scrum* emerges as an alternative to maintain and visualize artifacts used during the meeting. This yields visible benefits not only for students, who no longer will need to attend the course, but also for Universities, which will save on resources to carry out their software engineering courses. Fig. 2 (a) shows the inside of *Virtual Scrum*, in which 4 members physically distributed are sharing a virtual room through an avatar representation.

Fig. 2. Inside *Virtual Scrum:* (a) Meeting among Scrum members. (b) Virtual Poker Planning.

In order to hold a software meeting, several artifacts are mandatory to ensure that most software engineering practices are met. Thus, the *Virtual Daily Meeting* artifact is used by students to hold Daily Meetings. *Virtual Scrum* provides students with the *Virtual PDF Viewer* artifact to present reports or pictures, the *Virtual Browser* artifact to surf on the Web, and the *Virtual Calendar* to schedule events notified by the *Virtual Agenda*. In addition, a chat with videoconference support is provided through the *Virtual Chat* artifact.

During a daily meeting, the team reviews the estimations and considers the lessons learned so as to adjust the development velocity for the next Sprints. The Scrum Master, who is also a student, is responsible for starting the daily meetings taking into account the 15-minute time-boxing period. Within this period, the members of the Scrum Team answer the following questions: What have you done since yesterday? What are you planning to do today? And do you have any problems that would prevent you from accomplishing your goal? This information is used during the retrospective meeting at the end of each Sprint.

To sum up, by using *Virtual Scrum*, students will get a concrete picture of how to practically setup a suitable Team Room to implement the software practices of the Scrum framework and also to learn the different aspects related to the management of a software project in an agile methodology.

4   Experimental Results

The experiment focused on evaluating how much *Virtual Scrum* helps students in different aspects of the Scrum framework. Thus, we carried out a case study with 8 students of last year of System Engineering at UNICEN University of Argentine.

Students were of both sexes and were between 21 and 25 years old. They were given some lectures of Scrum in the context of Software Engineering course of the System Engineering BSc program at the Faculty of Exact Sciences (Department of Computer Sciences-UNICEN). Each student had a personal computer in order to simulate a geographical distribution. Before the experiments, we held a training course for the participants so as to provide them with the skills to interact with each artifact of the virtual world and its relationship with the Scrum framework. The experiment consisted in building a web-based system to manage purchase and sale of products so as to perform all the Scrum activities such as building the Product Backlog, estimating and planning the user stories, holding Daily Meetings and observing task progress. Professors, who played the role of Product Owner, gave students a list of 9 user stories. To evaluate the perception of the tool, we used a questionnaire based on Likert's approach [17] so as to collect student opinions about *VS* artifacts. The questionnaire items were statements based on a 3-point scale in which the students could either totally agree, agree, or disagree.

4.1   Analysis of Student Performance in Scrum Process

We observed students using *VS* artifacts. Particularly, we focused on estimating and disaggregating user stories. Most *VS* artifacts were suitable for discussing and supporting argumentations in user story estimation. Table 1 summarizes the user stories loaded in the *Virtual Product Backlog* artifact, the estimations in days for each user story obtained from the *Virtual Poker Planning* artifact, and the *Earned Value* (ER) for each user story. ER refers to the ratio between remain work decrease and amount of work done. Ideally, the remain work decrease between days d_1 and d_2 once Sprint started should be grater or equal to the amount of work done during this period. Thus, the goal value of this metric is greater or equal to 1. However, values much greater than 1 mean a poor planning. Equation (1) shows how to calculate ER, where ER_{dj} is the ratio between the amount of work done for the task j during the day i, $WS_{i,j}$, with $i=1, 2, ..., d-1$ and the total work $WS_{i,j} + WR_{d,j}$ (done and remain) [11].

$$ERd,j = \frac{\sum_{i=1}^{d-1} WSi,j}{\sum_{i=1}^{d-1} WSi,j + WR\,d,j} \qquad (1)$$

Table 1. Estimation and earned values of user stories

User Story	Execution time (in days)	Initial Estimation (story points)	ER_{tarea}
US 01	14	50	0,25
US 02	14	10	0,35
US 03	7	150	0,71
US 04	14	100	0,65
US 05	14	100	0,35
US 06	14	5500	0,35
US 07	14	100	0,43
US 08	14	100	0,35
US 09	7	100	0,55

For simplicity, user stories (USs) were comparable to each other, had the same level of granularity and began to be developed the same day. The USs were estimated to be ready within 1 to 2 weeks. The story point column of Table 1 shows the relevance of the US. For example, story points of *US 06* were high because students did not have enough knowledge about web front-end technology, which was a high priority requirement to the Product Owner.

When students reached the building phase, the execution days shown in Table 1 were more than they had estimated. Also, ER shows the percentage of completeness of each US in which the values for *US 01* and *US 02* show that students underestimated the importance of those features because they estimated few story points and they obtained low ER in that USs. During the retrospective session, students realized that all the estimations made with the Poker Planning technique did not reflect the complexity of the system. Then, they considered that the reason for underestimated and overestimated USs was the lack of experience in the technology and in the planning technique. To make matters worse, they did not acquire enough information from the Product Owner because they considered it unnecessary. In this light, we believe that the major obstacle the students faced was the lack of assistance in the decision making process, especially when they preformed the estimation of the user stories.

4.2   Questionnaire Evaluation of *Virtual Scrum* Perception

To better prepare the students to fill out the questionnaire, we included some general "warming up" questions placed at the beginning of the questionnaire, asking, for example, what Scrum is and how software projects actually benefit from it. Then, we added several query items designed to collect the students' opinions with respect to performance of *Virtual Scrum* according to decision making and coordination; usability; quality of tool features, and commitment.

According to Fig. 3, most students agreed that discussion processes were coordinated and efficient. Also, most students were satisfied with the meeting artifacts supported by the tool. Nevertheless, regarding decision making, the results showed that the amount of students who agreed to effectiveness of the decision making process was nearly the same as the amount of students who disagreed. So, it is necessary to work on decision making assistance related to user story disaggregation, estimating, prototyping, etc. Also, some issues related to usability caused problems in communication as it is shown in Fig.4.

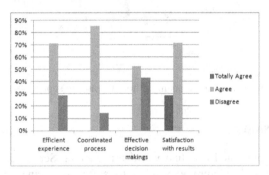

Fig. 3. Opinion about decision making and coordination supported by the tool

As regards tool usability, Fig. 4 shows there are some issues that affect the use of the tool like avatar movement controls and readability in the 3D scenario. On the contrary, most students agreed that face-to-face meeting can be replaced by *Virtual Scrum*. More than 80% of students will use the tool whenever it is not viable a face-to-face meeting.

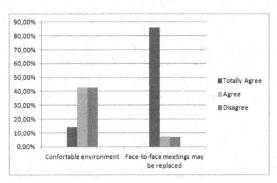

Fig. 4. Opinion about tool usability

Regarding tool features, Fig. 5 shows that more than 70% of students are satisfied with the quality of work supported by the tool. To measure the quality of work, we took into account the ease of students to interact with the tool. We concluded that problems in 3D interfaces do not affect considerably the Scrum process and member interaction. In addition, the figure shows high commitment to the solution obtained through the tool. Only less than 20% of students were little committed to the solution. Also, if usability improvements are implemented, there will be more commitment and responsible attitude of students in decision-making during meetings.

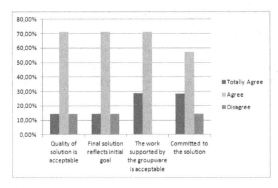

Fig. 5. Opinion about quality of tool features to support the process

5   Conclusion

In this work we presented a virtual world for teaching Scrum framework aiming at preparing students for future exposures to software engineering. *Virtual Scrum* represents a helpful tool for students to learn and exercise good software engineering practices. For instance, the Poker Planning technique is used to estimate efforts, the Product Backlog is used to manage user stories and Daily Meetings are used to perform peer reviews and progress checking.

The experiment carried out with students from last year of System Engineering at UNICEN showed that *Virtual Scrum* is also viable to support virtual meetings at different stages of Scrum life cycle during a real and controlled software development project. As a consequence, most students would use the tool again, and even replace a face-to-face meeting in case it cannot be held.

This finding provides an opportunity to use *VS* in a distributed software development context. Developers distributed all over the world make it difficult to apply Scrum due to the difficulty in coordinating a meeting and the lack of constant communication. Thus, *VS* emerged as an alternative to support virtual meetings in software environments using Scrum with members physically distributed.

However, there are some issues to be improved in order to enhance meeting performance like the interaction inside the tool and lack of traceability of real world software artifacts. On the other hand, there are a number of threats to validity in our evaluation of *VS*. The case-study was small to make generalization, even though it has shown positive feedback. In particular, students in the experiment had theoretical knowledge of Scrum but they had no real experience on it. Less than half of students were not involved in the software business. Regarding the size of the project, the case-study was performed by only one Scrum Team. Thus, we are interested in studying the coordination of multiple Scrum Teams in order to observe whether the tool is helpful to facilitate team coordination.

Finally, future work will be threefold: (1) to experiment with more students in larger software projects, (2) to integrate *VS* with software development tools like issue trackers and versioning systems, and (3) to apply profiling techniques to provide personalized assistance to students according to their observed problems such as decision making process at different stages of Scrum.

Overall, we concluded that *VS* helps students learn how to work on software development based on Scrum. In addition, *VS* provides effective communication among developers and coordination mechanisms among life cycle artifacts, in order to maintain the project synchronized. In this way, we confirmed the anecdotal evidence of Scrum as a framework used not only in the context of software development, but also in teaching software engineering.

References

1. Cohn, M.: Agile Estimating and Planning. Prentice-Hall (2006)
2. Mahnic, V.: Teaching Scrum through team-project work: students' perceptions and teacher's observations. International Journal of Engineering Education (2010)
3. Schwaber, K.: Agile Project Management with Scrum (2004)
4. Whitehead, J.: Collaboration in Software Engineering: A Roadmap. University of California, Santa Cruz (2007)
5. Kivi, J., et al.: Extreme Programming: A University team design experience. In: Proceedings of 2000 Canadian Conference on Electrical and Computer Engineering, pp. 816–820 (2000)
6. Mahnic, V.: A case study on Agile Estimating and Planning using Scrum. Electronics and Electrical Engineering (2011)
7. Reichlmayr, T.: The agile approach in an undergraduate software engineering course project. In: 33rd Frontiers in Education, vol. 3, pp. 13–18 (2003)
8. Diaz, J., Garbajosa, J., Calvo-Manzano, J.: Mapping CMMI Level 2 to Scrum Practices: An experience report. In: Software Process Improvements, vol. 42, pp. 93–104. Springer, Heidelberg (2009)
9. Sutherland, J., Ruseng Jakobsen, C., Johnson, K.: Scrum and CMMI Level 5: The Magic Portion for Code Warriors. In: Proceedings of the 41st Annual Hawaii International Conference on System Sciences (2008)
10. Herbsleb, J.: Global Software Engineering: The Future of Socio-technical Coordination. School of Computer Science. Carnegie Mellon University (2007)
11. Mahnic, V., Zabkar, N.: Introducing CMMI Measurement and Analysis Practices into Scrum-based Software Development Process. International Journal of Mathematics and Computers in Simulation (2007)
12. Nijholt, A., Zwiers, J., Peciva, J.: The Distributed Virtual Meeting Room Exercise. In: Proceedings ICMI 2005 Workshop on Multimodal Multiparty Meeting Processing (2005)
13. Reidsma, D., et al.: Virtual Meeting Rooms: From Observation to Simulation. Journal AI & Society, London (2007)

14. Stockdale, R., Parsons, D.: Agile in Wonderland: Implementing a Virtual World Workshop Activity. In: 20th Australian Conference on Information Systems, Melbourne (2009)
15. Whitehead, J.: Collaboration in Software Engineering: A Roadmap. University of California, Santa Cruz (2007)
16. Teyseyre, A., Campo, M.: An Overview of 3D Software Visualization. IEEE Transactions on Visualization and Computer Graphics 15(1), 87–105 (2009)
17. Likert, R.: A technique for the measurement of attitudes. Arch. Psychol. 22 (1932)
18. Kulpa, M., Johnson, K.: Interpreting the CMMI. CRC Press (2008)

Security of the Automatic Information On-Line:
A Study of the Controls Forbid

Francisco V. Cipolla Ficarra[1,2] and Andreas Kratky[3]

HCI Lab. – F&F Multimedia Communic@tions Corp.
[1] ALAIPO: Asociación Latina de Interacción Persona-Ordenador
[2] AINCI: Asociación Internacional de la Comunicación Interactiva
[3] Interactive Media Division – University of Southern California, USA

c/ Angel Baixeras, 5 – AP 1638, 08080 Barcelona, Spain
via Tabajani, 1 – S. 15 – CP 7, 24121 Bergamo, Italy
ficarra@alaipo.com, akratky@cinema.usc.edu

Abstract. We present a first set of automatic information which is generated in the Web 2.0 with regard to people, whether it is individually or in groups, totally distort reality through the data that are associated to it. Besides, we analyze for the first time cyberbullyism in some European and American regions which violates the safety controls in the servers and the execution void in the application of the national and international laws in the custody of the rights of the internet users. Finally is presented an experimental heuristic technique for the first evaluation of the profile of the cyberbully, with the purpose of quantifying the human and economic damage in the credibility of on-line information.

Keywords: Internet, Intranet, Extranet, Web 2.0, Cyberbullism, Security, Privacy, Human Factors.

1   Introduction

The safety of the digital information is one of the main goals in the creation of products and offer of services in the late 20th Century societies, and of the new millennium. These are societies that have focused 99,99% of their activities in digital support. Consequently, any inconvenience in the nets of the intranet, extranet and Internet, due to the energy cuts, computer viruses, destruction of the databases, etc., means the paralysis of services and products which generate wealth for the coffers of the institutions with a profit, in the public and private sector, whether it is national and/or international [1] [2] [3]. The opening of the intranet networks towards the outside of the labour institutions, for example, has been a long process due to issues related to safety and the associated human factor [4]. Sometimes, in certain working environments, it is necessary to start to analyze the human factors when the losses derived from safety rather than from the computer systems (that is, configuration parameters, programmes which control the traffic and the volume of the files inside

F.V. Cipolla-Ficarra et al. (Eds.): ADNTIIC 2011, LNCS 7547, pp. 151–164, 2012.
© Springer-Verlag Berlin Heidelberg 2012

and outside the network, the access to the confidential information files in the intranet network, etc.).

In the later years of the former millennium, novel and important projects related to sharing data on-line at a zero cost, were discarded by the heads of enterprises and industries, following the advice of the software and hardware outsourcing firms in the face of eventual computer attacks from outside its institutions [3]. It was in this way that some pioneering projects inside the graphic computing 2D and 3D aimed at mechanic, chemical, civil engineering, etc., where databases with millions of 2D and 3D components were put at the disposal of the users for free, didn't advance and were cancelled because the designers weren't authorized to navigate the Internet [5]. That is, instead of using for free three-dimensional objects of a bookshop, considerably cheapening the production costs of goods and services preferred to put the designers in the face of the CAD applications to generate them from zero, for computer safety reasons [6]. Obviously many of these small industries or product services for the automotive, naval, airspace, building sectors, etc., which also ceased their activities after following the lousy advice from the external technicians who gave their outsourcing services.

In the safety of the computer systems, the human factor is vital in the software and hardware outsourcing firms. Sometimes it is not the insider staff or attacks from outside the enterprise or industrial facilities, but rather those who give outsourcing services, through technicians experts in computing (software and hardware) whose fees paid per hours of service [3]. As a source, the source of the conflicts lies in the sale of new servers, software licenses for antivirus, renewal of computers and printers maintenance contracts, etc. Conflicts which grow in the periods of maximal industrial production and check or checkmate the activities of a firm forcing the directors to acquire the software and/or hardware suggested by the salesmen of the outsourcing firms. In few words, it is a sabotage since that who sells the antivirus is the same who has set the virus in the network of that industry, for instance. The behaviour of those technicians and their bosses is within the framework of cyberbullying. This is the modus operandi of many outsourcing firms in Southern Europe. A way to act that is complicated to prove legally because they have access to a key piece of security: the server that fulfils the role of firewall. In the case it is proven, the legal sanctions which are applied in those places of the EU are laughable, in face of the economic and human damage caused. So far we have considered as aspect of the banned actions, and which may be called local and relatively controllable, but hardly eradicated from the legal point of view.

In the international context, we also find behaviours belonging to the cyberbullying environment, especially when they refer to the social networks, where the "product" are the people [7]. In this case, generally in an anonymous way, or because of automatisms of the computer systems, alien to people's will, their personal, professional data, etc. may be included in certain portals. This inclusion may be agreeable or not, to the users at the moment of discovering its existence. Now the inclusion in some cases is automatic but the exclusion of those groups requires a red tape process. This process may consist in a simple communication through an email, to the heads of the portals, or through the reports to the competent authorities where the user dwells, so that they take it upon themselves to carry out the steps necessary for exclusion. Theoretically this second option should definitively exclude the user from deeds alien to his will, that is, banned. However, the cyberbuully's actions don't stop, and he takes shelter in the anonymity of the Internet. All of this makes some professionals of the sector of the new technologies of communication and information unable to participate in the social networks. In short, the excellent breakthroughs in the issues of safety and privacy of the information may be eclipsed by realities belonging to the sector of the human or social factors, inside the computing context.

In the current work we will analyze the origin of the cyberbully and the shelter inside the educational context in Lombardy and Catalonia. We will also describe other mechanisms which may control the users' activities, without previous knowledge or. authorization [8]. In both cases, we intend to establish the first profile of those who devote themselves to cyberbullying in Southern Europe with ramifications in the American continent, for instance. Starting from it, an evaluation technique will be perfected which may improve the safety and credibility of the on-line information, without resorting to the purchase of specialized software and hardware.

2   Cyberbullying: Main Characteristics in a True Example

One of the radical problems in the spread of cyberbullying since the start of the new millennium is when the people who practice it understand that they are in anomalous working structures (firms, industries, colleges, etc.) where those who have to exert authority or exerting control [8] [9] are sidelined due to the renewable working contracts or do not have the support of the rest of the academic staff, for instance. The model of garbage control in Southern Europe is the main cause why the phenomenon of cyberbullying has quickly spread among the students. That is, the future professionals of the factual or formal sciences. A fast expansion which starts in high school down to the colleges. Next we will describe a true example, removing direct references for privacy reasons. In the next figure we can observe how an institution where temporal or rubbish contracts are rife in a prestigious scientific portal such as ACM (Association for Computer Machinery).

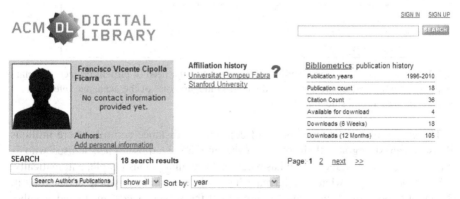

Fig. 1. Automatic information which does not reflect the professional's emotional reality (because of working relationship reasons) towards that university (?)

Another of the anomalies is that the Spanish, French, Italian, Portuguese etc. legal systems prevent on-line publication (a free access listing) of those who practice cyberbullying because of privacy reasons. In our case, we will only resort to Google Maps to locate the growth of the phenomenon along time and we will eliminate the names. We will also use square parenthesis *[ ]* to insert the important variables which may help the detection of a potential cyberbullying expert.

We have the origin of cyberbullying with a simple email. It makes apparent to the eyes of an expert in safety systems the presence of a potential cyberbully. Obviously, that an expert in communicability has the necessary knowledge and/or experiences to make quickly an analysis of the discourse of the message. Only in the first message received it can be detected a continuous insistence beyond normal in the relation professor-student, for instance, and the famous two letters that refer to Russia: "ru". In the log files of the portal constantly attacked, these two letters will be seen for a decade (figures 3 and 4), camouflaged in a myriad ways (in the figure 2 accompanied with a question mark). From that message, and thanks to the analysis of the discourse, the cyberbully has given a signature of his way to act.

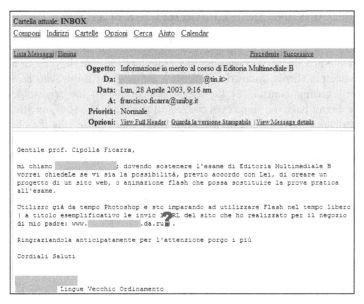

Fig. 2. First message received where is already apparent the need to present projects to obtain supposedly some kind of profits inside the democratic structure of the academic interrelations between professors and students

The emails are unwitting sources of constant far-distance control, where millions of users can strengthen their role of cyberbullying victims. When a user who is attacked erases a message he/she has received from anonymous people, automatically, he/she's indicating at what time he reads his mail and even from where he/she does it. (geographic position through the IP number of the server or computer) and whether he/she opens or not the enclosed files. In the latter case the risk is higher, since it can indicate a potential user to send them viruses. In our case, the person who sent the message of figure 2 was a Lombardy university student. Its author makes apparent the danger of the college portal in the face of external attacks *[self-denunciation]* and the possibility of reading the confidential data of the students *[self-intromission to the computer system]*. Student coming from the social sciences and besides lacking the computer knowledge or computer safety, in an autonomous way but *[belonging to an association of free or open software]* of the Linux environment. That is, he/she *[lacked the necessary self-knowledge]* but *[transmits plenty of other people's knowledge]*. That plenty of supplied information in a disinterested way and free is in order *[to draw attention]*. The goal is *[participating in projects]* and surpassing quickly the other mates.

As a rule, these people are *[highly individualistic]*. That is, they do not accept teamwork, and use it *[to reach the people who exert the controls]*. In the case of college it may start with the hired professors, then go to the associated professors and even to the dean himself. This escalade also allows him to boost his resume. For instance, when theoretically the access to the college working posts is frozen at national level because of financial restrictions, these people can get from the dean's office may get contracts as clerks. Also their immediate superiors, that is, the associated professors may strengthen their salary, through the hiring of their services as external specialists (a kind of pseudo outsourcing through projects, for instance, giving lessons, improving the safety of the college portal and incorporating elements of the Web 2.0, carrying out make-up operations to the interface, etc.) whose cost per hour is twice or three times as much, with relation to the university technical staff, who have been occupying similar steady posts for a decade.

One of the problems which is hard to evaluate in the case of cyberbullying is the behaviour of who is exerting it, that is, whether it is something fleeting or persists along time. With this goal our experiment consisting in including the author of the message in a project of a portal, where he would collaborate as a technician. The working group belonged to the environment of the social sciences. Now in this working group was applied the laissez-faire strategy in the systems aspects (the platform on which the portal can work is Windows and Linux), but without direct access to the provider of the Internet service. Little by little the professor and the members of the project started to work in Windows, placing the first beta versions of the on-line multimedia system. However, the cyberbully constantly was generating improvements that enriched the original project, such as the animations made with Flash, and needed *[to have access to the files and programs at any times]*. An access which should be made through FTP (File Transfer Protocol) to the portal that was in the server of the provider of the Internet dominion and hosting to gain speed of data transmission. In that sense, if he/she doesn't have the access to the passwords of the dominion provider, after previously consulting the Linux group, he/she conditions his continuity in the participation of the project to the change of platform (from Windows to Linux) and the installation of a small program "open source" to be able to directly access the files of the portal without using password. A software that just like the used tool to detect the failing in the college portal came from Russia. The Windows portal is shifted to Linux since the goal was to evaluate the behaviour of a cyberbully along

time. It was like that how periodically during ten long years he/she has been going in
and out of the system, periodically erasing not only the counter of the visitants, but
even the homepage of the portal (www.mondoguareschi.com).

Fig. 3. Area of the portal (www.mondoguareschi.com) which is constantly being attacked by
the cyberbully

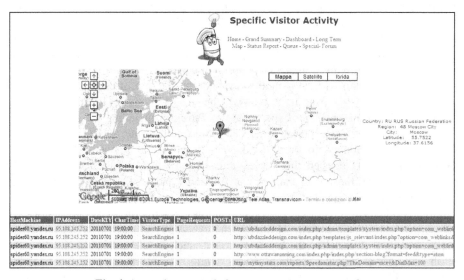

Fig. 4. A portal, apparently innocuous to computer attacks

Fig. 5. The reading of the log files is important to detect the intromission or attack to the server
and/or computer systems

Evidently the type of counter may need to be reinitialized now and then (figure 3), but not every day, as it can be seen in the accesses made by the cyberbully. Dates that coincide with activities out of Europe of the professor who coordinated the project. This behaviour demonstrates that the phenomenon of cyberbullying does not decrease with the passing of time. The financial risk is huge when his portal design or information architecture services are hired. Now they act in that way because *[they rely on an implicit or tacit support of the power in the national or international group to which they belong]* such as can be the open source of Linux or a group of university professors. Some of these professors, having a cyberbully as a colleague, present themselves to society as computer technicians, who advises legally or judicially the pertinent authorities in the courts. Here is one of the reasons why cyberbullying has exponentially grown in the last decade in Southern Europe. The victims of these attacks are invited to file reports to the local authorities. The modality of the reports is against anonymous. Now watching who are the working colleagues of the technicians who make the reports, one understands why these investigations turn into nothingness. This negative result prevails where *[parochialism]* is in force. The genesis of that way of acting lies in the process of enculturation inside the groups of the primary or secondary schools, especially non-secular, that is, religious [10]. This behaviour does not only not change in the *[temporal space]*, it doesn't change in the *[geographic space]* either, as it can be seen in figures 7, 8, and 9.

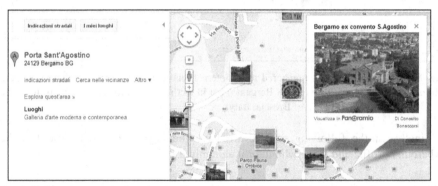

Fig. 6. College base of the Lombardy –Bergamo city, where cyberbullying has been exerted in the last few years

Fig. 7. Catalan college –Barcelona city, base where cyberbullying is currently exerted

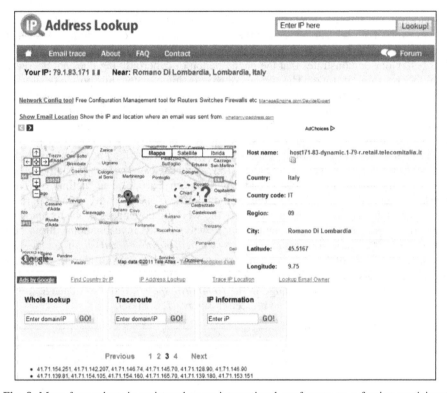

Fig. 8. Maps from where is registered to an international conference as a foreign participant (Romano di Lombardia, Province of Bergamo) but in fact it is few kilometres away from where the cyberbully lives (Province of Brescia, Italy)

Finally, in the following scheme we have the keywords which describes the cyberbully profile and those who tutor it along time.

Fig. 9. First set of keywords which make up the evolution cadre of the Cyberbullying in Southern Europe

A reality like that described prevents that some professionals may enjoy the advantages of the Web 2.0 because they are a constant target of attacks, immune from the legislative point of view. That is why in portals such as LinkedIn, Facebook,

Twitter, etc., we can easily find those who practice cyberbulling with their matching pictures and networks of friendships and acquaintances. In those networks it is always important to take into account the way in which the relationships among the members of the group are generated (circular, monodirectional, sequential, star, etc.), always avoiding the star [11]. In that structure, nests the dynamic persuader [12] who may boost cyberbullying to achieve one of his goals, such as being outstanding inside the network and occupying a higher position. Now there is an excellent exception to that modality of star-shaped structure, when we have the graphic information that sums up the relationships of scientists in regard to the works they share among themselves, as it can be seen in figure 8, content drawn from portal Arnetminer – www.arnetminer.com.

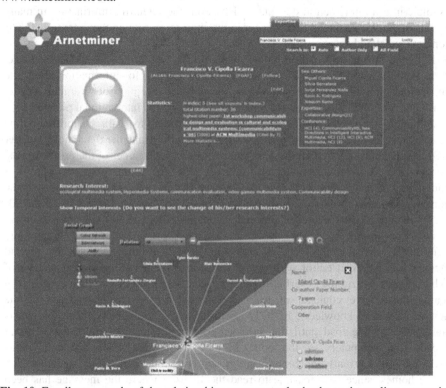

Fig. 10. Excellent example of the relationships among people thanks to the on-line automatic information

3   Automatic Information On-Line: Problems and Some Solutions

There are certain portals like that presented in figure 10, where the updating of the information is made in an automatic way and the purpose it serves is positive, since it allows to know quickly the intensity of the links among the other members of the network. The thickness of the lines denotes those relationships which are strongest along time given the volume of collaboration in the works of scientific research which have been published. However, in this kind of scientific automations, such as that which appears in the portal –www.informatik.uni-trier.de/~ley/db/indices/a-tree, we see how along time many publications are not considered, that is, they aren't automatically loaded in the databases. In that sense, it is also striking how the researchers of software engineering usually plump for publicly presenting a selection of the works, since many of them are rubbish and belong to the fritter junk. In this latter operation there is no automatism, but rather a manual selection of them. There aren't automatism either in many portals of the Web 2.0 related to the HCI, the design, interactivity, communicability, etc. where the author must register the publications, after the approval of the controller of contents of the portal. We have an example in www.interaction-design.org. However, the scientific information in many portals of the Web 2.0 tend to disappear in the short term, forcing the users to get their contents registered again.

In the automatic information online related to the web professionals, for instance, there is the possibility of knowing who has been looking for information about the curriculum vitae or the published works, through the reception of an email. In that sense, the portal "LinkedIn" –www.linkedin.com is one the international pioneers.

Although the automatisms are positive in order to gain visibility online immediately and the portals of prestige such as usually wants the dynamic persuader [13], in the hands of a cyberbully may mean the end of the career of the professionals. For instance, not having financial resources available to hire the services of a community manager and eradicate the infamy that circulates online against those honest and modest professionals. In the coast of the Spanish Mediterranean of the 90s the cyberbullism was exercised through anonymous messages to the management heads. For instance, in the specialized printed press in graphic computing, multimedia, virtual reality, etc., it was enough with sending periodically myriad messages to the chief editor with regard to the articles of one or several victims of cyberbullying, where the cyberbullies declared that they didn't serve their contents (in reality those were contents of technological avant-garde but the heads of the newsroom lacked knowledge of ICT, for instance). Automatically those journalists started the decline road until the disappearance of the team of journalists. In that decade, the computers of the colleges were a constant source of anonymous cyberbullying. Currently the controls are greater both in the educational structures and in the homes, since it is feasible to read the IP from where the message has been written. An example in this regard can be found in the following figure that refers to an online questionnaire (the same which has allowed the presence of the hometown of the cyberbully in figure 8): http://www.alaipo.com/conference-adntiic/Information/ Information_ALAIPO_ADNTIIC.html

Although we have enumerated so far individual examples, cyberbullying may also be corporative, national and international with a manual or manipulator automatism from apparently democratic institutions such as can be a public university. In that sense, the genesis may be in associations related to the human-computer interaction and the new technologies born in autonomic regions colleges and which automatically found other associations outside the university centres to exercise controls in the local and national press, and also branch out and diversity the pressure groups. We have a Catalan example in the University of Lleida, where from the early 90s is created a theoretically non-profit organization but cashing in association fees as if they were the international organizations ACM or IEEE. Allegedly they were at the same level as those associations. Simultaneously, it fosters and supports organizations like "alzado", "cadius", etc. whose purpose is to destroy all that which doesn't respect the rules they impose. That is, professors who didn't pay the yearly fees, or did not promote outside the borders of their autonomic region or state borders the expansion of the exclusivist model in usability issues, interactive design, etc., or did not follow their models or curricula (in reality rehashes of others coming from the American continent) were quickly sidelined and excluded.

These organizations have used their knowledge about interactive design of interfaces to present themselves for a long decade as the only specialists in the Internet inside Spain and in some economically speaking emerging Latin American countries.

That is, they have generated a star-shaped network in countries like Colombia, Mexico, Chile, Brazil, etc. Although they have used the instruments of the Web 2.0 for the circulation in Latin America, in Spain that modus operandi was oriented from Barcelona to the main newspapers of nationwide circulation, such as "El País" (www.elpais.com) or from Majorca from the SER radio station (www.cadenaser.com), or from the autonomous television of Catalonia (www.tv3.cat) to international television, etc. In few words, there is a merger of traditional media with the new media for the spread of the classic cyberbullying in the press, radio, television, etc. with the "automatic of the social networks on-line".

In Latin America the rapid circulation of the phenomenon is due to the way in which these operations have been disguised or the vested interests of some official covenants among educational institutions, such as can be the agreements among universities. The sign of those agreements in the 90s entailed a high academic status for those who achieved them (head of department, academic secretary, dean, etc.) on both sides of the Atlantic.

However, the European financial reality makes impossible a myriad aspects of said agreements. Those who have signed it in the American continent prefer to join European cyberbullying against their countrymen, under the principle "your enemies are my friends". The consequences of these deviations is the implementation of European academic antimodels in the Latin American university education and the lack of a legislation in keeping with the new realities deriving from the financial context.

In the face of the legislative void, or the lack of compliance of the current laws, the only solution is not to use the resources stemming from the social networks. Obviously that we are in situations where the estates do not take care of the dignity of people, and their licit activities. The behaviour of a few may bring about considerable financial damages, not only to those who suffer such injustices, but also to the rest of the international community.

Here is one of the reasons where the great set of multimedia contents, with free on-line access, has started to be reduced in the new millennium and break down into restricted access subsets. That is, paying to have access to contents which used to be totally free. Therefore, we are in the face of a new digital gap due to the access to contents by human and/or social factors. Finally, one of the legislative solutions in some countries of Southern Europe, is relating cyberbulllying to stalking. However, this topic remains open for future lines of research of the social factors.

4   Lessons Learned and Future Research

Without any doubt the breakthroughs in the issue of information safety to protect the privacy of the users, for instance, has grown exponentially with variegated solutions stemming from biometrics, mathematics, etc. However, the apogee of the automatic information, due to the development of the Web 2.0 makes these solutions be alien to the daily reality of those users who are victims of cyberbullying, individual or corporative, for instance. As it has been demonstrated, the scientific context is not excluded from this reality, with which is affected one of the cornerstones of the credibility of the on-line information. That's why every time the issue of computer safety is approached it is important to consider the human aspects, because many times the failings do not hail from the software or the hardware [14], but rather from the people who interact with the systems.

The strategy used on a potential cyberbully, seen and confirmed along a period of time, as it has been demonstrated in the current work, has allowed to get a first set of characteristics as well from his personal profile and his behaviour. The goal of the analysis is to establish some models in future researches, tending to generate metrics of human factors, which are aimed at computer safety. Also in these future works we will try to quantify the economic damage they cause.

The automatisms in generating portals with information by professionals may be positive if the information they store really depicts reality. In contrast, they are negative and foster the lack of credibility of the information when we are in the face of a mirage. The inclusion in portals in an automatic way is fast, but the exclusion of them may entail a long bureaucratic process, i.e., to write severals emails to webmaster or community manager. Furthermore, we are in the face of information that sometimes doesn't have the go-ahead from the author, and there isn't a mechanism either which balances what goes in and out of those portals.

5   Conclusion

The computer literature on the issue of safety has grown exponentially with the democratization of the Internet. New horizons have been opened from the technological point of view in order to increase the protection of the data and digital information. However, the studies in human factors are scarce. In the current work has been made apparent that the early integration of the future computer science professionals in groups prompted by unearthly precepts may be a constant source of destruction of freedom in the Web 2.0, the Web 3.0 and future versions. The members of the pressure groups, anonymous and destructive, as a rule, act freely out of non-earthly reasons, alien to the legislative rules of the national and international community.

Finally and inside the private, public or hybrid institutions, the person or people who have access to confidential information, where it is to look it up, including the technical environment, that is, those who set the safety parameters of the firewall, for instance, should enjoy the utmost confidence. The head of ICTs must enjoy the utmost freedom to communicate irregularities to the superior ruling board of the structure where they are immersed. Besides, it is advisable that periodically safety tests are carried out from outside the facilities, even geographically remote, so that third parties can act freely. The reports should be confidential and delivered simultaneously to the head of computer safety and also the member of the ruling board who oversees the correct functioning of the data in the internal and external network. The ideal thing is that said additional control function doesn't focus on the very responsible of ICTs, in order to prevent nasty and irreparable surprises, deriving from the human factors, in the context of computer safety.

Acknowledgments. The authors would like to thank to Maria Ficarra, Juri Hwang, Mabel, Luz, Cristian and Carlos for the helps.

References

1. Falcarin, P., Collberg, C., Atallah, M., Jakubowski, M.: Software Protection. IEEE Software 28(2), 24–27 (2011)
2. Karat, C., Brodie, C., Karat, J.: Usable Privacy and Security for Personal Information Management. Communication of ACM 49(1), 56–57 (2006)
3. Cipolla Ficarra, F.V., Ficarra, V.M.: Software Managment Applications, Textile CAD and Human Factors: A Dreadful Industrial Example for Information and Communication Technology. In: Cipolla Ficarra, F.V., de Castro Lozano, C., Pérez Jiménez, M., Nicol, E., Kratky, A., Cipolla-Ficarra, M. (eds.) ADNTIIC 2010. LNCS, vol. 6616, pp. 121–131. Springer, Heidelberg (2011)
4. Mead, N., Jarzombek, J.: Advancing Software Assurance with Public-Private Collaboration. IEEE Computer 43(9), 21–30 (2010)
5. Cipolla Ficarra, F.V: Evaluation of Interfaces and Portals for International E-commerce. In: Proc. ISAS-SCI 2001 –World Multiconference on Systemics, Cybernetics and Informatics: Information Systems Development, vol. 1, pp. 274–279 (2001)
6. Cipolla Ficarra, F.V., Cipolla Ficarra, M., Giulianelli, D.A.: Industrial E-Commerce and Visualization of Products: 3D Rotation versus 2D Metamorphosis. In: Salvendy, G., Smith, M.J. (eds.) HCI International 2009, Part II. LNCS, vol. 5618, pp. 249–258. Springer, Heidelberg (2009)
7. Lieberman, H., Dinakar, K., Jones, B.: Let's Gang Up on Cyberbullying. IEEE Computer 44(9), 93–96 (2011)
8. Curran, C.: Combating Spam, Spyware, and Other Desktop Intrusion: Legal Considerations in Operating Trusted Intermediary Technologies. IEEE Security & Privacy 4(3), 45–51 (2006)
9. Tamai, T.: Social Impact of Information System Failures. IEEE Computer 42(2), 58–65 (2009)

10. Cipolla-Ficarra, F., et al.: Handbook of Computational Informatics, Social Factors and New Information Technologies: Hypermedia Perspectives and Avant-Garde Experiencies in the Era of Communicability Expansion. Blue Herons Editions, Bergamo (2011)
11. Cipolla-Ficarra, F., et al.: Handbook of Advance in Dynamic and Static Media for Interactive Systems: Communicability, Computer Science and Design. Blue Herons Editions, Barcelona (2011)
12. Cipolla-Ficarra, F., et al.: Quality and Communicability for Interactive Hypermedia Systems: Concepts and Practices for Design. IGI Global, Hershey (2010)
13. Cipolla-Ficarra, F.: Persuasion On-Line and Communicability: The Destruction of Credibility in the Virtual Community and Cognitive Models. Nova Publishers, New York (2010)
14. Rostad, L., et al.: Learning by Failing (and Fixing). IEEE Security and Privacy 6(4), 54–56 (2008)

Communicability and Usability
for the Interface in e-Learning

Leda B. Digión and Mabel Sosa

Departamento de Informática
Facultad de Ciencias Exactas y Tecnologías
Universidad Nacional de Santiago del Estero (UNSE)
Avenida Belgrano (S) 1912, (4200), Santiago del Estero, Argentina
{ldigion,litasosa}@unse.edu.ar

Abstract. A quality attribute specification model for the development of e-learning systems is introduced. Quality issues are measured in terms of usability and communicability for the interface maintenance, defined in relation to the evolution of an apprentice or personalized student, according to learning styles and collaboration issues in the study group. This paper relies on the User Centered Design, and includes the stages of user interface analysis, design and evaluation for collaborative systems. We aim at attaining the best quality for educational processes inherent to the e-learning environment, by means of an early quality evaluation, based on the referred attributes. The model also allows the evolution from an apprentice to a personalized and cooperative apprentice, as a potential user and organizer of the learning processes in e-learning environment.

Keywords: Usability, Communicability, E-learning, Collaborative Systems.

1 Introduction

The technology should be considered as a mediator element in the different learning processes; as far as this becomes a socio-cognitive tool for the creation and appropriation of the socio-cultural environment. Besides, with the technology the individual cognitive processes become stronger, and above all a foundation is set for the building of new dialogues intended for the learning processes creation, reaching beyond the conception of the individual. This has been recently nominated as collaborative learning [1].

E-learning environments should generate spaces apt to facilitate the teaching-learning process; hence the importance of having usable systems which aim at attaining the desired educational goals. As much of the learning environment as the educational materials are designed in perfect articulation with a set of technological and educational requirements [2], considering the basic principles of Human Computer Interaction (HCI), which bestows a set of techniques and methodologies for the design of interactive systems [3].

An e-learning system is thoroughly interactive, and therefore, interaction should be its key element in its conception and its design, also taking into account the user necessities and characteristics.

F.V. Cipolla-Ficarra et al. (Eds.): ADNTIIC 2011, LNCS 7547, pp. 165–175, 2012.
© Springer-Verlag Berlin Heidelberg 2012

The term usability is mostly associated to the following propriety of an interactive system; "easy to use and to learn". It is defined on ISO 9241-11[26] as "the extent to which a product can be used to achieve specific goals with effectiveness, efficiency and satisfaction in a specified context of use".

Usability constitutes a key factor in the student skills when acquiring knowledge and competences in a satisfactory way.

From the e-learning instructive point of view, the learning activities should stimulate the student in the learning process, and those activities should be introduced which best fit in the student style, trying to satisfy the personal or educational expectations. In relation of these assumptions, the User Centered Design [3] is a philosophy of design and a process where the final user requirements and limitations constitute the center of each of the steps in the design process. The user is involved in each stage of the process, and it should be granted that the final product fulfill the needs and characteristics of the user, creating the possibility of a positive learning experience.

ISO Standard 13407 [4] establishes four user centered design activities: understanding and specifying the user context: identifying and specifying the user and organizational requirements; evaluating the designs considering the requirements and producing design solutions. Each stage of the model introduces the following characteristics: it is user addressed (experience and satisfaction); the model is directed with a user input; a substantial user participation (studies, experiences, feedback, motivation); user description and characteristics; design of an interactive prototype (software engineering); several processes (often casual or non specified processes); evolution through "trial and error" method [5].

Besides, to determine the usability of a system, three factors should be taken into account: user, content and the environment in which the system is used. In this context user includes its identification and the unveiling of its needs and characteristics; then educational content includes to establish design guides, techniques and requirements that should be fulfilled, and the various issues related with the separation of the content and the visualization of the content; and finally the educational environment which takes into account the requirements identification and the learning environment characteristics, the tasks analysis and the interaction design. These three factors give a closer view of the e-learning process with usability characteristics and contribute to place it in the user centered design [6].

In the area of collaborative learning mediated by technology it is clear that this system promotes the collaborative work, develops new cognitive processes and modifies certain attitudes. That is why it is considered as a "preparation with the netware and for the netware, allowing the social construction of the knowledge through the development of competences for knowledge construction and elaboration" [7].

In this paper a conceptual model of usability and communicability specifications is introduced aiming at the maintenance of the user interface with focus to the proper competences of the student, mainly the learning styles and the characteristics of collaborative learning, within the general frame of user centered design, applied to e-learning systems.

2   Collaborative Usability and Communicability

Teaching and learning virtual environments or e-learning are informatics applications developed for educational needs. Their aim consists in facilitating communication among participants, mainly teachers and students, and is implemented in different modes: distance e-learning or a combined mode of distance and presential e-learning (blended) [8].

Considering the goals and broad applications of e-learning, it should be provided with properties related to the user centered design approach [9]; also, it must be usable and take into account the user characteristics and skills, when interacting with the learning virtual environment and educational contents.

Usability [10] is an attribute consisting in user interface facility of use, and it is defined with five quality components: learnability or capacity of being learned, efficiency, memorability or capacity of being remembered, user errors avoidance and user satisfaction generation.

In an educational context, where elements of mediation are to be found, such as objectives and goals, learning strategies, pedagogical resources, contents, etc., usability is not exclusively an inner attribute of the software, but it should be defined as another element of mediation within a certain context of use with, among others, educational goals, user expectations and motivation.

Besides, encouraging the collaborative group work in this kind of environments, group members are prepared to develop fluent communication and ideas or information exchange between them, whether in synchronous or asynchronous way; they are also prepared to facilitate coordination, cooperation and collaboration for developing activities and attaining conflict resolution; with the scope of attaining individual and group objectives. To summarize, the proper and characteristic elements of a collaborative system are: communication, coordination and cooperation [11].

In this perspective, collaborative usability is defined from the process point of view, as the effectiveness as effectiveness and satisfaction with which a certain product facilitates the attainment of user group specific objectives in a specific use context; and from the point of view of the product is defined as the software capacity of being understood, learned and used, being friendly for a user group, in specific conditions of use [12].

Besides, communicability is synergically related to usability, even though they are two totally different disciplines [21]. While from an interaction perspective, usability is related to the construction and modeling goals of the information. Communicability has to do with the information architecture as a foundation of the visual layouts, which facilitate the recognition of the interaction elements.

According to that, interface constitutes an element related to the user expectations, which are important to be explained. It is said that an interface, to be meaningful for an user, should articulate in a balanced way the efficiency of visual stimuli, in order to create a communicational channel, to be able to deal with the aroused sensitiveness produced in the interaction, and firmly and clearly communicate the usage functions of the system. Therefore, in the area of interface design, emotion should fulfill an important role, since it creates a context as message channel and facilitates interaction. An interface design cannot be figured out unless the stimuli control are considered as part of the communication goals.

Any interface fulfills the communicative functions according to the goals with which the user should be satisfied. These goals are transferred in the various visual stimuli of the message and they spur a reaction in accordance to the personal behavior and the cognitive area. Thus, the visual stimuli are the orientation "lights" which guide the behavior in the user conscious reflection channel.

The proposed Communicability Model [13], defines the various stages to the development of graphic interfaces with communicative effectiveness. It is shown in the model that both disciplines, communicability and usability are considered in Cognitive Ergonomics, facilitating the evaluation of the development from a user centered approach: how the proposed system will cogitate and perceive, which will be the reactions against the layouts, etc.

Following the development process of both disciplines, the usability of contents is found as a common issue. It is oriented to determine if information and interactions meet the standards of the system. By means of Cognitive Ergonomics the human issues of interaction and system usability are evaluated.

Also communicability is included in the development of the interface visual level, where verb-iconic elements are articulated. These elements are needed to establish an effective and efficient communication with the user through perception fusion, semiology, image retorics and image syntax.

3   Learning Styles and Collaborative Learning

The definition of the term learning style has great importance, because it deals with a factor that has influence in the effectiveness of the teaching-learning process. Learning activities related to the student style are intended to stimulate the student in the learning process, and those activities should be offered to a particular student which better adapt to her/his needs [25].

Learning style is related to the different ways of learning, namely with the various strategies for gathering, interpreting, organizing and thinking about the referred information [14]. Various learning styles are recognized [15]:

- Alva Learning Systems: three different styles are recognized, visual, kinesthetic and auditive.
- VARK: four types are recognized, visual, auditive, kinesthetics and the read/write strategy.
- Myers-Briggs Type Indicator (MBTI): defines different styles derived from personality preferences, namely extraversion/introversion, sensing/intuition, thinking/filling and judgment/perception, etc.
- Felder and Silverman: identifies learning preferences in four dimensions: active/reflective, sensing/intuitive, visual-verbal, and sequential-global, related to the student preferences of learning modes.

An e-learning system generally promotes and offers the user different alternatives for group or team work, oriented to collaborative work with peers. In the case of e-learning design, the main task of the user is to learn, which is by nature a tacit and abstract task [16].

It is said that e-learning evaluation can bring the usability participants out of their "comfort zone", what brings to the perception of the necessity of integrating usability and learning [17]. It is therefore outlined here the necessity of developing models which take part in the process, such as the user model (apprentice and facilitator/author), content model, communication model and evaluation model (service quality evaluation).

Therefore, collaborative learning construction comes up as a set of pedagogical mediations, digital or not digital, that aim at uniting the effort of a certain group toward the goal of being able of learning together; in this scenario enters the technology for the generation of new spaces or environments leading to the construction of knowledge and learning. Small and heterogeneous groups are referred [18], working together in a task in which each member is individually responsible for a part of the activity, which cannot be completed but with a collective work and within a state of interdependency.

Collaborative learning [19] is defined as certain situation in which a group establishes a mutual commitment in order to develop some task in which the coordination and relation of interactions compels the achievement of a common goal.

Four principles can be identified in collaborative learning structures: simultaneous interaction, equal participation, positive interdependency and individual responsibility, which positively influence in the student competences development [20].

Collaborative learning initiates with the understanding of the potential which lays in the diversity and the comprehension of the essential nature of the community. It requires of planning developed by the educators, and strategies to approach activities apt to attain good and enhanced interaction, personal commitment and individual and collective reflective actions.

Computer supported collaborative learning (CSCL) is an environment to improve teaching-learning processes mediated by information and communication technology. It is absolutely certain that students attain a high level of success when they collaborate in the process of achieving learning activities [21].

Hence, it is necessary to distinguish two vital ideas to express the mediated collaborative learning:

- The idea of learning in a collaborative way. The apprentice do not feel to be an isolated person, but in interaction with the others, sharing objectives and distributing responsibilities in a friendly way, proper of this kind of learning.
- It is outlined the role of the computer as a mediation element, supporting the learning process.

Environment [7] should be understood as a set of interrelated elements which constitutes a system which facilitates the learning process. Besides, the generation of educational spaces based on a computer mediated communicational system is properly named learning environment. This system is empowered as a specifically designed tool able to support collaborative knowledge production.

That is why the tasks designed for collaborative environments have the purpose of guiding the group towards the performance of the proposed goals. And therefore, the design turns to be the fundamental base towards the knowledge collaborative construction.

4   Proposed Conceptual Integration

A specification of usability and communicability of e-learning interfaces is proposed. The evaluations of attributes are made according to the analysis of the apprentice user and the analysis of the collaborative type group tasks, made by a specialized apprentice called cooperative apprentice.

The specifications of learning styles are obtained from the user analysis, and the group roles specifications are obtained from the tasks analysis. From the specifications data an apprentice profile is defined, which will be used as a reference for the required usability and communicability specifications (user requirements).

The user requirements and defined tasks will be used as a guide for the design stage and prototype creation, and the output product will be evaluated as a function of the usability and communicability [21].

In figure 1 a model is introduced, which includes user centered design activities (analysis, design and evaluation), and also the techniques that can be applied in each activity.

When a software project is initiated, usability specifications [22] should be elaborated, trying to actually reflect the usability level of the system in those specific issues that are of more importance. These specifications will rule the iterative process of development, although for its creation it will be needed to previously identify the users and the tasks that they will develop with the system.

To attain these usability specifications [22], it is proposed to make the user and tasks analysis. As for the user analysis, since the aim is to create a usable software system, it is needed first to know the specific users for which it is conceived in order to establish its main characteristics. The user analysis consists in defining a set of indicators which influence the quality of the virtual environments. Therefore, these indicators will also influence in the academic performance of students whose learning styles better adjust with the details of the environment, and in this way they will facilitate the mechanisms for the acquisition, storage and reutilization of the information.

Usability principles are focused to a set of elements which will transform the educational environment into an attractive scenario apt to retain the student. These elements are related to the information organization, readability, connection with learning elements, reply time, multimedia elements selection, net browsing. All these elements should be adapted to the predominant cognitive styles of the students. For instance, a predominantly active cognitive style will make the learning process feel more comfortable in a flexible and open instructive scenario; a reflective style needs virtual environment full of relevant information, through hypertext links which generate reflection and analysis of the introduced information contents. In the case of pragmatic students, since they are looking for the possibility of a practical application of the acquired knowledge, they will need designed spaces where demonstrations could be made, with introduction of practical examples, etc.

In task analysis a description of a set of tasks is made to understand in detail how people do when they bring about a certain task. In this context a task is a user meaningful activity, something the user considers that is needed or pleasant to bring forth. Generally, in an e-learning environment the apprentice does not work alone, but integrates a group where they together try to reach foreseeable goals. Therefore it is required to establish certain characteristics in the interface to achieve group collaborative work.

Besides, for the apprentice to engage in collaborative work and fulfill the assigned task, it is necessary to determine the skills and competences in order to assign the best role in the group. This role can be attained starting from the formal recognition of the behaviors which are most adequate to the group work and interrelation, according to peer compatibility. To achieve this purpose the introduced procedure [23] will be chosen which has as a goal the work group organization within a conformed team in the project. This procedure is based on the work role identification of the apprentice, and from this starting point the ideal model for group organization will be determined. Thus the task performance of each individual in the group and of the whole team will be enhanced.

For the communicability specifications the concept affordance is applied [21], indicating the inner characteristic of an object for showing all the actions the user can achieve with it. In other words, the user will recognize through visual representation the function of the object, what is it for, and what purpose has the object. Thus, every media object of the interface explains its function through shapes, dimensions, colors and content with which they have been designed, and no further explanation will be needed. Thus, the media object affordance is obtained through the relations of the inner object characteristic, applying two proprieties: visibility: the media object should be outstanding and so the user will realize its existence and should be able to perform actions on it; and intuitive comprehension, meaning that actions than can be achieved with the media object are evident.

At last, in the specification it is considered that media object visibility and comprehension are design traits intended to satisfy the user goals, and for that reason the learning object interfaces should be self-explaining interfaces, without further explanations or instructions about how to interact with media objects. In addition, media objects should be descriptive, as much in other objects context as in its visual composition, to attain consistency between the design and the actions which are represented.

In a second cycle of the e-learning environment development and going forward with the User Centered Design vision, it is proposed to consider the site interface maintenance as part of the site production stage, starting from the introduction of a cooperative apprentice. This cooperant should implement support tasks for collaborative learning.

Communications between cooperants will be based on the exchange information of the apprentices according to their social role (what is defined in a previous analysis); synchronization actions will be based on the site operative restrictions, for instance the access, security, concurrency requirements of petitions. Each one of these restrictions will be present according to the assigned role.

In other words, now the apprentices constitute a technical and organizational team in charge of the site production, with a specific collaborative role also to accomplish tutoring actions. So the aim is to have cooperants working on the interface in proactive collaboration, performing design corrections, requirement updates, and added information accumulation (content).

These cooperants can almost be considered as site "developers". They will work on the composition, writing and supervision of the site, in accordance with the information core of the application and calling for new apprentices to work on the interface. The presence of the initial developer is needed to control the work of collaborative users.

Paying attention that "protocol and organizational schedules should be defined among different members which work in the site maintenance" [24], the existence of a cooperative apprentice is proposed for this background.

Inside the Usability and Communicability Specification "cooperant views" can be generated. This requirement can be visible in the site when the cooperant logs in the site to fulfill a certain task, for instance, debate about inner conceptions, feedback reception, variable manipulation to revise hypotheses and models. The cooperative interaction environment should also be studied (analysis); screens and controls organization (design); and ergonomic standards to cover unpredictable occurrences; do not skip the study of organizational and cognitive factors.

With the purpose of developing strategies to enhance learning in virtual environments and multimedia systems, outstanding research works are reviewed [27] from various authors. With this background a set of principles is established which approach multimedia learning from a cognitive point of view. From this result a reorganization of the information [28] is proposed in seven categories in relation to their application in the educational multimedia material design, and all these principles are shown [29]:

1. Principles of multimedia character: Includes the split attention, mode, and spatial and temporal contiguity principles, and they pay special attention to the way of integrating one or more media to aid the individual to learn.
2. Principles that derive from cognitive overload: consist of the principles related to overloaded work memory prone to interfere with learning process, the redundancy, segmentation, previous training, coherence and signalization principles.
3. Principles which deal with the way the multimedia material is presented to the user: voice and image presentation principles are gathered.
4. Principles related to the user activity: consist of those principles which allow student activities planning toward the knowledge construction, such as the principle of assisted discovery, worked example, collaboration and self-explanation.
5. Principles related to the instructional animation: they deal with educational animations, including principles of apprehension, congruence, interactivity, focused attention and flexibility.
6. Principles which support navigation: they are related to navigation and site mapping.
7. Principles related to user specific characteristics: such as previous knowledge and cognitive principle of aging.

Between the position of a tutor and an apprentice as final user, it is proposed here a more expert cooperant, as a designer and interpreter of the educational message, operating with these principles. Understanding the human mind and memory, the way information is processed, and also knowing and applying the multimedia learning principles is fundamental to design, develop and enable a virtual environment or an educational multimedia system. In a User Centered Design background, evaluation measures taken during the design stage should be oriented to acquire more information needed for its own activities. To evaluate usability, an "evaluation of characteristics" [10] could be performed. This is a particular heuristic evaluation, of the characteristics of a prototype for its availability and comprehension, exclusively focused in one trait of the interface. In the proposed framework it would be for each cooperative user view (role of the cooperative work). Finally, we try to enhance the interface with the active participation of the cooperative user, which should develop not only the tasks related to the "production" of the site but also has tutoring functions for collaborative learning, to optimize the reutilization, combination, edition and visualization of the educational material.

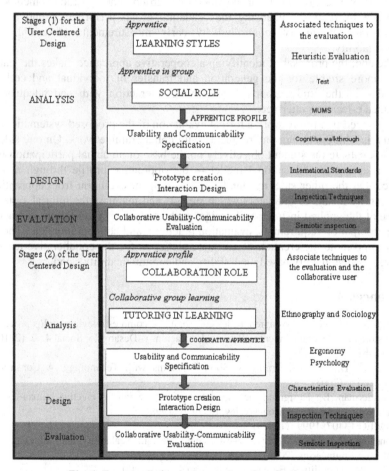

Fig. 1. Framework for the integration of quality issues

5   Conclusion

A poor interaction design system, especially in e-learning processes, cannot improve in usability by merely changing its graphic interface. For that reason, this model, centered in the apprentice user, is inclined to prioritize usability evaluation, and then to recognize and identify the apprentice in a virtual teaching-learning environment, based on collaborative learning preferences and styles.

Usability and communicability specifications, taking into account learning styles, group collaboration issues and participation in learning tutoring through interface maintenance, constitute an important influence in the educational process, what afterwards will facilitate the system validation according to the expectation fulfillment and the user needs.

On the base of a quality specification framework, a working plan can be designed for the e-learning project management, which considers, according to the cooperative apprentice, the evolution in a collaborative group, the operative methods of appropriate instruction, enhancing the academic group performance and also the software product quality, controlled by early measurements of usability and communicability.

In the end, the proposal of identifying a cooperative apprentice makes the learning process more simple for the generation and transfer of individual and collective knowledge in the study group, if conserving interaction with and adequate and maintained e-learning interface.

It is planned in a future work a formal evaluation of the proposed systematic model in virtual teaching-learning environments with collaboratuive work. On one side, the aim is to evaluate the student objectively on the base of an actual participation in the model, adapting the educational model to the apprentice profile through a proper interface. On the other side, to monitor the participant evolution from apprentice to cooperant, by means of indicators which support and maintain the tutorial system on the base of the applied instructional design, such as content organization, interactivity level, participation requiremnts, evaluation practices, and collaboration, etc. The final goal is to promote the creation of adequate platforms for the collaborative teaching-learning practice, mainly based on usability and communicability standars.

References

1. Cardozo-Cardone, J.: Los aprendizajes colaborativos como estrategia para los procesos de construcción de conocimiento. Revista Educación y Desarrollo Social 4, 2 (2010) (in Spanish)
2. Jonassen, D., et al.: Learning to Solve Problems with Technology. A Constructivist Perspective (2003)
3. Shneiderman, B.: Designing the user interface. Strategies for efective human-computer interaction, 3rd edn. Addison-Wesley, Reading (1998)
4. ISO/IEC 13407: 1999 E (1999)
5. Constantine, L., Windl, H.: Usage-Centered Design: Scalability and Integration with Software Engineering (2000)
6. Miller, M.: Usability in E-Learning. Learning Circuits (2005)
7. Gros, B.: Aprendizaje, conexiones, y artefactos: La producción colaborativa del conocimiento. Editorial Gedisa, Barcelona (2008) (in Spanish)
8. Ferreira Szpiniak, A., Sanz, C.: Hacia un modelo de evaluación de entornos virtuales de enseñanza y aprendizaje. La importancia de la usabilidad. TE&ET. In: Revista Iberoamericana de Tecnología en Educación y Educación en Tecnología, pp. 10–21 (2008) (in Spanish)

9. Hackos, J., Redish, J.: User Interface Task Analysis. John Wiley & Sons, New York (1998)
10. Nielsen, J.: How to conduct an Heuristic Evaluation (on-line). Useit.com-usable information technology (1994), Access, http://www.useit.com/papers/heuristic/heuristic_evaluation.html (reference : June 05, 2003)
11. Grudin, J.: Groupware and social dynamics: Eight challenges for developers. Communications of the ACM 37(1), 92–105 (1994)
12. Tobarra, M., Montero, F., Gallud, J.: Usabilidad Colaborativa: Caracterizando la Usabilidad en Entornos Colaborativos. Grupo de investigación LoUISE. Universidad de Castilla-La Mancha. Albacete. España. IX Congreso Internacional Interacción, Albacete (2008) (in Spanish)
13. Correas, J.: Comunicabilidad, paradigma de la Interacción Humano-Computador (2009) (in Spanish), http://www.nosolousabilidad.com/articulos/comunicabilidad.htm
14. Duque, N., Jiménez-Ramírez, C.: Modelo de generación de cursos virtuales adaptados al perfil del estudiante. Universidad Nacional de Colombia, Medellín (2002) (in Spanish)
15. Hazel, P.: ¿What can we learn from Learning Styles? (2002), http://www.paulhazel.com/docs/styles.html
16. Zaharias, P., Poulymenakou, A.: An Implementing Learner-Centered Design: The interplay between usability and instructional design practices. Journal of Interactive Technology and Smart Education (2006)
17. Squires, D.: Usability and Educational Software Design: Special Issue of Interacting with Computers. Interacting with Computers 11(5), 463–466 (2005)
18. Johnson, D., Johnson, R., Stanne, M.: Cooperative Learning Methods: A Meta–Analysis. University of Minnesota (2000), http://www.clcrc.com/
19. Cabrera, M.: La colaboración en el aula: más que uno más uno. Bogotá. Magisterio (2008) (in Spanish)
20. Kagan, S., Kagan, M.: The structural approach: six keys to cooperative learning. In: Handbook of cooperative learning methodspp, pp. 115–133. Greenwood Press, Westport (1994)
21. Cipolla-Ficarra, F.: Quality and Communicability for Interactive Hypermedia Systems: Concepts and Practices for Design. IGI Global Editions, Hershey (2010)
22. Ferré-Grau, X.: Integration of usability techniques into the software development process. In: International Conference on Software Engineering (Bringing the Gaps Between Software Engineering and Human-Computer Interaction), pp. 28–35 (2003)
23. Digión, L.: Procedimiento de formación de grupos de trabajo en el proceso software. Facultad de Ciencias Exactas y Tecnologías. Universidad Nacional de Santiago del Estero. Anales de CACIC (2005) (in Spanish)
24. Trevor, J., Koch, T., Woetzel, G.: Metaweb: Bringing synchronous groupware to the World Wide Web. In: Proceedings of the European Conference on Computer Supported Cooperative Work (2002)
25. Gentry, J.: Using Learning Style Information to Improve the Core. Financial Management Course & Financial Practice and Education (Spring-Summer 2000)
26. ISO 9241-11 Ergonomic requirements for office work with visual display terminals (VDT)s. Part 11 Guidance on usability (1998)
27. Mayer, R.: The Cambridge Handbook of Multimedia Learning. Cambridge University Press, New York (2005)
28. Herrera, B., Latapie, V.: Diseñando para la educación. No solo Usabilidad. Revista multidisciplinar sobre diseño, personas y tecnología (2010) (in Spanish) ISSN: 1886-8592

Towards Software Architecture Documents Matching Stakeholders' Interests

Matías Nicoletti, J. Andrés Diaz-Pace, and Silvia Schiaffino

ISISTAN Research Institute, CONICET-UNICEN
Campus Universitario, Paraje Arroyo Seco (B7001BBO), Tandil, Argentina
{mnicolet,adiaz,sschia}@exa.unicen.edu.ar

Abstract. Architecture documentation is a crucial activity in any software development project. In practice, architecture documenters face two problems: how to generate relevant documentation contents for the main stakeholders, and how to avoid documenting too much about the architecture. We propose a personalization approach based on stakeholders' interests to tackle these problems. The expected contribution is to facilitate the documenter's tasks, while making the resulting documentation useful to the stakeholders. We specifically describe a user profiling tool that builds stakeholders' profiles, which serve to link the stakeholders to sections of the architectural documents. These links help the documenter to prioritize sections that are potentially relevant to those stakeholders. The tool has been implemented as a semi-automated pipeline based on text mining techniques. The results, although preliminary, show that our proposal is helpful for a stakeholder-centric architecture documentation process.

Keywords: Architecture Documentation, User Profiling, Text Mining, Stakeholders.

1 Introduction

Documentation is a common activity of any software development project, and it is important in early development stages because the decisions made at those stages will shape the rest of the development and the quality of the software product. Documentation is also useful for knowledge sharing and communication among project stakeholders. A relevant documentation artifact is the so-called *Software Architecture Document (SAD)*, which captures the key *design decisions* that enable the system to satisfy its main quality attributes, and therefore, the business goals posed by the system stakeholders [3]. Basically, architectural decisions refer to a number of high-level software structures and patterns (e.g., layers, client-server, etc.), normally depicted via *architectural views*, and their justification in terms of quality-attributes and functional requirements.

Producing good architectural documentation and keeping it up-to-date is challenging, particularly in the context of iterative development processes. On one

F.V. Cipolla-Ficarra et al. (Eds.): ADNTIIC 2011, LNCS 7547, pp. 176–185, 2012.

side, documentation consumers (e.g., stakeholders) want to access to the "right architectural contents" of the SAD, with as less information overloading as possible. Unfortunately, these consumers are often swamped with architectural knowledge that not always satisfies their *information needs*. Recent studies [8, 11] have shown that many individual stakeholder concerns are addressed by a fraction (less than 25%) of the SAD, but for each stakeholder a different SAD subset is needed. On the other hand, the documentation writer (or *documenter*) faces several forces that constraint his/her task, such as: how to generate timely documentation for the main stakeholders, how to keep up with the features being added in development iterations, and how to avoid documenting "too much" about the architecture. In addition, the value of documentation writing is often not clearly perceived by upper levels of management.

In this context, we see the SAD management process as a balancing act between having "good enough" documentation (for the stakeholders) and creating it in a cost-effective manner. By good enough, we mean the degree to which the documentation supports the stakeholders' tasks, while also exposing concerns such as architectural risks or quality-attribute tradeoffs. By cost-effective, we imply that the documentation is delivered incrementally, and its contents are prioritized according to some economic strategy. Over the last years, several architecture documentation approaches have been developed [12] and tool support has become a key asset (e.g., CASE tools, Wikis, collaborative platforms). These efforts have mainly targeted the consumer's perspective of the documentation process. In this article, we focus on the documenter's perspective, that is, how the documenter can produce SAD contents that are actually informed by the stakeholders' information needs.

Certainly, having a SAD with the necessary architectural views to satisfy all the stakeholders would be ideal, but this is seldom the case in real projects, due to economic reasons, schedule pressures, and also conflicting stakeholders' interests, among others. A more practical approach is to select a set of views addressing the concerns of the most relevant stakeholders, and then adjust the view contents and level of details accordingly [2]. In order words, we argue for a *personalization* of the SAD contents. To do so, we propose capturing the main characteristics of each stakeholder by means of *user profiling techniques* [9]. The expected contribution of our approach is to facilitate the documenter's tasks, making the documentation process both cost-effective and more useful to the stakeholders. In this article, we specifically describe a tool approach that builds stakeholders profiles based on topics of interest, which serve to link the stakeholders to sections of the architectural documents. Along this line, we have implemented a semi-automated pipeline based on text mining techniques. The outputs of this pipeline help the documenter to prioritize the sections of a SAD based on their stakeholder relevancy. The results, although preliminary, show that our approach is helpful for the whole architecture documentation process.

The rest of the article is organized around 4 sections. Section 2 discusses background and related work. Section 3 presents the main components of the proposed approach. Section 4 describes the current prototype for the detection of stakeholders' interests and their linkage to architecture documents. This section also includes an experimental evaluation of the prototype. Finally, section 5 gives the conclusions and outlines future work.

2   Related Work

Several approaches have investigated how to codify and make (better) use of architectural knowledge. In fact, the IEEE Standard 1471-2000 about Recommended Practice for Architecture Description of Software-Intensive Systems [6] recognizes the need of supporting the understanding of the SAD. However, few approaches have targeted the personalization of these documents by means of user profiles.

Farenhorst et al. [4] analyzed the requirements for a tool to capture architectural knowledge and share it among a group of architects. Based on these requirements, the authors also created a web portal called JIT AK Portal that includes some personalization functions. These functions are mostly oriented to the documentation reader, and particularly to a single stakeholder type (i.e., the architects). In JIT AK Portal, the documenter is responsible for providing a web interface with structure and contents that match the architects' interests. The approach provides no guidelines for this task. Another related tool is Knowledge Architect [7], developed by Jansen et al. The goals of this approach are to facilitate the access to a base of architectural knowledge and the search for specific issues in the knowledge base. A difference with JIT AK Portal is that Jansen's approach uses a codification strategy that supports the retrieval of knowledge for multiple types of stakeholders, although still concentrated on the reader's side. In addition, Knowledge Architect does not consider personalization techniques regarding the generation of documentation contents.

In [11], the authors propose an automated approach to deal with chunks of architectural information. These chunks are the result of specific exploration paths followed by a stakeholder when reading a SAD. The relevance of a given chunk is determined by factors such as the time spent by a reader on a section, or the access frequency for a section. The idea is to recommend candidate sections to new stakeholders by reusing previous (similar) exploration paths of the SAD. A prototype supporting the approach has been recently published [10]. This approach is interesting in the sense that assists a reader to find relevant information. However, the characteristics of that reader are neither explicitly captured nor used in the assistance.

A limiting aspect of the approaches above is that they are general-purpose in that they do not leverage on available architectural documentation methods. Currently, there are several documentation methods available for software architectures. A few relevant examples include: Views and Beyond (V&B) developed by the Software Engineering Institute, Viewpoints and Perspectives proposed by Rozanski and Woods, and Siemens' 4 Views [3]. These methods basically prescribe the structure of the SAD (i.e., a template), the kind of views to be used, and sometimes the relationships of these views with stakeholder types. Guidelines about the documentation process are usually not part of these methods. One exception is the V&B method, which provides a few rules for combining views or adjusting the level of detail of these views, based on the different stakeholders' roles [2]. A drawback of V&B is that the view templates are general and the stakeholders' roles are static. In practice, the documenter is expected to determine the "right contents" in order to fill in those view templates. V&B is often viewed by practitioners as being bureaucratic (or high-ceremony) with respect to the amount of documentation to be generated.

There have been experiments with Wikis as a mechanism to support architecture documentation. JIT AK Portal and the Knowledge Architect are examples of this kind of tool support. In fact, the V&B method has been also implemented on top of a Wiki. Some lessons learned of this experience are discussed in [1].

3   Proposed Approach

A well-known rule for producing good documentation is to write its contents from the reader's perspective, rather than from writer's perspective [3]. In the architecture documentation process, we interpret this rule as a feedback loop in which the documenter produces incremental versions of the SAD to fulfill the information needs of (most of) the stakeholders. Figure 1 shows a conceptual schema of our approach.

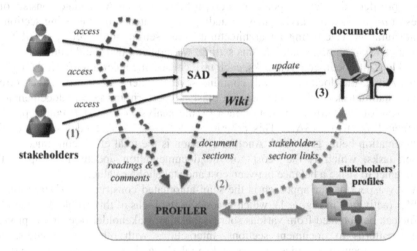

Fig. 1. Actors and components of our approach

We assume a community of stakeholders working on a given project, and interacting with each other through a collaborative platform (including tools such as: chat, forums and shared repositories). For their daily work, these stakeholders have access to a Wiki that contains the architectural documentation (i.e., the SAD) of the project. The documenter periodically delivers new SAD versions in the Wiki. The stakeholders may send feedback about a given SAD version, which will trigger updates in subsequent versions. Along this line, the main goal of the documenter is to decide which documentation tasks should be prioritized (and performed) for the next SAD version, in such a way the most relevant stakeholders are satisfied.

The approach involves three activities. First, the stakeholders access different sections of the current SAD hosted by the Wiki. We assume the SAD is structured around templates for predefined architectural views (e.g., module views, allocation views) and accompanying text. We base our approach on the V&B method, which already provides templates for the SAD. Stakeholders playing different project roles will have different concerns with respect to the SAD. For instance, project managers are mainly interested in allocation views, whereas developers need extensive information about views of modules and components-and-connectors.

Second, as the stakeholders read different Wiki sections and eventually leave textual comments about the SAD contents, the platform in background collects this feedback and passes on to a profiler. The profiler also receives information about the structure of the SAD. Based on these inputs, the profiler applies text mining techniques in order to identify relevant *topics* in the stakeholders' comments as well as in the documents. The idea here is to infer stakeholders' interests and match them with specific sections of the SAD. Those topics coming from the stakeholders will serve to build (or update) *user profiles* of these stakeholders. Those topics extracted from the SAD will serve to establish *links* between a given stakeholder and a number of SAD sections, meaning that the stakeholder is potentially interested in those sections. These links will be used as recommendations to the documenter.

Third, the documenter takes both the user[1] profiles and recommendations produced by the profiler, in order to update the current SAD version. An update consists of a series of *documentation tasks*, such as: adding new contents to an existing section or architectural view, creating an architectural view, setting the level of detail for a section or view, among others. In this setting, we envision that the documenter keeps a "backlog" of documentation tasks, each task consuming a certain effort. At a given point in time, the documenter will combine several criteria to prioritize the current documentation tasks and select a subset of tasks to perform in the next documentation cycle. One of such criteria is determined by the analysis of the stakeholder profiles and their links to the SAD. This criterion reflects the "stakeholder value" of the documentation being generated. Another criterion is the total effort consumed by the chosen tasks, which is the "cost" of the documentation update. It is up to the documenter to strike a balance between cost and stakeholder value.

A key aspect of our approach is the semi-automated construction of stakeholders profiles (activity 2 in Figure 1), which is actually the focus of this article. In general, a profile can be obtained from various sources, such as: stakeholder roles in the project, access patterns to document sections, interactions with other stakeholders, and analysis of recurring topics in the stakeholder's activities. Information can be collected explicitly, through direct stakeholder intervention, or implicitly through agents that monitor user activity [9]. Initially, we define the stakeholders' profiles based on predefined interests derived from typical project roles. In fact, V&B characterizes several types of stakeholders regarding their use of architectural views. We can think of these characterizations as static profiles. However, these profiles will certainly change over time. For these reasons, we have designed our profiler to augment the static profiles given by V&B with topics of interest. These interests can be derived from the stakeholders' comments, reflecting the particularities of each stakeholder, so as to provide more accurate recommendations to the documenter.

4   Profiling Stakeholders via Text Mining

The Profiler component (see Figure 1) implements two processing stages, namely: profile building, and user-section linking. The first stage executes a mining procedure

---

[1] The terms 'stakeholder' and 'user' are used interchangeably.

to extract *human-knowledge concepts* from the users' text (see sub-section 4.1). A similar mining procedure is applied on the SAD contents. The outcomes of this stage are: a set of user profiles and a document representation (of the SAD).

Each user profile has a static and a dynamic aspect. The static aspect is taken from the stakeholders' characteristics provided by the V&B method (as the degree of interest of a stakeholder on a given architectural view). They also provide a list of predefined concepts for each stakeholder type (e.g., manager, architect, tester, etc.). The dynamic aspect of the profile contains a list of specific user's interests. In more detail, this list will have concepts and categories that were referenced by each user or that were mentioned in the architecture documents. Categories represent concepts with different levels of abstraction. We preferred the usage of concepts (instead of terms), because concepts describe the context in which terms are used (i.e., semantic knowledge), and are hence more informative regarding stakeholders' interests.

For the second stage, the SAD is divided into related units of text, called *document sections*. These sections are already predetermined by the SAD template structure. Then, the Profiler computes a similarity measure between the profiles and the sections matching those profiles (see sub-section 4.2). The output is a set of links between the users and parts of the original document. We model each link as a weighted relation. Relations can be grouped per user and sorted in descending order by their weights. The resulting ranking of relevant sections per stakeholder is shown to the documenter.

4.1   The Concept-Mining Pipeline

We have designed a technique for extracting concepts from unstructured text. This technique is mainly oriented to address the dynamic aspect of the stakeholder profile. The inputs can be any kind of textual information generated by the target users, such as electronic conversations, opinions on the Web, or comments on Wiki pages. The output is a set of user profiles, each one containing a ranking of the most relevant concepts (for that user) as well as categories for those concepts. Since this profile is based on topics that are regularly mentioned by the user, the information can be considered as an approximation of the user's interests.

The technique is implemented as a semi-automated pipeline with six filters (Figure 2). In step 1, a parsing module identifies the involved users and their messages. In step 2, noisy text is pre-processed to prepare the user messages for future analysis. This processing involves: i) deletion of references to users by their names, ii) filtering of stop-words, and iii) application of a Porter's based stemming algorithm.

In step 3, entities are identified from messages. An entity can be seen as a group of semantically-related terms. To this end, we use two text mining tools provided by the Stanford NLP Group[2]: a named entity recognizer and a POS (Part-Of-Speech) tagger. The recognizer relies on a classification-based approach to detect named entities, like persons, institutions, artifacts or any kind of proper nouns. The POS tagger automatically assigns a grammatical label to every word in a sentence. We are focused on nouns and their modifiers. By grouping the results of both techniques, each user's message is associated to a set of entities.

---

[2] See http://nlp.stanford.edu/

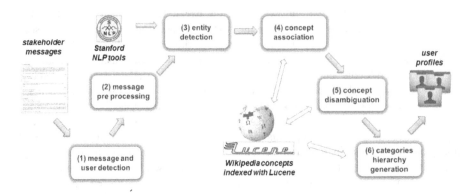

Fig. 2. The concept mining pipeline

In step 4, the concept association is performed. We use a semantic dictionary containing concepts of human knowledge based on Wikipedia. The unstructured information from Wikipedia is indexed with Lucene[3]. Since the domain is limited to Software Architecture concepts, we customized the indexes to work on Software Engineering topics (e.g., categories like: software architecture, software quality, and concepts such as: design pattern, performance, etc.). The entity names are matched against the Wikipedia concepts, using the TF.IDF measure for comparison. For a given entity, the first N concepts returned by the search are mapped to that entity.

In step 5, ambiguous concepts are handled using a disambiguation index. We use an adapted version of Lesk's algorithm, which considers a window of N nearest concepts to the ambiguous one (with N=2). The description of each disambiguation concept is compared to the descriptions of the nearest concepts using the cosine comparison function. The most related concept replaces the ambiguous one.

Finally, in step 6, a category hierarchy is built for each concept. Initially, we associate first-level categories to concepts, and then, we establish relations with higher level categories in order to build the hierarchical structure. Since categories can be quite general (e.g. SOFTWARE) and it takes considerable time to compute them, we decided to limit the hierarchy tree depth to 3 levels.

4.2   Linking Users to Document Sections

The first module of the pipeline was adapted to take a textual document as input in order to produce a document description, which actually resembles a user profile. We refer to such representation as a *section profile*. After the pipeline is executed, the representation will contain the concepts and categories involved in each document section. By doing so, we treat the problem of linking users to sections as the computation of a similarity function between two profiles: a user profile and a section profile. To compute the similarity, we apply the CF.IDF measure. Based on TF.IDF, the CF.IDF measure uses the concept frequency and the inverse document frequency

---

[3] See http://lucene.apache.org/

to determine the relevance of a concept in a collection of documents (or sections, in this case). A variation of this measure is used for dealing with categories.

For each user profile, we compute its similarity with the section profiles. The similarity score between the user profile and one section profile is estimated using Equation 1:

$$sim(up,\ sp) = \sum_{i \in N} confidf(ucon_i) + \sum_{j \in M} catfidf(ucat_j) \qquad (1)$$

with N: number of concepts, M: number of categories, $confidf(x)$: CF.IDF value for concept x, and $catfidf(y)$: CF.IDF value for category y. Then, we sort the associated sections (in descending order) according to the similarity scores. Using a threshold strategy, we finally define the number of sections that are considered relevant for each user. The best value for the threshold was determined through the evaluation procedure (see sub-section 4.3).

4.3 Experimental Evaluation

We empirically evaluated the pipeline above with the goal of assessing how well the user-section links were generated. To simulate architectural documents, we selected 2 articles (called dataset A and dataset B) from InfoQ.com related to software architecture topics. The dataset A was a document that contained 18 sections and 2095 words, and 14 users participated in the discussion. Data set B contained 14 sections, 1126 words, and 17 users participating in the discussion.

Both datasets were tagged in advance. For each user, an expert annotated the potentially relevant sections according to the user's comments in the discussion thread. Afterwards, we ran our pipeline on the two datasets and computed the confusion matrixes for both cases. To assess the results, we worked with standard measures such as: accuracy, precision, recall, and F-measure [5]. We also studied the effects of two parameters: the relevancy threshold and the inclusion of categories for the CF.IDF measure. If the categories are excluded from this measure, the similarity between two profiles is computed by Equation 2 (a simplification of Equation 1).

$$sim(up,\ sp) = \sum_{i \in N} confidf(ucon_i) \qquad (2)$$

On the other hand, we developed a term-based approach in order to have reference results for our concept-based technique. The approach used the TF.IDF measure to compute the similarity between user messages and section contents. We estimated the same measures mentioned above. Table 1 shows the results for the two experiments. The table rows are the approaches grouped by different threshold values. The table columns are the measures per dataset. At first sight, the F-measure reached the highest values using a threshold of 0.2-0.3 in both datasets (see Figure 3). Therefore, by considering the first 20-30% of the linked sections as relevant, we achieved a balance in the tradeoff between precision and recall. In all the cases, the performance of the CF.IDF techniques was better than that of the TF.IDF one, although no major differences were observed. The precision improvement with CF.IDF was around 4-7%, whereas the accuracy was improved by 2-4 %. As regards the F-measure, CF.IDF outperformed TF.IDF by 3.5-6.5%.

Table 1. Experimental results for data sets A and B

		A - Are you a software architect?				B - SOA certification			
		accuracy	precision	recall	fmeasure	accuracy	precision	recall	fmeasure
threshold 0.1	TF-IDF	0.706	0.821	0.252	0.564	0.580	0.706	0.114	0.345
	CF-IDF(-C)	0.722	0.893	0.272	0.611	0.588	0.765	0.124	0.374
	CF-IDF(+C)	0.714	0.857	0.262	0.587	0.580	0.706	0.114	0.345
threshold 0.2	TF-IDF	0.738	0.732	0.445	0.647	0.613	0.647	0.308	0.529
	CF-IDF(-C)	0.770	0.804	0.491	0.711	0.630	0.686	0.334	0.564
	CF-IDF(+C)	0.754	0.768	0.471	0.68	0.588	0.588	0.282	0.481
threshold 0.3	TF-IDF	0.738	0.686	0.522	0.644	0.634	0.647	0.408	0.578
	CF-IDF(-C)	0.754	0.714	0.542	0.67	0.626	0.632	0.407	0.567
	CF-IDF(+C)	0.754	0.714	0.546	0.671	0.576	0.544	0.351	0.488
threshold 0.4	TF-IDF	0.738	0.633	0.677	0.64	0.609	0.569	0.543	0.562
	CF-IDF(-C)	0.762	0.663	0.705	0.67	0.601	0.559	0.536	0.552
	CF-IDF(+C)	0.683	0.561	0.597	0.567	0.567	0.520	0.498	0.513

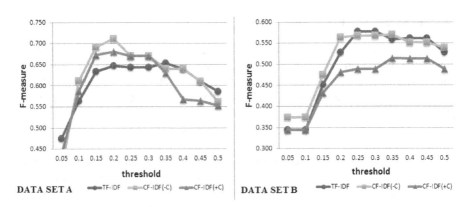

Fig. 3. F-measure comparison

The inclusion of the CF.IDF measure for categories seemed to affect the computations, as evidenced by the slightly lower results with CF-IDF(+C) than with CF-IDF(-C) ones. Despite this difference, having categories in the user-section linking process was supposed to perform better than the standard CF.IDF measure for concepts. We believe this problem might have been caused by the use of categories with a high level of abstraction (currently 3 levels). Overall, the proposed pipeline achieved reasonable results. For a threshold of 0.2, the CF.IDF technique obtained a precision of 68-80%, and a recall of 33%-49%. Thus, we plan to further develop this technique in the context of our general approach (see Figure 1).

5   Conclusions and Future Work

In this article, we proposed a general approach for implementing a stakeholder-centric and agile architecture documentation process. At the core of our approach is the personalization of architectural documents based on the profiles of the stakeholders consuming those documents. These profiles are built on top of existing stakeholders' characterizations (with respect to architectural knowledge) as well as on text mining techniques. To this end, we have presented a tool that executes a topic-based mining process for constructing user profiles and for ranking the sections (of potential interest to these users) of an architectural document. We argue that such a mining process has advantages in terms of understandability and semantic information for the profiles, when compared to traditional keyword-based mining techniques.

A preliminary tool evaluation using topics has shown promising precision and recall, allowing us to conjecture that the stakeholders' profiles can really assist the documenter in his/her documentation tasks. Nonetheless, our profiling tool is at a prototype stage, and it still needs improvements, mainly on aspects of performance and architecture-related knowledge. We are currently testing the topic-based mining technique with different datasets and types of stakeholders. We are also exploring alternative strategies for handling the concepts and their categories.

As future work, we will integrate the profiling tool with the remaining components of the approach. To feed the profiler, we will investigate techniques and technologies for monitoring stakeholders' activities within a network and collect more data about them. We will also consider the application of Artificial Intelligence planning techniques to support the documenter in selecting the right tasks for the next version of the architecture documentation.

Acknowledgments. This work has been partially supported by ANPCyT (Argentina) through Project PICT Bicentenario 2010 No. 2247.

References

1. Bachmann, F., Merson, P.: Experience using the web-based tool wiki for architecture documentation. Technical Report TN-041, CMU-SEI (2005)
2. Clements, P., et al.: A practical method for documenting software architectures. In: ICSE (2003)
3. Clements, P., et al.: Documenting Software Architectures: Views and Beyond, 2nd edn. Addison-Wesley Professional (2010)
4. Farenhorst, R., et al.: A just-in-time architectural knowledge sharing portal. In: Proc. of WICSA 2008, pp. 125–134. IEEE, Washington DC (2008)
5. Goossen, F., et al.: News personalization using the CF-IDF semantic recommender. In: Proc. of WIMS 2011, pp. 10:1–10:12. ACM, New York (2011)
6. IEEE Std 1471-2000: Recommended practice for architectural description of software-intensive systems (2000)
7. Jansen, A., et al.: Enriching software architecture documentation. Journal of Systems and Software 82(8), 1232–1248 (2009)
8. Koning, H., Vliet, H.: Real-life IT architecture design reports and their relation to IEEE Std 1471 stakeholders and concerns. Automated Software Eng. 13, 201–223 (2006)
9. Schiaffino, S., Amandi, A.: Intelligent User Profiling. In: Artificial Intelligence, pp. 193–216. Springer, Heidelberg (2009)
10. Su, M.T., Hosking, J., Grundy, J.: Capturing architecture documentation navigation trails for content chunking and sharing. In: The 9th IEEE/IFIP (WICSA), pp. 256–259 (2011)
11. Su, M.T.: Capturing exploration to improve software architecture documentation. In: Proceedings of ECSA 2010, pp. 17–21. ACM, New York (2010)
12. Tang, A., et al.: A comparative study of architecture knowledge management tools. Journal of Systems and Software 83, 352–370 (2010)

An Architecture for Resource Behavior Prediction to Improve Scheduling Systems Performance on Enterprise Desktop Grids

Sergio Ariel Salinas[1], Carlos García Garino[1,2], and Alejandro Zunino[3]

[1] Instituto para las Tecnologías de la Información y las Comunicaciones (ITIC), UNCuyo, Mendoza, Argentina
{ssalinas,cgarciag}@itu.uncu.edu.ar
[2] Facultad de Ingeniería, UNCuyo, Mendoza, Argentina
[3] ISISTAN, Facultad de Ciencias Exactas, UNICEN, Tandil, Argentina
azunino@exa.unicen.edu.ar

Abstract. An Enterprise Desktop Grid (EDG) is a low cost platform that scavenges idle desktop computers to run Grid applications. Since EDGs use idle computer time, it is important to estimate the expected computer availability. Based on this estimation, a scheduling system is able to select those computers with more expected availability to run applications. As a consequence, an overall performance improvement is achieved. Different techniques have been proposed to predict the computer state for an instant of time, but this information is not enough. A prediction model provides a sequence of computer states for different instants of time. The problem is how to identify computer behavior having as input this sequence of states. We identify the need of providing a architecture to model and evaluate desktop computer behavior. Thus, a scheduling system is able to compare and select resources that run applications faster. Experiments have shown that programs run up to 8 times faster when the scheduler selects a computer suggested by our proposal.

Keywords: Enterprise Desktop Grid, Resource Discovery System, Computer Behavior Prediction, Scheduling System, Classification Algorithms.

1 Introduction

In recent years, Enterprise Desktop Grids (EDG) [1] have become a less expensive alternative to traditional Computational Grids. This technology gathers desktop computers spread over different institutions all over the world such as universities, schools or enterprises. An EDG makes use of desktop computer idle time to run computation intensive applications with independent tasks. Platform maintenance costs are highly distributed among the participant institutions. For these reasons, considering the technological infrastructure of the region, an EDG might be of interest for Latin American institutions.

A distributed computing system requires two important components: a resource discovery system and a scheduling system. The RDS is responsible for searching

F.V. Cipolla-Ficarra et al. (Eds.): ADNTIIC 2011, LNCS 7547, pp. 186–196, 2012.

computational resources over a distributed system. The scheduling system organizes and distributes user processes over different computational resources based on the information provided by the RDS. Both components have been studied in depth by the research community.

Advances in the RDS research area makes it possible to find different solutions to improve the search process of computational resources [9, 14, 7, 13]. However, the literature does not discuss how the information provided by the RDS may affect the scheduling system performance. Let us consider the following situation: a scheduler queries a RDS for available computers to run a set of distributed applications according to computational capabilities constrains. Based on this information, the scheduler starts a matchmaking process to select a set of computers where to run the applications. Since the RDS does not provide information about the computer availability, there is a risk of failure in the running process. For instance, some of the computers selected might be no longer available or maybe they are already turned off.

Computer availability prediction techniques have been applied for different purposes: to improve load balancing, to prevent failures or to predict computers availability. These techniques perform better if the events being analyzed respond to certain patterns. It is possible to observe this situation in EDGs where most participant resources are computers placed at different offices and computing laboratories for teaching. Computers at the same office stay on at the same time interval, for instance from 08:00 a.m. to 06:00 p.m. On the other hand, computer usage at laboratories is organized according to a teaching scheduling. For these reason, we argue that it is possible to predict with a good precision the desktop computers states in EDGs.

Different prediction techniques estimate the expected computer state for an instant of time. Possible states are: available, busy, turned on, turned off, etc. For each computer it is possible to calculate a sequence of expected states for a time interval. We use the concept of resource behavior to denote changes in the computer states over the time. Let us consider a computer that constantly switches its state from available to busy in a time interval i. Its behavior is unstable and it is not suitable for running applications in the interval i. The possible resource behavior is useful in the computer selection process made by a scheduler.

In this paper, we propose an architecture to predict, calculate and evaluate the behavior of desktop computers in EDGs. The architecture improves the computer selection process made by the scheduling system. As a consequence, the application runtime is reduced leading to an overall performance improvement. To validate the architecture, we monitored a set of desktop computers at UNCuyo[1] University 4 over a month. After that, we simulated the execution of distributed applications over different computers. We evaluated two situations: i) the scheduler selects computers randomly and ii) the scheduler selects computers based on the information provided by our architecture. Experiment results showed an improvement up to 8 times faster running applications under different scenarios. The contributions of this work are twofold: i) an architecture to compute information required for a scheduling system to

---

[1] http://www.uncu.edu.ar

perform applications faster and ii) an heuristic to model computer behavior in such a way that the comparison between computers behavior is simple.

This paper is organized as follows. Section 2 introduces related works on prediction techniques. In section 3 the proposed architecture is presented. In section 4 the simulation process used to evaluate our proposal is explained followed by an analysis of the experiment results. Finally, in section 5 the conclusions and future works are presented.

2   Related Works

Different prediction techniques have been used for various purposes: load balancing, failure prediction, performance system prediction and performance improvements on the scheduling system. In general, prediction techniques use statistical models and time series analysis. Next, we introduce the most representative works.

The Network Weather Service (NWS) provides accurate forecasts of dynamically changing performance characteristics from a distributed set of metacomputing resources [17, 16]. The prediction mechanism uses a mixture of experts forecasting methods, each having its own parameterization. Based on the performance history, every model performs a forecast for a set of measurements. The system uses a set of sensors to gather observable measurements, which are stored in a persistent storage. The data collected are: fractions of CPU time available for new processes, TCP connection time, bandwidth and end-to-end round-trip network latency values. A forecaster process requests the relevant measurement history from a persistent storage to generate a forecast.

In addition to performance prediction, an accurate failure prediction mechanism is critical in computational Grids for efficient application running completion. Although statistical methods can be used, they are based on assumptions such as time homogeneity not always present in Grids. A mechanism for failure prediction that overcomes this drawback is presented in [8]. It uses a filtered failure prediction model (FFP) that consists of series of UP/DOWN events. Periodic events are tagged and filtered out. The remaining events are used by a traditional statistical method. The strategy used in the discussed work outperforms exponential and Weibull distributions by more than a factor of 10.

Analysis of time series data has been used for prediction. For instance, the exponential smoothing technique has been tested to compute forecasts. An extensive set of experiments over a real Grid environment named PlanetLab [2] demonstrated that a dynamic load balancing based on prediction via exponential smoothing led to a significant reduction of parallel applications runtime [6]. Experiments in this work showed a speed-up factor on average 1.8 using a dynamic balancing based on prediction in comparison with equal load balancing.

Prediction techniques have also been used in scheduling systems. The real-time scheduling advisor (RTSA) [3] is a user-level system that advices on how to schedule real-time tasks. The goal of the RTSA is to help client application to meet deadlines and to report when deadlines cannot be met. The resource prediction is based on statistical time series analysis documented in [5, 4]. The system suggests a resource from a set of computers such that a task with nominal runtime t_{nom}, if started now, will be completed in time $(1+sf)\ t_{nom}$ or less with a confidence *conf* where *sf* is the slack factor. The system response consists of a copy of the request t_{nom}, *sf* and *conf* values, the selected host and an estimated task runtime.

A decentralized approach for volunteer computing systems based on resource availability prediction is presented in [11]. Resource availability prediction is computed considering three input factors: i) resource availability, ii) group availability and iii) current group availability. The first factor is computed from a historical resource activity register. It represents the probability of individual machines availability at a given time of the week. The second factor quantifies the number of resources available at a given time. Finally, the third factor is calculated based on the number of busy and idle computers. This model reduces the number of job interruptions in a distributed system of non-dedicated desktop computers.

In contrast to existing works, our proposal performs an evaluation of the evolution of different computer states over a time interval. Although it is possible to use any of the prediction techniques mentioned before, we propose to use classification algorithms from the Artificial Intelligence area. These algorithms are selected because statistical models perform a poor accuracy in scenarios where there are periodic events [8]. For instance, desktop computers are turned on/off every day or periodically are off-line for maintenance reasons. Classification algorithms showed in preliminary tests a high accuracy to predict future computer states. Based on the prediction performed, we propose a heuristic to model the computer behavior through a set of metrics. Thus, it is possible to compare different computers behavior. This architecture is expected to be part of a resource discovery system to provide comprehensive resource information that improves the overall Desktop Grid performance. For this reason, this architecture considers components to manage information about computer features. In the next section, we introduce the proposed architecture and a detailed explanation of its components.

3   Proposed Architecture

The main goal of the proposed architecture is to provide comprehensive information about desktop computers in EDGs. This information includes: i) computational power features, ii) applications installed, iii) computer availability prediction and iv) a set of metrics that defines the resource expected behavior for a given time interval. The architecture acts on each computer and is composed of the following modules: i) *resource activity sensor*, ii) *preprocessing*, iii) *predictor,* iv) *analyzer,* v) *descriptor* and vi) *registry.* The interaction between modules is shown in figure 1. The resource activity sensor monitors and records data about each computer activity. The preprocessing module creates a training dataset based on data generated by the sensor module. The predictor module uses this dataset to estimate the resource behavior pattern in the past. Based on this information, it predicts the expected behavior for a future time interval. The analyzer module takes as input the prediction previously computed to calculate a set of metrics that defines the computer expected behavior. The descriptor module scans hardware and software computer features. Finally, the information generated by the analyzer and descriptor modules is sent to the registry module. The registry is responsible for the resource information management. Next, a more detailed explanation of the architecture components is introduced.

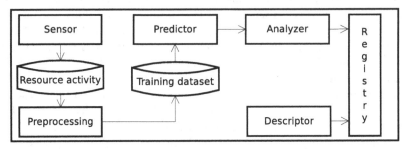

Fig. 1. Proposed architecture

3.1   Resource Activity Sensor

The resource activity sensor is a software component that periodically collects information about the computer activity. The data recorded are the following: i) date and time, ii) percentage of free RAM and iii) CPU load. To keep consistent information, computers date and time are synchronized with a central server. The sensor at a configurable sampling frequency records the resource activity. Then, it stores this information for a further analysis. The resource monitoring process is non-invasive and user-transparent. In general, the storage space required to record the information monitored does not exceed a megabyte size per day. Regularly, oldest records are erased to limit the volume of the information stored.

3.2   Preprocessing Module

Classification algorithms from the Artificial Intelligence area require a training dataset with labeled data to classify new data instances. The preprocessing module is responsible for generating this dataset. It has the following information: i) month, ii) day, iii) hour, iv) minute, v) CPU state, vi) RAM state and vii) computer state. The training dataset is computed based on the data collected by the sensor activity. The labels for the CPU, RAM and computer state are determined based on different thresholds. For instance, if the percentage of free RAM is above 90% the label used is "*free*". The possible states for the RAM are: "*free*" or "*full*". The labels used for the CPU are: "*busy*" or "*idle*". The computer states are determined based on the CPU and RAM states. The possible values are: "*available*", "*busy*" and "*off*". For instance, if the CPU state is idle and the RAM state is free then the computer is available to process Grid applications.For each record created by the activity sensor, a dataset record is computed. This process runs in a few seconds and is triggered with a certain configurable frequency.

A dataset represents changes in the computer states over a time interval. For each instant of time t_1, t_2, ... t_n there is a record in the dataset that is computed on the basis of the activity sensor information. For those instant of time where there is no data monitored by the activity sensor, the computer state considered is *"turn off"*. The training dataset is used for the predictor module to estimate the computer state for a certain instant of time. Each computer stores its own dataset and activity records.

3.3   Predictor Module

The predictor module aims at estimating the possible computer states for a time interval. We propose to use classification algorithms from the Artificial Intelligence area because they showed in preliminary tests an accuracy of 90 %. However, it is possible to use any prediction model presented before. Weka [10] framework makes it possible testing different classification algorithms, for a further analysis please refer to [15]. The testing process used a training dataset computed having as input monitored information from desktops computers at the UNCuyo University. The C4.5 algorithm [12] showed the highest average accuracy, about 90 %. For this reason it was used in the testing process. The state prediction is represented by a resource behavior prediction array (RBPA). Every RBPA has associated a resource behavior prediction header (RBPH). A RBPA is a sequence of computer states $state_{t1}$, $state_{t1}$, ..., $state_{tn}$, which were predicted for a time interval between t_1 and t_n. The possible states are computed by the preprocessing module. The RBPH provides information about the resource behavior prediction array. This information is important for the evaluation module to process the RBPA and includes: i) the computer time zone, ii) the date and time when the prediction was computed, iii) start date, iv) end date, v) sampling frequency, vi) predictive method and vii) predictive method accuracy.

3.4   Analyzer Module

The analyzer module is responsible for computing a set of metrics that model the computer expected behavior for a time interval. This module is the main component of the proposed architecture. It implements a heuristic model to predict the computer behavior based on the resource behavior prediction array. This heuristic model characterizes the computer behavior that facilitates the comparison of different computers. Thus, the scheduling system is able to select those computers with a higher probability to finish running an application efficiently. The set of metrics are introduced next:

— *Statecount*: is the number of instances of certain state in the RBPA.
— *Clustering*: is the number of clusters of the selected state in the RBPA.
— *Cohesion*: this value represents how spare are the clusters of the state being analyzed in the RBPA. This metric is calculated according to the following formula:

$$Cohesion = Statecount/Clustering$$

— *Statescope*: this value counts the number of instants ti from the first to the last state occurrence.
— *Stability*: this value provides a measure that represents how volatile is the state being analyzed according to the RBPA. Computers that show higher values are more likely to run applications faster. This metric is computed as follows:

$$Stability = Cohesion/Statescope$$

Next, we introduce an example that represents how this module operates. Let us consider the following situation. The scheduling system requires two desktop computers to run an application that requires 4 units of time for its execution. There are seven computers that fulfill application requirements. The RBPA for each computer is showed in table 1.

Table 1. Example of metrics computed by the analyzer module from different computers for the state *available*

	R1	R2	R3	R4	R5	R6	R7
t_1	available	available	available	available	available	available	busy
t_2	available	available	available	available	available	busy	available
t_3	available	available	available	busy	busy	busy	busy
t_4	available	busy	available	available	available	available	available
t_5	available	busy	busy	available	available	available	busy
t_6	busy	busy	available	busy	busy	busy	available
t_7	busy	busy	busy	available	busy	busy	busy
t_8	busy	busy	busy	busy	busy	available	available
t_9	busy	busy	busy	busy	busy		
t_{10}	busy	available	busy	busy	available	available	available
State_count	5	5	5	5	5	5	5
Clustering	1	2	2	3	3	4	5
Cohesion	5	2.5	2.5	1.7	1.7	1.3	1.0
State_scope	5	10	6	7	10	10	10
Stability	1.0	0.25	0.42	0.24	0.17	0.13	0.10

Although any of the seven computers are available for five units of time, it is possible to observe how the metrics computed varies. Those computers with higher stability metric value are more likely to run an application faster than others. In the example above, the heuristic evaluate the state available but it is possible to calculate the same metrics for other states.

3.5   Descriptor Module

The descriptor module is a stand-alone component that scans and gathers automatically hardware and software features from a computer. The main goal of this module is to publish the resource computational capability. This information is managed by the registry module and may include: processor frequency, RAM available, hard disk capability, installed network card, operating system, applications installed, etc. Computational capabilities are required for the scheduling system to select resources that fulfill software and hardware requirements to run applications. Any changes in the computer features are periodically update and send to the registry module.

3.6   Registry

The registry module is responsible for the management of the information provided by the descriptor module and the analyzer module. As mentioned before, this information is required by the scheduling system to run distributed applications. The RDS is responsible for managing this information from participant resources in an EDG. Interaction details between a registry module and the RDS is part of future works.

4   Experiments and Results

The testing process of the proposed architecture aims to evaluate improvements on the scheduling system performance. For this purpose, two scenarios were simulated: i) the scheduling system selects randomly a computer where to run a process and ii) the scheduling system selects a computer suggested by our proposal. The metric used is the overall average time for running an application under both scenarios. The predictor module used the C4.5 classification algorithm from the Artificial Intelligence area.

The simulation process uses information collected from 30 computers at UNCuyo University. For twenty days, a software application monitored and recorded every ten seconds computer CPU load and RAM available. This information was integrated into a main database for a further analysis. According to the data obtained computers are available from 8:00 a.m. to 4:00 p.m. From the data collected, it is possible to observe that computers usage is more intensive during the morning than in the afternoon. For this reason, experiments were split into two period of time: i) from 8:00 a.m. to 12:00 p.m. and ii) from 12:01 a.m. to 4:00 p.m.

To simplify the simulation process we consider the following assumptions:

- An application can be run on any computer i.e. there is no computational power constrains.
- An application runs any time the computer is available according to its monitoring information.
- If a computer is turned off and an application has not finished, it will continue running when the computer be available again.
- Computers manage a buffer to enqueue different applications tested.

The number of applications that run simultaneously was calculated as a percentage of the participant computers. The percentages considered included: 30%, 60%, 100% and 120%. In the latter case the number of applications was 20% greater than the number of computers. This variation makes it feasible the simulation of different workload. Runtime is computed as the difference between the start up and finish timestamp regardless how many times the computer was turned off.

The simulation included 8.607 application instances with a runtime randomly generated between 600 and 3600 seconds. The application start up time was also randomly selected from one of the time intervals mentioned before. The simulation process performed the following steps. The start up time and runtime required for the application were generated randomly. The application running process was simulated on a randomly selected computer. Then, the same application was simulated on a computer selected according to our proposal. Finally, the time required to run the application was calculated for both scenarios.

The simulation process was repeated around one hundred times. Results shown in table 2 considered the average runtime for each workload configuration. The first three columns include the period of time assessed, workload and number of simulated applications. The fourth column shows the performance of a scheduler that uses the proposed architecture. The fifth column shows results for the random selection strategy. Finally, the last column represents the percentage of applications where both strategies performed the same runtime.

Table 2. Simulation process results

Period evaluated	Workload	Applicat ions number	Our proposal	Random	Equal
08:00 a.m. to 12:00 p.m.	30%	500	**49%**	19%	32%
	60%	1000	**42%**	26%	32%
	100%	1500	**40%**	27%	33%
	120%	1942	34%	29%	**37%**
12:01 p.m. to 04:00 p.m.	30%	363	**57%**	15%	28%
	60%	734	**48%**	22%	30%
	100%	1112	**43%**	25%	32%
	120%	1456	**38%**	27%	35%
Total		8607	**41%**	25%	34%

Results show that from 8.607 applications simulated on average our proposal outperforms a random selection. In some cases, improvements achieved in the runtime are up to 8 times faster in comparison with a random selection strategy.

5   Conclusion and Future Works

We proposed an architecture to model, to evaluate and to predict computer behavior. The information provided by the architecture improves the scheduling system performance. Existing works are focused on providing an accurate computer state prediction for an instant of time. We argue that a computer behavior is defined by a sequence of changing states over a time period. For this reason, we propose a heuristic to model computer behavior. In practice, it is represented by a set of metrics computed from a sequence of predicted states.

To validate our proposal, we monitored 30 desktop computers at UNCuyo University for a period of twenty days. A software component recorded every ten seconds each computer CPU load and RAM available. This information was used to test our proposal and to assess different classification algorithms. The proposed architecture is able to use any prediction technique presented in this work. In a preliminary stage, we assessed different algorithms from the Artificial Intelligence area using Weka framework. C4.5 algorithm was selected because computer state prediction showed an accuracy of 90%.

A simulation process was used to evaluate how the information provided by our proposal improves the scheduling system performance. For this purpose, two computer selection strategies were compared: i) random selection and ii) selection based on our proposal. The process simulated 8.607 application instances under different workload scenarios including: 30%, 60%, 100% and 120%. The latter case the number of applications was 20% larger than the number of computers. The runtime required for different application instances varied from 600 to 3600 seconds. Our proposal performed better than random selection up to 57% of applications and makes it possible an average runtime up to 8 times faster.

In future works, we expect to include in our experiments a larger number of computers. In addition, we will compare how different prediction techniques may affect our proposal accuracy and performance. We also will consider scenarios where it is possible migrating applications to different computers.

References

1. Choi, S., et al.: Characterizing and classifying desktop grid. In: Proceedings of the Seventh IEEE International Symposium on Cluster Computing and the Grid, CCGRID 2007, pp. 743–748. IEEE Computer, Washington (2007)
2. Brent, C., et al.: Planetlab: an overlay testbed for broad-coverage services. ACM SIGCOMM Computer Communication Review 33, 3–12 (2003)
3. Dinda, P.: The statistical properties of host load. Sci. Program. 7, 211–229 (1999)
4. Dinda, P.: Online prediction of the running time of tasks, vol. 5, pp. 225–236. Kluwer Academic Publishers, Hingham (2002)
5. Dinda, P.: A prediction-based real-time scheduling advisor. In: Proc. International Parallel and Distributed Processing Symposium, IPDPS 2002, Abstracts and CD-ROM, pp. 10–17 (2002)
6. Dobber, M., Koole, G., van der Mei, R.: Dynamic load balancing experiments in a grid. In: Proceedings of the Fifth IEEE International Symposium on Cluster Computing and the Grid (CCGrid 2005), vol. 2, pp. 1063–1070. IEEE Press, New York (2005)
7. Edwards, W.: Discovery systems in ubiquitous computing. IEEE Pervasive Computing 5(2), 70–77 (2006)
8. Kang, W., Grimshaw.: Failure prediction in computational grids. In: 40th Annual Simulation Symposium, ANSS 2007, pp. 275–282 (2007)
9. Meshkova, E., et al.: A survey on resource discovery mechanisms, peer-to-peer and service discovery frameworks. Computer Networks 52(11), 2097–2128 (2008)
10. Weka Machine Learning Project. Weka, http://www.cs.waikato.ac.nz
11. Ramachandran, K., Lutfiyya, H., Perry, M.: Decentralized approach to resource availability prediction using group availability in a p2p desktop grid. Future Generation Computer Systems (2010)
12. Salzberg, S.: C4.5: Programs for machine learning by Quinlan, R. Morgan Kaufmann. Machine Learning 16, 235–240 (1994)
13. Trunfio, D., et al.: Peer-to-peer resource discovery in grids: Models and systems. Future Generation Computer Systems 23(7), 864–878 (2007)

14. Vanthournout, K., Deconinck, G., Belmans, R.: A taxonomy for resource discovery. Personal and Ubiquitous Computing 9, 81–89 (2005)
15. Witten, I., et al.: Weka: Practical machine learning tools and techniques with java implementations (1999)
16. Wolski, R.: Experiences with predicting resource performance on-line in computational grid settings. Sigmetrics Perform. Eval. Rev. 30, 41–49 (2003)
17. Wolski, R., Spring, N., Hayes, J.: The network weather service: a distributed resource performance forecasting service for metacomputing. Future Generation Computer Systems 15(5-6), 757–768 (1999)

Discrete Sequences Analysis for Detecting Software Design Patterns

Juan Francisco Silva Logroño[1], Luis Berdún[1], Marcelo Armentano[2], and Analia Amandi[2]

[1] ISISTAN Research Institute, Fac. de Cs. Exactas, UNCPBA
Campus Universitario, Paraje Arroyo Seco, Tandil, 7000, Argentina
[2] CONICET, Consejo Nacional de Investigaciones Científicas y Técnicas, Argentina
{juanf.silval}@gmail.com,
{lberdun,marmenta,amandi}@exa.unicen.edu.ar

Abstract. A design pattern names, abstracts and identifies the key aspects of a common design structure that make it useful for creating a reusable object-oriented design. Designers with little or no experience in this area are forced to read long catalogs of patterns to acquire this knowledge, missing the learning that is only obtained from practice. In this paper we propose to analyze the sequence of actions needed to be executed in a CASE tool in order to model different design patterns. The purpose of this analysis is to create a model that can be used by an interface agent to detect the design pattern an inexperienced user is trying to create in the tool and to assist him/her in this procedure.

Keywords: Interface Agents, Design Patterns, Discrete Sequence Analysis.

1 Introduction

Interface Agents [9] arise in order to provide users with proactive and reactive support in a personalized way in the use of a software application. To provide assistance, interface agents own a user model that is built according to the interests, preferences, priorities and needs demonstrated by the user through their interaction with the agent. However, the task of an interface agent is not only to learn the preferences and habits demonstrated by the user during use of the application, but it also must consider the user's goal previous to start interacting with him/her.

In order to provide a recommendation service two main factors must be considered in the design of an interface agent: first, the focus of attention with regard to the activities being undertaken by the user and second, the uncertainty regarding the user's current goal. With these premises in mind, the need to create an agent capable of performing an early detection of the user's current goal arises, so that the assistance provided by the agent is adapted to the context of the tasks performed by the user.

For the reason expressed above, and because of the difficulty of predicting the user's goal when designing a software system is that the use of interface agents in CASE tools (Computer Aided Software Engineering) has been an almost unexplored field. In several applications approaching this task [12, 5, 14, 6, 2], the means used by

F.V. Cipolla-Ficarra et al. (Eds.): ADNTIIC 2011, LNCS 7547, pp. 197–207, 2012.

the agent to advise the user require a computation time that is generally not available in an application with these characteristics.

The purpose of this article is to analyze the sequences of actions performed by a user when using a CASE tool in order to achieve early detection of the design pattern that the user is trying to model. We propose the use of Variable Order Markov (VOM) models, to reduce computational time needed to identify the user's goal and to formulate a set of possible actions to take. These models enable an early detection of the user's goal based on the actions he/she performs in a CASE tool. For our experiments, we used an AI planning algorithm, called Ag-Ucpop [8], to automatically generate the plan corpus needed to train the VOM models representing each design pattern.

The rest of this article is organized as follows: Section 2 describes some related work. Section 3 provides a brief overview on design patterns. Section 4 provides an introduction to Variable Order Markov models and its learning algorithms, and Section 5 describes how VOM models can be used to detect design patterns. Section 6 presents Markov Models as a case in point for use with the previously mentioned Design Patterns, describing one by one the aspects to be taken into account when combining them. Section 7 presents our experimental results and finally Section 8 presents our conclusions and some observations on future work.

2   Related Work

Design patterns have been widely researched and a variety of tools supporting them have arisen [12, 5, 14, 6, 10]. Among the features supported by these tools we can mention: extraction of patterns from source code, manipulation of patterns as first-class entities, formalization of patterns and generation of pattern instances from a collection of pattern templates, among others. Nevertheless, few attempts to incorporate AI techniques have been reported.

As far as we know, there exist in the literature few approaches to help the user in the selection of appropriate patterns for a given design context. In general, these approaches try to detect scenarios in which it could be useful to apply a pattern to improve some aspect of the design. In contrast, we only focus on the detection of the design pattern from a limited set of actions performed by the user. It is up to the interface agent to use this information in order to assist the user during the design process. For example, the approach presented in [2] introduces an interface agent that helps the user during the software design process. In this work, Bayesian networks are used to model the user's actions in order to detect the design pattern being modeled. One of the limitations of this approach is that an expert training is needed in order to improve the model. Our approach overcomes this limitation since VOM models are trained with a plan corpus generated computationally. Both the above mentioned work and our present work take a similar computational time to make a decision, but the advantage of our approach is that good results can be obtained only by modeling the final structure desire for a given design pattern.

Regarding the generation of plan corpora using planning algorithms, Blaylock & Allen [3] proposed the use of an AI planner and Monte-Carlo simulation to stochastically generate artificial plan corpora. They modified a planning algorithm (SHOP2 [11]) to randomly generate one of a set of all possible plans for a given goal and start state. The output generated by this approach in several cases results in valid but redundant information. In our case, we avoid this situation with the filtering process we apply and with the transformation from a partial order plan to a set of total order plans over the output obtained with ag-Ucpop. The use of redundant information during the training process of the PSAs results in misvalued transition probabilities.

3   Software Design Patterns

Design patterns are descriptions of communicating objects and classes that are customized to solve a general design problem in a particular context. A design pattern names, abstracts and identifies the key aspects of a common design structure that makes it useful for creating a reusable object-oriented design. Design patterns identify the participating classes and instances, their roles and collaborations, and the distribution of responsibilities [4].

Table 1. Design patterns space

Category	Creational	Structural	Comportamental
Patterns	Abstract Factory, Builder, Factory Method, Prototype, Singleton	Adapter, Bridge, Composite, Decorator, Facade, Flyweight, Proxy	Chain of Responsability, Command, Interpreter, Iterator, Mediator, Memento, Observer, State, Strategy, Template Method, Visitor

Design patterns capture solutions that have developed and evolved over time. Different design patterns vary in their granularity and level of abstraction. In 1995 Eric Gamma and a group of designers presented one of the most cited design patterns catalogs, commonly known as GoF catalog (Gang of Four). In this catalog, they present 23 design patterns classified according to their purpose (Table 1). Patterns can have creational, structural, or behavioral purposes. Creational patterns are concerned with the process of object creation. Structural patterns deal with the composition of classes or objects. Finally, behavioral patterns characterize the different ways in which classes or objects interact and distribute responsibility.

4   Variable Order Markov Models

Variable-Order Markov (VOM) models are an important class of models that extend the well known Markov chain models. These models consider that in realistic settings, there are certain realizations of states (represented by contexts) in which some future states are independent from the past states, leading to a great reduction in the number of model parameters. Algorithms for learning VOM models over a finite alphabet Σ create a probabilistic finite state automaton (PFA) which can model sequential data of considerable complexity. In contrast to N-order Markov models, which attempt to estimate conditional distributions of the form $Pr(\sigma|s)$, with $s \in \Sigma^n$ and $\sigma \in \Sigma$, VOM algorithms learn such conditional distributions where context lengths $|s|$ vary in response to the available statistics in the training data. Thus, VOM models provide the means for capturing both large and small order Markov dependencies based on the observed data. Ron et al. [13] introduced an algorithm for learning VOM models from data. This model is described using a subclass of Probabilistic Finite Automata, which they called Probabilistic Suffix Automata (PSA). For the construction of the PSA, a construction called Prediction Suffix Tree (PST) is used. PST preserves the minimal sub-sequences of variable length that are necessary for precise modeling of the given statistical source. The empirical probabilities are computed as follows. Let $e^1, e^2, \ldots,$ e^m, be the set of m training examples over the alphabet Σ. The length of the *i-th* training example is given by l_i, that is $e^i = e^i_1, e^i_2, \ldots, e^i_{li}$. The empirical probability of a sequence s with length l is computed using *Equation 1*.

$$\tilde{P}(s) = \frac{\sum_{i,j} \chi_s^{i,j}}{\sum_{i \, s.t. \, l_i \geq |s|} l_i - (|s|-1)} \tag{1}$$

$$\text{where } \chi_s^{i,j} = \begin{cases} 1 \, if \, s_1, s_2, \ldots, si = e^i_j, e^i_{j+1}, \ldots, e^i_{j+l_i-1} \\ 0 \, \, otherwhise \end{cases}$$

The numerator is the number of times the sequence s was observed in the sample and the denominator is the maximal number of possible overlapping occurrences a pattern of the same length could have. The conditional empirical probability of observing an action σ right after a given sequence s is given in *Equation 2*.

$$\tilde{P}(\sigma \, | \, s) = \frac{\tilde{P}(s \cdot \sigma)}{\tilde{P}(s)} \tag{2}$$

The training algorithm builds a probabilistic suffix tree where each node is labeled by a sequence of symbols shorter than a maximum value L. A pruning procedure is then applied to the tree aiming at eliminating those nodes whose prediction function is similar to other nodes modeling shorter contexts, and at eliminating nodes modeling very uncommon contexts (with probability lower than a given parameter γ_{min}). This pruning procedure prevents over-fitting the training data. Finally, a smoothing procedure is applied to consider all observations that did not occur in the training examples, but that might occur when using the PST as a predictor. The smoothing procedure used consists of collecting a probability mass equivalent to $|\Sigma|\gamma_{min}$ and distributing it among all possible symbols in each given context.

5   Detecting Software Design Patterns with Variable Order Markov Models

In order to detect the design pattern the user might be willing to use, the agent will own a set of PSTs modeling the sequences of actions that the user might perform to model the corresponding design pattern using a CASE tool.

The process of detecting the design pattern the user intends to model consists then in classifying the observation sequences, after each observed action in one of the possible PST modeling each design pattern. With this purpose, when a new action is observed, the probability that each PST assigns to the observation sequence is given by *Equation 3*, where $\gamma(s_{i-1}, \sigma_i)$ corresponds to the probability value assigned by the node s_{i-1} to action σ_I, being $s_0 = \varepsilon$ (the tree root) and for $1 \leq j \leq |r|$, s_j is the sequence labeling the deepest node reached by taking the walk corresponding to $\sigma_i, \sigma_{i-1}, \ldots, \sigma_1$, starting at the tree root.

$$PSA_k(r = \sigma_1, \cdots, \sigma_{|r|}) = \prod_{i=1}^{|r|} \gamma(s_{i-1}, \sigma_i) \qquad (3)$$

Then, the pattern modeled by the PST assigning the highest probability to the observed action sequence will be selected by the agent to provide assistance to the user.

In order to avoid the underflow problem that might arise when the observation sequence gets longer, instead of applying *Equation 3* directly to the observation sequence, we apply an exponential moving average. The exponential moving average (EMA) is a statistics that allows monitoring a process giving more importance to recent observations and gradually forgetting older observations. This smoothing technique also enables a better performance under noisy actions performed by the user while interacting with the CASE tool.

EMA is based on a smoothing constant λ in the range $(0, 1)$ that represents the aging of the process. EMA_t represents the exponential moving average for time period t. EMA_1 corresponds to the a priori probability of the first observed action and for every time period $t>1$, EMA_t is computed as shown in *Equation 4*.

$$EMA_t = \lambda \cdot \gamma(s_{i-1}, \sigma_i) + (1 - \lambda) \cdot EMA_{t-1} \qquad (4)$$

It is easy to see that a value $\lambda=1$ implies that only the most recent observation is considered, ignoring any previous observations, while a value $\lambda=0$ only considers the first observation and the process does not evolve. λ can be expressed as a percentage or as a N periods of times, where $\lambda=2/(N+1)$. The value of λ is usually set to 0.2 or 0.3 [7], but these values are somehow arbitrary and should be estimated empirically for each application domain.

After each observed action, the pattern recognizer will compute the EMA for each PST modeling a design pattern and will make a ranking with the most probable patterns the user might be willing to model in the CASE tool. Whenever the EMA value for some PSTs is over a given threshold τ a prediction is made.

6   Software Design Patterns as Discrete Sequences of Actions

In previous sections we briefly introduced software design patterns and Variable Order Markov models as a convenient representation for modeling discrete sequences. In this section we describe how we can represent software design patterns as discrete sequences of actions in such a way that they can be modeled using PSTs.

6.1   The Alphabet

Software design patterns are usually modeled with Class Diagrams since they offer a simple visualization of the relations among different classes in an object-oriented design. CASE tools offer the user the possibility of selecting different artifacts such as abstract or concrete classes, and interfaces and to connect these artifacts with different kind of relations, such as dependencies, generalizations, associations, etc. The use of all these artifacts will be the base for the alphabet used to represent design patterns as sequences of actions needed for training the PSTs. Table 2 shows the actions we considered along with the symbol assigned for the alphabet.

Table 2. Actions considered as part of the alphabet for building PST models

Action	Symbol
Interface added	AddInterfaz
Abstract Class Added	AddAbstractClass
Class Added	AddClass
Aggregation relation added	DefAggregation
Composition relation added	DefComposition
Generalization relation added	DefGeneralization
Association relation added	DefAssociation
Dependency relation added	DefDependency
Implementation relation added	DefImplementation

6.2   Representation of a Design Pattern as a Sequence of Symbols

Once we have defined the alphabet, we need to build the sequences of actions needed to model a design pattern. Consider for example the class diagram shown in Figure 1, corresponding to the Factory Method design pattern.

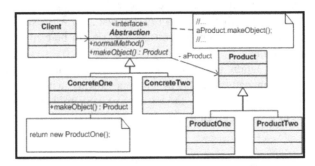

Fig. 1. Class diagram for the Factory Method design pattern

Each artifact in the class diagram in Figure 1 is created after the user performs one of the actions described in Table 2. These actions must be performed in a specific order according to the syntax of the class diagram. For example, it is impossible to create a relation between two classes if these classes are not created beforehand. With these restrictions in mind the following three alternative sequences of actions might be performed to achieve the class diagram shown in Figure 1:

1. AddAbstractClass, AddClass, AddClass, DefGeneralization, AddAbstractClass, AddClass, AddClass, DefGeneralization, DefGeneralization, DefGeneralization, DefAssociation, AddClass, DefAssociation
2. AddAbstractClass, AddClass, AddClass, AddAbstractClass, AddClass, DefAssociation, DefAssociation, DefGeneralization, AddClass, AddClass, DefGeneralization, DefGeneralization, DefGeneralization
3. AddAbstractClass, AddClass, DefGeneralization, AddClass, AddAbstractClass, AddClass, AddClass, DefGeneralization, AddClass, DefGeneralization, DefAssociation, DefGeneralization, DefAssociation

The first sequence, for example, indicates that the user first adds an abstract class to the diagram, and then he/she adds two concrete classes and connects them with a generalization relationship. After this, the user repeats the process with a new abstract class and two concrete classes with the corresponding generalization relationships. Finally, the user connects the two abstract classes with an association relationship and creates a new concrete class connected to the diagram with another association relationship.

6.3   Building the Plan Corpus

The term Plan Corpus is used to name the consistent training data from a goal list and the actions performed by the user to reach them. In our particular case, each goal will refer to the construction of a model of a particular design pattern, and the actions considered are those listed in Table 2. The quality of the Variable-Order Markov model developed to represent the patterns depends on the correctness and completeness of this plan corpus.

For our experiments, we used an AI planning algorithm, called Ag-Ucpop [8], to automatically generate the plan corpus. We selected the Ag-Ucpop algorithm due to the simplicity to obtain all the plans to achieve a particular goal. The planner's input are 1) the definition of the final state desired, that is the design pattern being modeled, and 2) the set of actions that can be performed in the CASE tool. The planner's output is a set of feasible plans that allow the user to achieve the given final state, and consequently to model the corresponding design pattern. Each of these plans is a partial order plan. This fact allows us to obtain several total order plans from a single plan found by the algorithm. A total order plan defines a feasible sequence of actions that when executed in any world satisfying the initial state description will let the user achieve the goal [15].

Figure 2 shows the planning actions we used with their corresponding pre- and post-conditions. In this figure it is possible to see the different domain constraints mentioned above. For example, the action defDependency needs the pre-existence of class A and class B.

```
action( addInterface( I ), [], [], [interface( I )] ).
action( addAbstractClass( C ), [], [], [class( C ), type(C, abstract), free( C)]
).
action( addClass( C ), [], [], [class( C ), type(C, concrete), free( C )] ).
action( defAgregation(A, B ), [], [class( A ), class( B )], [aggregation(A,B)] ).
action( defComposition(A, B ), [notEqual(A,B)] , [class( A ), class( B )],
[composition(A,B)] ).
action( defGeneralization(A, B ), [notEqual(A,B)] , [class( A ), free( A ),
class( B )], [generalization(A,B), not (free( A) )] ).
action( defAssociation(A, B ), [] , [class( A ), class( B )], [association(A,B)]
).
action( defDependency(A, B ), [notEqual(A,B)] , [class( A ), class( B )],
[dependency(A,B)] ).
action( defImplementation(A, B ), [] , [class( A ), interface( B )],
[implementation(A,B)] ).
```

Fig. 2. Action definition to the planning process

A planning problem consists of a 3-upla $<S_0, S_\infty, A>$, being S_0 the initial state, S_∞ the desire final state, and A the set of available actions. In our case the initial state is empty because we assume that the user begins with an empty diagram; the available actions are those defined in Figure 2. The final state is defined according to the specific pattern design we want to model. We describe each pattern using a set of objects and relationships among them. Figure 3 shows an example of how the design pattern Factory Method was defined using this notation. With this information we execute the algorithm and collect the set of possible plans needed to achieve the desired design patterns. For more information about the planning algorithm, please refer to [8].

```
class(AbstractFactory), type(AbstractFactory,abstract), class(ConcFactory1),
generalization(ConcFactory1,CbstractFactory), class(ConcFactory2),
generalization(ConcFactory2,AbstractFactory), class(Client),
association(Cliente,AbstractFactory), class(AbstractProduct),
class(ConcProduct1), generalization(ConcProduct1,AbstractProduct),class(ConcProduct2),
generalization(ConcProduct2, AbstractProduct), association( AbstractFactory,
AbstractProduct)
```

Fig. 3. Final state for the Factory Method

As mentioned above, the planner's output is a sequence of partially ordered actions that when performed enables the achievement of the corresponding goal. The plan is a partial order plan, i.e. there are several actions at the same level that could be executed at different times. From this plan it is possible to obtain several different total order plans that allow achieving the same goal.

7   Experimental Results

In the experiments shown in this section we use three different metrics to evaluate the results obtained for a model Q given a testing sequence $Seq=\sigma_1, \sigma_2,..., \sigma_n$: *error* (*Equation 5*), online accuracy (*Equation 6*) and convergence (*Equation 7*). These metrics are used to test the efficiency of the model to predict a pattern, not to measure the computational efficiency of the model.

$$error_q(Seq = \sigma_1, \sigma_2, \cdots, \sigma_n) = \frac{\sum_{i=1}^{n} |Q(\sigma_i) - Q_{best}(\sigma_i)|}{\sum_{i=1}^{n} Q_{best}(\sigma_i)} \qquad (5)$$

$$precision_q(Seq = \sigma_1, \sigma_2, \cdots, \sigma_n) = \frac{\sum_{i=1}^{n} best_Q(\sigma_i)}{n} \qquad (6)$$

$$convergence_q(Seq = \sigma_1, \sigma_2, \cdots, \sigma_n) = \frac{n - t + 1}{n} \qquad (7)$$

$$not\_best_Q(\sigma_{t-1}) \text{ and } best_Q(\sigma_j) \ \forall j \text{ s.t. } t \leq j \leq n$$

$$\text{where } best_Q(\sigma_i) = \begin{cases} 1 \text{ if } Q(\sigma_i) = Q_{best}(\sigma_i) \\ 0 \text{ if } Q(\sigma_i) \neq Q_{best}(\sigma_i) \end{cases}$$

The error level is calculated as follows: First we sum all absolute values obtained by subtracting the probability value calculated for the PSA for a sequence at each timestamp i, $Q(\sigma_i)$, from the best value given by all models for the same timestamp. Then, we normalize this value with the sum of all best values for each timestamp. The *online accuracy* for a model Q is calculated as the division of the number of times the target model Q is present in the N best predicted result, with the number of predictions made, m. A prediction is presented when the probability value of a PSA, in a given moment, is higher than a confidence threshold τ. Finally, convergence metric measures the number of observations needed to identify a given pattern. The time t in *Equation 7* is known as the convergence point.

7.1   Evaluation

For the experiments, we took a subset of the categories presented in [4] (3 creational patterns, 4 structural patterns, and 4 comportamental patterns). We codified an example for each pattern, and specified a class diagram to see it in a simple and concise way. Following the mechanism described in Section 5.3 we computationally generated a set of plans needed to achieve each pattern. Finally, with the resulting sequences provided by the planner, we created the corresponding PSTs modeling each pattern.

We performed a Leave-One-Out cross validation with the training sequences for each pattern. To determine the most adequate EMA value to be used during these tests, we made a full evaluation of the domain using values for λ ranging from 0.1 to 1.0, using intervals of 0.1. With these results we concluded that the appropriate value for λ was 0.2.

Table 3 shows the results of the experiment. The table shows that the online accuracy values for each model is around 65%, with some special cases in which the value is close to 30%. These particular cases result from the way the pattern is implemented. The Class diagrams used to represent these patterns use basic structures used in Object Oriented Programming; therefore, this simple structure was present in several of the patterns used in the experiments.

The average error obtained was 7.8%. We have to bear in mind that this metric is independent of the number of models considered to make the prediction. It is calculated using the distance between the probability value of the actual user's goal and the top value of the plan recognizer. The average convergence was of 53%, with some values lower than 34%, similar to the results obtained for the online accuracy.

With these results, we conclude that combining a planning algorithm with VOM models to formulate plans and make predictions in the domain of software patterns give us high levels of certainty about the user's goals at the moment of designing a software pattern.

Table 3. Experimental Results

Category	Pattern	Online Accuracy	Error	Convergence	Sequences length (average)
Creational	Abstract factory	0,78509964	0,02891106	69,1803	23
	Factory Method	0,95139217	0,00324753	78,8108	13
	Prototype	0,33333333	0,18535306	16,4683	7
Structural	Adapter	0,47037441	0,15656416	34,1058	6
	Bridge	0,80208333	0,06706767	70,3125	12
	Composite	0,26956107	0,15291051	20,9924	8
	Decorator	0,60063437	0,04938729	42,3299	12
Comportamental	Command	0,71853189	0,04900221	60,4813	15
	Iterator	0,83858521	0,02541061	73,1404	15
	Mediator	0,67768595	0,09292792	67,7686	11
	Observer	0,71040243	0,05159191	54,9127	15
Average values		0,65069853	0,07839763	53,5003	12,45

8   Conclusion

In this paper, we made use of Variable Order Markov models to model sequences of actions needed to create a design pattern. The models obtained are then used to detect the pattern that the user is trying to design so that an interface agent can provide assistance to non experienced users. The results shown in Section 7 give us high levels of certainty about the user's goals at the moment of designing a software patterns.

Other issue addressed in this paper is the creation of the Plan Corpus needed to train these models in a purely computational way, using a planning algorithm. With this approach we can build the plan corpus only with the knowledge about the design patterns being modeled. This allows us to easily increase the number of patterns being considered and also include anti patterns.

As future work, we propose the study of all design patterns defined in GoF catalog, using not only class diagrams to represent them but also sequence diagrams and the definition of methods and variables within classes, which we expect will improve the results presented in this paper. Also we plan to include anti patterns as a way to predict known mistakes at design time.

References

1. Armentano, M., Amandi, A.: Modeling sequences of user actions for statistical goal recognition. User Modeling and User Adapted Interaction 22(3), 281–311 (2012)
2. Berdún, L., Díaz-Pace, J.A., Amandi, A., Campo, M.: Assisting novice software designers by an expert designer agent. Expert Syst. Appl. 34(4), 2772–2782 (2008)
3. Blaylock, N., Allen, J.: Generating Artificial Corpora for Plan Recognition. In: Ardissono, L., Brna, P., Mitrović, A. (eds.) UM 2005. LNCS (LNAI), vol. 3538, pp. 179–188. Springer, Heidelberg (2005)
4. Gamma, E., Helm, R., Johnson, R., Vlissides, J.: Design patterns, elements of reusable object-oriented software. Addison-Wesley, New York (1994)
5. Florijn, G., Meijers, M., van Winsen, P.: Tool Support for Object-Oriented Patterns. In: Aksit, M., Auletta, V. (eds.) ECOOP 1997. LNCS, vol. 1241, pp. 472–495. Springer, Heidelberg (1997)
6. Hautamäki, J.: Pattern-based tool support for frameworks: Towards architecture-oriented software development environment. Ph.D. Thesis (2005)
7. Hunter, J.: The exponentially weighted moving average. Journal of Quality Technology 18(4), 203–209 (1986)
8. Berdun, L., Amandi, A.: Planning para agentes inteligentes. In: Proceedings del 7° Simposio Argentino de Inteligencia Artificial, ASAI 2005, Rosario, Argentina, pp. 12–23 (2005) (in Spanish)
9. Maes, P.: Agents that reduce work and information overload. Communications of the ACM 37(7), 31–40 (1994)
10. Meijler, T., Demeyer, S., Engel, R.: Making design patterns explicit in face: a frame work adaptive composition environment. SIGSOFT Softw. Eng. Notes 22, 94–110 (1997)
11. Nau, D., et al.: Shop2: An Htn Planning System. J. Artif. Intell. Res. (JAIR) 20, 379–404 (2003)
12. Roberts, D., Brant, J., Johnson, R.: A refactoring tool for smalltalk. Theory and Practice of Object Systems 3(4), 253–263 (1997)
13. Ron, D., Singer, Y., Tishby, N.: The power of amnesia: Learning probabilistic automata with variable memory length. Machine Learning 25(2-3), 117–149 (1996)
14. Tokuda, L., Batory, D.: Evolving object-oriented designs with refactorings. Automated Software Engineering 8, 89–120 (2001)
15. Weld, D.: An Introduction to Least Commitment Planning. AI Magazine 15(4), 27–61 (1994)

A Programming Model for the Semantic Web

Marco Crasso[1,2], Cristian Mateos[1,2], Alejandro Zunino[1,2], and Marcelo Campo[1,2]

[1] ISISTAN Research Institute, UNICEN University, Tandil, Buenos Aires, Argentina
[2] Consejo Nacional de Investigaciones Científicas y Técnicas (CONICET), Argentina
mcampo@exa.unicen.edu.ar

Abstract. This year the concept of "Semantic Web" celebrates its tenth anniversary since it was coined by prominent researchers Tim Berners-Lee, James Hendler and Ora Lassila. To date, there are many technologies to describe, in a *machine-understandable* way, information and services available in the Web. An incipient research area is focused on solving the issues related to building applications for truly exploiting semantically-described resources. In this paper, we present an approach to upgrade a software application into a Semantic Web-enabled one. The approach builds on the Aspect-Oriented Programming (AOP) paradigm to allow developers to incorporate ontology management capabilities into an ordinary object-oriented application without modifying its source code. The paper also discusses related works and presents case studies.

Keywords: Semantic Web, Software, Model, Aspect-Oriented Programming.

1 Introduction

From its beginnings, the Web was conceived as a system of computer networks sharing linked HyperText documents. Later, applications become Web resources as well upon the arrival of Web Services technologies. Nowadays, the Semantic Web is an extension of the traditional Web, in which resources and services are described in such a way that a machine can understand it [1]. The goal of this extension is that applications become "users" of the Web. In this sense, it is expected that once every Internet resource will be properly, and semantically, described, applications will be able to compose different resources to achieve their goals, without human intervention. Accordingly, software applications needing external information or services to solve everyday problems, such as meeting or flight arrangement, supply-chain management, and so on, will reach unprecedented levels of automatism [2].

For the vision of the Semantic Web to become a reality, standards and ontologies should converge, and in turn applications should be turned from systems that assume a closed world to ones that will operate by composing Web resources. On one hand, standards play a pivotal role in developing and connecting heterogeneous functionality, specially when different providers offer and distribute their services over the Internet. In this sense, Web Services standards, such as Web Service Description Language (WSDL) and Simple Object Access Protocol (SOAP) [15], represent a big push in the right direction. WSDL is an XML format for describing

F.V. Cipolla-Ficarra et al. (Eds.): ADNTIIC 2011, LNCS 7547, pp. 208–218, 2012.

the intended functionality of a Web Service by means of an interface with methods and arguments, in object-oriented terminology, and documentation in the form of textual comments. For example, a provider may describe the interface of a service operation for retrieving the temperature of a certain region as getTemperature (zip:string):double.

In the context of information sciences, an ontology defines a set of representational primitives by which a domain of knowledge or discourse is modeled [5]. Ontologies are crucial for abstracting away syntactical differences, e.g. those present at WSDL documents, which may hinder the utilization of the corresponding services. To clarify the importance of ontologies, let us suppose that another provider uses getFahrenheitTempFor(regionCode:long):string to describe the signature of a service operation similar to getTemperature(zip:string):double. Clearly, these operations are syntactically different. Therefore, if either a human discoverer or a software agent looks for all services that retrieve the temperature of a certain region, they will have to infer that the aforementioned operation signatures have equivalent semantics. Indeed, the W3C (www.w3.org) encourages developers to describe ontologies by using the Ontology Web Language (OWL), an XML-based language having constructors for defining classes and properties, with cardinality, range and domain restrictions among others.

Ontologies allow providers to define each part of a service, i.e. its functionality, inputs and expected results, with an unambiguous description of its semantics. From now on, we will refer as annotation to the task of linking service descriptions with concepts represented in a machine-understandable model that explicitly defines the semantics of operations and data-types. There are different approaches to combine ontologies and standards for describing services and, in turn, build Semantic Web Services, such as OWL-S [8] and WSDL-S [12]. For the sake of exemplification, although their many differences, with these approaches developers can annotate the aforementioned services input with the ZipCode concept from Schema Web ontology[1], by extending the associated WSDL input definitions with the unique and public URI of ZipCode (http://www.daml.org/2001/10 /html/zipcode-ont #ZipCode).

Annotating a service may be a cumbersome task, specially when it requires building ontologies from scratch and training development team members on OWL and WSDL-S and their surrounding technologies. To cope with this problem, researchers have been investigating on approaches to facilitate ontology construction along with service annotation, e.g. by automatically suggesting ontologies for a given service description in WSDL [3]. In this paper we explore the annotation problem, but from the perspective of Semantic Web applications, i.e. those applications that consume external services to accomplish their goals. In essence, the approach for turning an ordinary application into an application that automatically discovers, selects and invokes Semantic Web Services, is to annotate its business object definitions with ontologies. This is because such an application not only requires to semantically express its functional needs, but also to "talk" with Semantic Web Services through ontologies. For example, to automatically call a service expecting a ZipCode concept as input, an application must upgrade its internal representation of ZIP code, possibly a variable of type long, into an OWL class instance.

---

[1] http://www.schemaweb.info/schema/SchemaInfo.aspx?id=20

Until now, unlike the case of service annotation, there is not a consensus about how to annotate applications. In some clean cases, the approach to decorate business objects classes with special proxy objects has shown to be useful for maintaining annotations in accordance with dynamic objects states [14]. One limitation of this approach is that it is feasible only when business objects are modeled and implemented in accordance with specific design conventions. Besides, to incorporate such special proxies to an application, its source code must be modified.

Undoubtedly, it is not always possible to refactor existing applications for accommodating business object designs and implementations or adding proxies. This paper presents an approach that copes with the aforementioned limitations. The approach bases on the Aspect-Oriented Programming paradigm to treat the requirement of semantic annotations as a cross-cutting concern. In computer science, a cross-cutting concern is a requirement that traverses different parts of an application, and it is complex to decouple from other application components. With this approach, management of annotations is encapsulated in modules, called semantic aspects, which can be plugged in any specific point of an application, without modifying its source code. Therefore, the opportunity for transparently turning an ordinary application into a Semantic Web-powered one, comes at expenses of learning and implementing the semantic aspects. Section 2 presents an overview of related work. Section 3 explains the proposed approach to annotate applications. Case studies and comparisons are shown in Section 3.1. Finally, Section 4 concludes the paper.

2   Related Work

The problem of ontology-application integration has been mainly approached by translating ontologies to source code files in any object-oriented language. The basic idea is to create an application programming interface (API) that represents a given semantic model [6]. Furthermore, when a business object is programmatically modified, the API forwards the associated changes to a database of ontological annotations, a.k.a. semantic repository [14]. This approach bases on bridging semantically equivalent object constructors of Description Logic (DL) and Object Oriented (OO) systems. For example, an instance of a Java class represents an instance of a single OWL class with most of its properties maintained.

RDFReactor [14] is an approach to transform a given ontology into an OO Java API. The approach receives its name since it accepts as input an ontology in Resource Definition Framework (RDF), the baseline for W3C ontology languages like OWL. For each business object definition found in the input ontology, RDFReactor generates a special stateless proxy object that delegates all method calls to semantic repository queries and updates. A proxy represents business objects by exposing the methods that would expose a plain object designed for representing the same business object. The proxies are responsible for querying the semantic repository when an accessor method is called, or for updating the repository when the call refers to a method used to control changes to a variable, i.e. a mutator method. To clarify this, let suppose that books are modeled as instances of a class named Book, which has associated isbn instances as well. Then, a special proxy for such an instance would set a relationship between a concept Book and another concept ISBN when the association is programmatically set, for example by calling setISBN method.

Figure 1 depicts the resulting classes and messages that have been produced after translating an ontology for the mentioned book domain. In the Figure, a specific business object, i.e. the b:Book, is created by a client. The approach replaces business object instantiation (let suppose a new statement in Java) with proxy instantiation. Then, the client indirectly updates the semantic model when calling the mutator method named setISBN, a typical Java setter method.

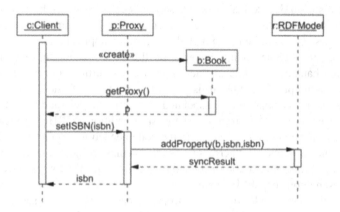

Fig. 1. RDFReactor's proxy example

Furthermore, there are a handful of tools implementing the same approach followed by RDFReactor, such as Jastor [13] and ActiveRDF [9]. A complete list of similar projects can be found in http://semanticweb.org/wiki/Tripresso. This Web site groups several researchers that discuss issues related to translation of ontology languages to OO languages.

All in all, though with the approach described in the previous paragraphs developers might bootstrap any OO application into a Semantic Web ready application, the approach has some limitations. Particularly, a major limitation is that the approach forces developers to introduce design and implementation-level changes into target applications, which is clearly an undesirable situation.

3   An AOP-Based Approach to Annotate Applications with Semantics

Separation of Concerns (SoC) [11] is both a principle and a process for building software applications, which states that each constituent part of an application should be free of behaviors not inherent to its functional nature. Traditionally, SoC has been achieved by using modularity, encapsulation and information hiding techniques in the context of Object-Oriented programming, or layered designs in an architectural one.

The AOP paradigm has shown to be quite effective in increasing application modularity and reducing inter-module coupling by allowing the separation of *cross-cutting* concerns, i.e. a concern that affects many parts of an application [4].

With AOP, the logic of cross-cutting concerns is encapsulated in modules called aspects, which can be joined to specific points of an application, called join-points. Aspects inhabit a special plane, whereas application components constitute the base plane. Weaving is the act of activating the aspects of the aspects plane that are associated with join-points at the base plane. Most AOP materializations allow one of two types of weaving: dynamic and static. The difference between both types of weaving stems from the moment at which aspect code is linked to the code of its join-points. With static weaving, the code is woven at compilation time, whereas dynamic weaving allows aspects to be incorporated into running applications.

Having explained the main concepts of the AOP paradigm, we propose an approach that handles semantic annotation as a cross-cutting concern. The rationale behind this assumption is that it is out of the scope of most business object representations to manage their associated semantic model, and clearly business objects represent most application parts, at least in traditional CRUD applications.

Our approach proposes to encapsulate the code needed to interact with a semantic repository into aspects. Furthermore, every business object mutator method is conceived as a join-point. Static or dynamic weaving, indistinctly, produces business object representations capable of managing their semantic annotations without having to modify their source code. In contrast to proxy-based approaches such as [14], our approach is not invasive for applications, since it maintains business objects encapsulation. This is because business object classes remain untouchable, even having instance variables for holding objects states. Aggregated code blocks, i.e. those sentences needed for updating a semantic repository, are concealed by the aspects.

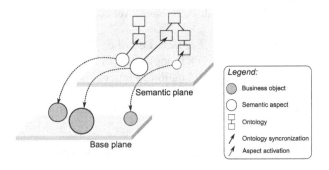

Fig. 2. Base and Semantic AOP planes

Figure 2 depicts the conceptual overview of the approach, in which business objects constitute the base plane of an application, which are not responsible for nothing apart from modeling the application business logic. Alternatively, the modules of the semantic plane (semantic aspects) keep business objects and ontologies updated.

To systematically annotate applications business objects with the proposed approach, the next steps should be followed:

1. identify business objects,
2. map the identified business objects onto ontological elements,
3. build semantic aspects for programmatically updating ontologies,
4. identify join-points,
5. weave aspects into join-points.

The first step refers to analyze the applications under study looking for the minimal set of business objects that need to be annotated, possibly to interact with external Web Services. Step 2 is intended for identifying to which classes or properties of an ontology should the business objects be mapped. At the next step, the implementation of semantic repository updates should be provided. This step requires to select technologies for materializing the AOP paradigm and the semantic repository, or in other words choosing among different AOP frameworks such as AspectJ or SpringAOP [7], and ontology containers, such as Jena [10]. Once proper technologies have been selected, the specific lines of codes for updating the ontology elements identified at step 2 should be encapsulated into aspects, which is done at step 3. Moreover, step 4 deals with analyzing the whole application and seeking in which parts of it the business objects are modified. Finally, the fifth step is for gluing aspects and the application.

The next sub-sections explain how to annotate particular business objects that belong to two real world applications that we are porting to the Semantic Web as an initial attempt to assess the feasibility of the proposed approach. The application domains and the employed AOP technologies are described.

3.1   Case Study I

In this section the five steps previously described will be applied for annotating an application belonging to the library domain. The application has been implemented in Java. Broadly, the application manages books and their authors. Books and authors are the business objects required to be annotated, which are represented as JavaBeans classes. JavaBeans is a programming convention that states that for each instance variable there is an accessor method named using the prefix "get", and a mutator method having the "set" prefix in its signature name. For example, the **Book** class has an instance variable called **author** of type **Author**, and it has two methods accordingly: **getAuthor()** and **setAuthor(Author)**, the accessor and mutator, respectively. The **Book** class has another instance variable, a **String** named **title**, and two more methods **getTitle()** and **setTitle(String)**. At the same time, books and authors are semantically represented using the next part of the library ontology:

```
<owl:Class rdf:ID="Book"/>
<owl:Class rdf:ID="Person"/>
<owl:ObjectProperty rdf:ID="isAuthorOf">
  <owl:inverseOf>
```

```
  <owl:ObjectProperty rdf:ID="hasAuthor"/>
 </owl:inverseOf>
 <rdfs:domain rdf:resource="#Person"/>
 <rdfs:range rdf:resource="#Book"/>
</owl:ObjectProperty>
<owl:ObjectProperty rdf:about="#hasAuthor">
 <rdfs:domain rdf:resource="#Book"/>
 <owl:inverseOf rdf:resource="#isAuthorOf"/>
 <rdfs:range rdf:resource="#Person"/>
</owl:ObjectProperty>
```

The association between books and authors for the business objects is semantically represented via the **isAuthorOf** property, which is defined as **inverseOf** the **hasAuthor** property, by annotating **x isAuthorOf y** the relationship **y hasAuthor x** holds.

Returning to the steps needed to employ the proposed approach, at this point business objects have been identified (step 1), and these objects have been mapped onto concrete ontology elements (step 2). With regard to step 3, the fact that the JavaBeans convention was followed allows for rapid identification of join-points, since aspects in charge of updating the semantic repository should be activated every time a setter method is called. To implement the aspects (step 4) for this application we have employed the well-known AspectJ support, and Jena for ontology annotations persistence. AspectJ has been designed as an extension of the Java language. One of the design drivers of AspectJ was that it should allow Java developers to intuitively incorporate aspects to their Java applications. On the other hand, Jena is a software library for manipulating ontology repositories programmatically. The next code illustrates the resulting aspect. As the reader can observe, we have used an aspects extension mechanism similar to regular class inheritance, and thus the generated aspect inherited from another aspect called SemanticAspect. This is because the boilerplate code needed for Jena initialization tasks has been abstracted for clarity reasons.

```
public aspect BookSemanticAspect extends SemanticAspect {
  pointcut setAuthor(Book b):
    target(b) && call (public * setAuthor(..));

  before(Book b): setAuthor(b) {
      if (m.getIndividual(ns+b.getISBN()) == null) {
        m.createIndividual(nsa.getISBN(),baseClass);
      }
    }

  after(Book b): setAuthor(b) {
    Individual ai=m.getIndividual(ns+b.getAuthor());
    Individual bi = m.getIndividual(ns+b.getISBN());
    bi.setPropertyValue(m.getProperty(ns+"hasAuthor"),ai);
    }
  }
```

To sum up, two instance variables, namely **author** and **title**, of the book business object have been mapped onto a semantic model in OWL. Then, proper synchronization mechanisms to mirror object changes onto a semantic repository have been implemented using AspectJ and Jena. Table 1 summarizes the application join-points and their corresponding aspects.

Table 1. Aspect composition summary

Join-Point	AspectJ
class: Book method: setAuthor	pointcut setAuthor(Book b): target(b) && call (public * setAuthor(..))
class: Book method: setTitle	pointcut setTitle(Book b): target(b) && call (public * setTitle(..))

3.2   Case Study II

We employed the proposed approach with another case study, namely a warehouse management Java application that uses a relational database through JDBC to persist warehouse article data. One peculiarity of the application's design is that business objects are represented by a single **Warehouse** object, which updates and queries the database. From a semantic perspective, we have employed an ontology having a class named **Article**, which has a property named **hasQuantity**. The range of this property is an integer, and its domain is an instance of the OWL class named **Article**. Therefore, when an article's quantity is modified in the **Warehouse** object (i.e. within the Java code), the associated **hasQuantity** property in the corresponding article is updated in the semantic repository.

To implement the semantic aspects we have employed the SpringAOP framework. This framework allows developers to implement aspects as any other ordinary Java method, but according to specific signatures defined by certain hook methods. Concretely, we have implemented the required hook method afterReturning as follows:

```
public void afterReturning(Object o, Method m, Object[] args,
Object target) throws Throwable {
        String code = String.valueOf(args[0]);
        if (model.getIndividual(ns + code) == null)
           model.createIndividual(ns+code,baseClass);
        Individual i = model.getIndividual(ns + code);
        long quantity = Long.parseLong(String.valueOf(args[1]));
        Property p=model.getDatatypeProperty(ns+"hasQuantity");
        i.setPropertyValue(p, model.createLiteral(quantity) );
}
```

As the reader can see, this application design is not as clean as that of the case study presented previously, since business objects and mutators were not evident. Here, business objects have been represented using the primary key of a relational table, i.e. in a conventional, database-like style. Moreover, one class has mutators, but no code convention was followed to name them. The next code presents for example the **incArticle** mutator method:

```
class Warehouse{
    public void incArticle(String code,long quantity) throws
Exception {
        conn.setAutoCommit(false);
        PreparedStatement stmt = conn.prepareStatement(
        "UPDATE ARTICLE SET QUANTITY=? WHERE CODE=?"
        );
        stmt.setLong(1,quantity);
        stmt.setString(2,code);
        stmt.executeUpdate();
        conn.commit();
    }
}
```

The semantic aspect should be activated every time the **incArticle** method successfully returns. Having identified business objects, mapping them onto ontology elements, implementing the semantic aspects, and detecting join-points, the missing step was to configure the SpringAOP framework for weaving the aspect and the join-point at run-time. The following XML code belongs to the SpringAOP configuration file:

```
<!- After advise declaration ->
<bean id="myAfterAdvice" class="MySemanticAfterAdvise"/>

<!- Proxy with interceptors stack declaration ->
<bean id="businesslogicbean" class="#aop#.ProxyFactoryBean">
  <property name="proxyInterfaces">
    <value>Warehouse</value>
  </property>
  <property name="target">
    <ref local="beanTarget"/>
  </property>
  <property name="interceptorNames">
    <list>
        <value>myAfterAdvisor</value>
    </list>
  </property>
</bean>
```

```
<!- Join point declaration ->
<bean id="myAfterAdvisor"
class="#aop#.RegexpMethodPointcutAdvisor">
  <property name="advice">
    <ref local="myAfterAdvice"/>
  </property>
  <property name="pattern">
    <value>Warehouse.incArticle</value>
  </property>
</bean>
```

4   Conclusion and Future Research

This paper presented a novel approach to incorporate ontology management into conventional applications. The main difference among related approaches is that application code is not modified. In most cases, running applications and ontologies may be integrated by re-launching the former ones. The main limitation of the approach, however, is that application developers should be trained in AOP.

In the near future, we will use performance metrics for evaluating different technologies for implementing the approach. The goal of this task is to have evidence about the overhead introduced by the semantic aspects over ordinary applications. Besides, we are employing the proposed approach with the reference Web application provided by Oracle to illustrate how developers can apply various Java Enterprise Edition technologies for implementing Web Services.

We are planning to extend the proposed approach in several directions. First, one line of research will investigate on facilitating semantic aspects generation. In parallel, we are designing heuristics for assisting developers in performing the second step of the proposed approach, which deals with mapping identified business objects onto ontological elements. In this sense, we will test the hypothesis that OO business objects specifications contain information –e.g. the names and comments of classes and methods– that is useful for guiding the ontology mapping process. Lastly, we will investigate the applicability of the extended approach in the context of SWAM [2], a Prolog-based programming language that allows the construction of mobile agents that are able to interact with RDF-described Web services and resources. Although SWAM is aimed at exploiting separation of concerns concepts, to a certain extent the language still forces users to mix agent code with the code in charge of interacting with semantic resources.

References

1. Berners-Lee, T., Hendler, J., Lassila, O.: The semantic Web. Scientific American 284(5), 34–43 (2001)
2. Crasso, M., Mateos, C., Zunino, A., Campo, M.: SWAM: A logic-based mobile agent programming language for the Semantic Web. Expert Systems with Applications 38, 1723–1737 (2011)

3. Crasso, M., Zunino, A., Campo, M.: Combining document classification and ontology alignment for semantically enriching Web Services. New Generation Computing 28, 371–403 (2010)
4. Enriquez, J.G., Vidal, G., Casas, S.: Design Configurable Aspects to Connecting Business Rules with Spring. In: Cipolla Ficarra, F.V., de Castro Lozano, C., Pérez Jiménez, M., Nicol, E., Kratky, A., Cipolla-Ficarra, M. (eds.) ADNTIIC 2010. LNCS, vol. 6616, pp. 92–101. Springer, Heidelberg (2011)
5. Gruber, T.: Ontology. In: Encyclopedia of Database Systems, pp. 304–307. Springer-Verlag New York, Inc. (2008)
6. Kalyanpur, A., et al.: Automatic mapping of owl ontologies into java. In: Maurer, F., Ruhe, G. (eds.) SEKE, pp. 98–103 (2004)
7. Mak, G., Long, L., Rubio, R.: Spring AOP and AspectJ support. In: Spring Recipes, pp. 117–158. Apress (2010)
8. Martin, D., et al.: Bringing semantics to Web Services with owl-s. World Wide Web 10(3), 243–277 (2007)
9. Oren, E., Heitmann, B., Decker, S.: ActiveRDF: Embedding Semantic Web data into Object-Oriented languages. Web Semantics 6, 191–202 (2008)
10. Reynolds, D.: Jena 2 inference support (2011), http://jena.sourceforge.net (last accessed June 2011)
11. Richardson, C.: Untangling enterprise Java. Queue 4(5), 36–44 (2006)
12. Sivashanmugam, K., et al.: Adding semantics to Web Services standards. In: The 2003 International Conference on Web Services, pp. 395–401. CSREA Press, Las Vegas (2003)
13. Szekely, B., Betz, J.: Jastor: Typesafe, ontology driven RDF access from Java (2011), http://jastor.sourceforge.net (last accessed June 2011)
14. Völkel, M.: RDFReactor – From Ontologies to Programatic Data Access. In: Proc. of the Jena User Conference 2006. HP Bristol (2006)
15. Weerawarana, S., et al.: Web Services Platform Architecture: SOAP, WSDL, WS-Policy, WS-Addressing, WS-BPEL, WS-Reliable Messaging and More. Prentice Hall PTR, Upper Saddle River (2005)

Combining Semantic Web Technologies and Rule-Based Systems for Building Advanced Medical Applications

Vili Podgorelec and Mitja Gradišnik

University of Maribor, FERI, Institute of Informatics,
Smetanova ulica 17, SI-2000 Maribor, Slovenia
{Vili.Podgorelec,Mitja.Gradisnik}@uni-mb.si

Abstract. In this paper we discuss the possibility of building advanced medical knowledge-based applications using a combination of two promising technologies: semantic web technologies for the representation of domain knowledge and known facts, and rule-based systems for the definition of rules for knowledge base. We developed a prototype web application *GeneMap*, which enables browsing on diseases and related genes, which are known to influence the development of a disease; the publicly available *Diseasome Dataset* is used as a source of semantically-annotated medical data. The prototype is used to show how the two technologies can be efficiently combined to improve both the performance of such applications and the possibility of discovering new patterns that could lead towards new medical knowledge.

Keywords: Semantic Web Technologies, Rule-based Systems, Medical Knowledge Representation, Knowledge-based Medical System, Disorder-gene Associations.

1 Introduction

Medicine is one of the domains, where the utility of semantic web technologies, especially ontologies, are widely accepted [1]. Medical ontologies have already been deployed at large scale in many medical domains, especially in biomedicine [2]. Semantic web technologies (i.e. ontologies) can be used for knowledge representation (representing information and semantically annotated data) within a specific domain [3], they can also be used to bridge two or more domains, to integrate medical data resources [4], to perform automatic inferring, etc. However, there are some fundamental problems regarding the efficient use of semantic web technologies in medicine, because of which there are many attempts to combine them with another existing technology [5].

The inferring mechanisms on real medical ontologies (which are quite large) are computationally highly complex and efficient reasoning on real-world ontologies containing a large set of individuals is still a very challenging task with current Description Logics-based technologies [6]. Furthermore, the languages for defining inferring rules are far from natural (using description logic as a formalism to define inferring rules), which makes them very difficult to use by domain experts

F.V. Cipolla-Ficarra et al. (Eds.): ADNTIIC 2011, LNCS 7547, pp. 219–229, 2012.

(physicians, medical and health-care experts, medical researchers), not possessing the high level of technical knowledge of this kind [7]. Finally, while using this kind of formalisms it is possible to represent the knowledge base for a domain (having all the troubles mentioned above in mind), it is still only possible to represent already known relations and facts. Namely, the semantic web technologies are primarily intended for the automation of knowledge-related processes and knowledge-based tasks, but not for the discovering of new knowledge itself, which is one of the main goals of medical research.

Based on these propositions, there are two important research questions, which we would like to answer. First, is there a more natural way of defining inferring rules on semantic data that could be efficiently used with existing technologies? And second, can be in this way also potentially new knowledge discovered?

The latest trends in knowledge and software engineering show that semantic web technologies is a major approach to represent static knowledge (concepts, their inter-relations and properties, operational data with meaning) and to define and implement an advanced information model for an application. On the other hand, rule-based systems are re-emerging as a technology to handle the dynamic aspects of knowledge representation. They enable an efficient and a more natural way of defining inferring rules. Until now, the two were used almost exclusively apart of each other, as they are somewhat overlapping. Namely, semantic web technologies include their own way to define inferring rules (in a form of description logic) and rule-based systems provide their own way to represent data (in a form of facts). However, we suggest that the combination of both can be efficiently used to solve the problems stated above. For this purpose, we decided to use a rule-based system for the definition of domain rules which are used to infer on semantically annotated data from an existing ontology without a need to convert or transform this data. Additionally, the approach should also enable one to search for new knowledge with semantic data.

2   Advanced Knowledge-Based Medical Applications

The domain of medicine has been always attractive realm for researchers of the artificial intelligence because of its vast amounts of specific domain knowledge, which can be usefully used to derive potential new knowledge. It seems that an ultimate method which would achieve human-level intelligence cannot be expected in near future, so researchers have to use existing methods, technologies and approaches, and properly combine them to get as effective intelligent solutions as possible. In this paper we present an approach to building advanced medical applications which are based on rule-based production systems (rule engine) and are capable of dynamically gaining data from semantic information sources, such as different semantic knowledge bases (i.e. medical ontologies) on the web. The conceptual architecture is presented on Figure 1. Using the proposed approach we have built such an advanced medical expert system for reasoning about related diseases based on their relation to genes, disorder-gene relations and the use of common drugs.

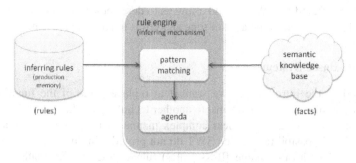

Fig. 1. The conceptual architecture of two combined technologies

2.1   Semantic Web Technologies (SWT)

Semantic web represents an evolutionary step in the development of information systems we know and brings new ways to share and use information. According to Passin [8], the vision of semantic web is that computers would be able to find, read and understand the meaning of data. In this manner, the SWT are able to represent knowledge in the form of semantically annotated, interconnected data. As such, SWT can replace in these days most used keyword search with very exact inquiring.

To achieve that goal a whole stack of technologies is required. SWT are based on XML language that enables them to be platform and program language independent. They are built in layers, where each upper layer provides additional functional aspects and is based on the lower one, with which is fully compatible[1]. The layers, from bottom up, include URI, XML and namespaces, RDF as the core technology for the semantic annotation of data [9], RDFS and OWL being languages for describing ontologies [10], Sparql a language for querying semantic data and RIF as a rule interchange format for describing logical rules of the data being semantically described.

The central part of a semantic web system is an ontology that describes some knowledge domain using notions of concepts, instances, attributes, relations and axioms – in the form of semantic data [11]. It is a useful way to organize and share information while offering means for enhanced semantic search. The syntax, needed to define a domain information (or knowledge) model in ontology, is defined by an ontology language; the most common being the Web Ontology Language (OWL).

A typical SWT system is based upon RDF, OWL and a rule language compatible to RIF – SWRL is widely used [12]. In this manner, RDF is mainly considered as a data backend and a data interchange technology. Concepts that are defined in ontology represent the useful information or knowledge. Rules enable encapsulation of logic – based on defined rules, new knowledge is being inferred according to concepts defined in ontology and RDF data. A query language (like Sparql) is used to query the semantic data. These building blocks represent the core SWT and comprise a typical SWT architecture which provides fairly expressive formalisms for knowledge representation and inferring on_ this knowledge. The use of all

---

[1] http://www.w3.org/2001/sw/

functionality, offered by SWT, would allow us to describe an information model very precisely, but would consume a lot of time and effort to solve a problem.

2.2   Rule-Based Systems

As outlined in the introduction, we wanted to replace some of the functionalities, offered by complex SWT formalisms, to another technology, which would allow us to perform the intended tasks in a less complex manner, with better performance, and some additional possibilities, which SWT do not provide. In this manner, we decided to use Drools (with other name JBoss Rules) rule engine [13]. Actually, it is more than just rule engine because it allows us to store, manage and validate rules. According to that it can be classified as a production rule engine.

Drools is fully Java based rules system. It implements the standard rule engine API, JSR-94 (Java Specification Request), which is standard runtime API for rule engines by providing a simple API to access a rule engine from a Java code similar to JDBC (Java Database Connectivity) providing the way of connecting to databases. Because Drools rule engine is built on Java technology stack, it can be easily used in combination with vast range of other technologies that support Java. In case of our prototype application we have used Drools rule engine combined with Jena Semantic Web framework for dealing with semantic data [14].

It has turned out that building expert systems on business rules was successful method in the past. Building a rule based expert system is a complex task which aims to capture the knowledge of a specific domain in form of business rules and therefore requires collaboration of programmers and domain experts. In mainstream computer engineering we usually use procedural programming. That means that programmers in computer programs encode what has to be done, how it has to be done and in what order it has to be done. On the other hand writing business rules represents declarative approach to programming. A declarative approach, in contrast, describes what the program should do, but omits much of the instructions on how to do it. Because declarative programs include only important details of a solution, they can be easier to understand than procedural programs. So, this approach of thinking is much closer to domain experts, who are usually not so technically oriented. An important advantage of Drools is also its built-in support of defining domain specific language which enables writing business rules in a syntax that is much closer to natural language and allows developers to express domain logic in terms of their domain jargon. It allows domain experts to productively participate in the development and maintaining processes of an expert system.

Drools rule engine consists of three fundamental components: production memory, working memory and inference engine [15]. Business rules are stored in production memory and are matched against facts stored in the working memory. In case of our prototype application the required data are on user's request retrieved from distant semantic knowledge bases, loaded into engine's working memory and processed in real time by the inference engine.

3   Web Application *GeneMap*

There has been a lot of research in medicine undertaken on identifying the causes of a development of specific diseases. The results have shown the importance of specific genes, which are known to influence the development of a disease [16]. The analyses of an individual's genome with the intention of determining the levels of individual predisposition to certain diseases are becoming very common. Recently, studies have shown the importance of SWT for the representation of genes-related knowledge in biomedicine [17].

We developed a web application called *GeneMap* that enables user to browse the diseases and relations between disorders and the related genes, known to influence the development of a disease. Besides showing the basic information about a disease and the related genes, the application provides also all the information about other diseases related to the selected one (Figure 2).

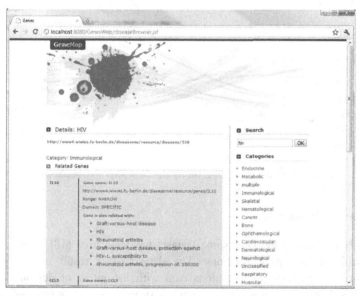

Fig. 2. Web application screenshot: it represents a page where the details of a specific disease (disorder) are shown together with the related genes

Technologically speaking, the web application is implemented using the JSF (Java Server Faces) technology. It can be deployed on any Java web container or application server. The Drools Expert rule engine is integrated within the application, which ensures loose coupling between web application and used semantic data source. Additionally, the rule engine is used to execute the defined domain rules, which are able to infer on basic semantic data to acquire additional relevant facts and patterns. The basic semantic data is retrieved from publicly available Diseasome Dataset using the SPARQL semantic queries. The UML class diagram of the web application is represented on Figure 3.

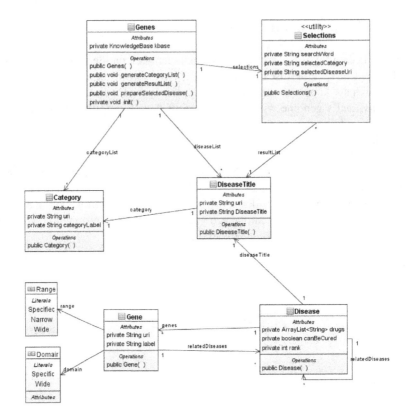

Fig. 3. The UML class diagram for the *GeneMap* web application

3.1   Semantic Data Source

In our web application the Diseasome Dataset has been used [18]. It is a semantic dataset with disorder-gene relations. The dataset is a result of a project for visualization of disorder-gene relations data with the intent of demonstrating the concept of scientific and research information systems of the future. The dataset is available to regular users in a form of a web page containing tabular data[2]; the information can also be viewed in a form of an interactive map[3].

For the advanced users and developers, however, it is convenient that all the information is also provided in the form of semantically annotated data, publicly available as a semantic data endpoint[4]. Currently the dataset contains information about 4213 diseases, representing altogether 91.182 triples in the semantic network. Dataset also contains a rich selection of links to external data sources.

---

[2] http://www4.wiwiss.fu-berlin.de/diseasome/
[3] http://diseasome.eu/map.html
[4] http://www4.wiwiss.fu-berlin.de/diseasome/sparql

3.2   Defining Inferring Domain Rules

The semantic dataset represents all the basic information needed to develop a medical application, so called static knowledge (within rule-based systems such information is called facts). The dynamic knowledge (inferring) is within rule-based systems, such as Drools, represented in a form of production rules. A production rule in Drools is represent in a form of

```
WHEN <condition> THEN <action>
```

Such a rule can be interpreted in the following manner: when some condition is met then some related action can be performed. This approach is a natural equivalent to human reasoning (some reason causes some related consequence). Furthermore, in this manner the single rules are independent of each other, which reduces the complexity of defining the whole set of inferring domain rules.

3.3   The Application of the Method: Some Examples of Inferring Rules

To demonstrate the possibilities the combination of semantic data and rule-based system provides a developer with, we will present and explain one such a rule, defined within the scope of our application.

The task is to search for all the related diseases. To relate two diseases, there should exist (at least one) gene that influences the development of both the diseases. In majority of cases, the related diseases are the consequence of the failure of the same genes; for such diseases also the symptomatic is similar.

Let's take gene UGT1A1 as an example: its mutation is usually related to the development of Gilbert and Crigler-Najjar syndrome. In both disorders the mutation of this gene affects the metabolism of bilirubin. Nevertheless, the both are two different disorders. While the Gilbert syndrome is classed as a minor inborn error of metabolism found in up to 5% of the population and is considered harmless, the Crigler-Najjar syndrome, on the other hand, is considered a much more harmful, often leading to severe brain damage in infants.

It is important to stress out that the used dataset does not provide explicit information on how the diseases are related. The given relations between genes and diseases are rather used to infer on related diseases. In the above example the related diseases are caused by failure of gene UGT1A1. In other cases the relation may be based on different aspects. For example, HIV is related to genes CCR2 and CCR5 but in such a way that it uses healthy genes; the failure of those two genes would cause the immunity by not allowing HIV to enter a cell. From the two examples it can be concluded that related diseases are not necessarily related due to a failure in common genes.

The list of related diseases is therefore composed by combining all the diseases, related to a specific disease in question. A set of related diseases is thus computed by iterating over all the genes related to a specific disease. A resulting production rule is presented on Figure 4.

```
rule "find related diseases"

    when

        $s:  Selections()

            $d:  Disease($genes: genes, $sdt: diseaseTitle ,
                    $relatedDiseasesSet: relatedDiseases) from
                    $s.selectedDisease

        $g:  Gene($rd: relatedDiseases) from $genes

        $dt: DiseaseTitle(this != $sdt) from $rd

    then

        $relatedDiseasesSet.add($dt);

end
```

Fig. 4. A production rule, used for finding the related diseases based on disorder-gene relations

Because the information on how the diseases are related is not explicitly available in semantic dataset, it is also possible to search for related diseases in a different manner. Although in a very modest form, some information on drugs (if available) used for the treatment of specific diseases is also provided in the used semantic dataset. However, the dataset only provides some links to a different dataset, namely the DrugBank Database [19].

Although quite modest, this additional information can be used to further improve the inferring on possibly related diseases, by exploring the use of (at least some) common drugs. The following rule (Figure 5) compares the two lists of possible drugs between potentially related diseases (using the rule from Figure 4). According to the number of common drugs it is possible to find the relation between diseases more accurately.

```
rule "rank related diseases"

    when

        $s:    Selections()

            Disease($relatedDiseasesSet: relatedDiseases) from
                    $s.selectedDisease

        $al:   HashSet(size>0) from collect (HashSet() from
                    $relatedDiseasesSet)

        $dis: Disease($drugs: drugs ) from $al

        $str: String() from $drugs

            Disease(drugs contains $str) from s.selectedDisease

    then

        $dis.setRank($dis.getRank() + 1);

end
```

Fig. 5. A production rule, used to determine the relation between diseases based on common . drugs

The next production rule (Figure 6) can serve as an example on how to determine the influence of a specific gene to the range of diseases, related to this very gene. Many genes are related to a narrow range of diseases – they only influence a set of diseases from a certain category.

For example: the above mentioned gene UGT1A1, the mutation of which affects the synthesis of a specific metabolism enzyme, only influences a small number of diseases, which are caused by the reduced activity of this enzyme. Some other genes are related to a broader range of diseases, as they influence diseases from different categories.

```
rule "select range"

    when

        $s:  Selections()

        $d:  Disease($genes: genes) from $s.selectedDisease

        $g:  Gene($rd: relatedDiseases) from $genes

          $al: HashSet(size>1) from collect (HashSet() from
                                    generateCategorySet($g))

    then

        $g.setRange(Range.WIDE);

end
```

Fig. 6. A production rule, used to determine the range of diseases for a specific gene

4   Discussion and Conclusion

As stated in the introduction, with the research presented within this paper we wanted to find out whether the combination of SWT and rule-based systems is appropriate for developing advanced medical applications. The design and implementation of such an application was not too complex (regarding the complexity of such solution itself). We may say that combining SWT (i.e. ontologies) for representing medical data and rule-based systems (i.e. production rule engine) enabled us to develop an advanced solution in an efficient manner, both regarding the development process itself, as well as the performance of the resulting application. Especially, this combination is appropriate for medical domain, where datasets are large and the users do not possess the technical expertise.

Using the Drools rule-based system all kinds of rules can be defined. When combined with the use of semantic data, this represents the fundament for an expert system, aimed at finding new knowledge based on semantic data using inferring rules. In our application, the system was able to fully automatically find a set of related diseases based on different conditions (both by exploring the disorder-gene relations and the drugs used for the treatment of a specific disease).

In this manner, both research questions from the introduction are adequately answered. We have shown that by combining the SWT and rule-based systems it is possible to develop advanced medical applications in an efficient manner. The presented medical application, demonstrating the combined use of SWT and rule-based systems, leaves and opens several topics and challenges for future research. The advantages of the presented approach would be even more noticeable when more semantic information sources would be used, providing further good chances to discover new and important medical patterns. Another possibility, that would most certainly attract medical experts to experiment with the proposed setting, is the definition of domain specific languages within Drools system for specific medical domains. When equipped with the possibility of defining inferring rules in a very natural way (almost natural language-like) medical experts would be able to realize all the advantages such an approach offers. Finally, there is an intriguing option of introducing the data mining principles for the discovering of new knowledge from semantic data.

References

1. Stevens, R., Goble, C.A., Bechhofer, S.: Ontology-based knowledge representation for bioinformatics. Brief Bioinformatics 1, 398–416 (2000)
2. Stephens, S., LaVigna, D., DiLascio, M., Luciano, J.: Aggregation of bioinformatics data using Semantic Web technology. Web Semantics: Science, Services and Agents on the World Wide Web 4(3), 216–221 (2006)
3. Pasquier, C.: Biological data integration using Semantic Web technologies. Biochimie 90(4), 584–594 (2008)
4. Podgorelec, V., Grasic, B., Pavlic, L.: Medical diagnostic process optimization through the semantic integration of data resources. Computer Methods and Programs in Biomedicine 95(2), S55–S67 (2009)
5. García-Sánchez, F., Fernández-Breis, J.T., Valencia-García, R., Gómez, J.M., Martínez-Béjar, R.: Combining Semantic Web technologies with Multi-Agent Systems for integrated access to biological resources. Journal of Biomedical Informatics 41(5), 848–859 (2008)
6. Mei, J., Bontas, E.P., Lin, Z.: OWL2Jess: A Transformational Implementation of the OWL Semantics. In: Chen, G., Pan, Y., Guo, M., Lu, J. (eds.) ISPA-WS 2005. LNCS, vol. 3759, pp. 599–608. Springer, Heidelberg (2005)
7. Ceusters, W., Smith, B., Flanagan, J.: Ontology and medical terminology: Why description logics are not enough. In: Proceedings of Towards an Electronic Patient Record, TEPR 2003, Boston, MA (2003)
8. Passin, T.B.: Explorers guide to Semantic Web. Manning, Greenwich (2004)
9. Manola, F., Miller, E. (eds.): RDF Primer. W3C Recommendation (2004)
10. McGuiness, D.L., Harmelen, F. (eds.): OWL Web Ontology Language Overview. W3C Recommendation (2004)
11. Lacy, L.W.: OWL: Representing Information Using the Web Ontology Language. Trafford Publishing (2005)
12. Horrocks, I., Patel-Schneider, P.F., Boley, H., Tabet, S., Grosof, B., Dean, M.: SWRL: A Semantic Web Rule Language Combining OWL and RuleML. W3C Consortium (2004), http://www.w3.org/Submission/SWRL/
13. Browne, P.: JBoss Drools Business Rules. Packt Publishing, Birmingham (2009)

14. Jena - A Semantic Web Framework for Java, http://jena.sourceforge.net/
15. Friedman-Hill, E.: Jess in Action: Java Rule-Based Systems. Manning Publications, Greenwich (2003)
16. Rawlings, C.J., Searls, D.B.: Computational gene discovery and human disease. Current Opinion in Genetics & Development 7(3), 416–423 (1997)
17. Gudivada, R.C., Qu, X.A., Chen, J., Jegga, A.G., Neumann, E.K., Aronow, B.J.: Identifying disease-causal genes using Semantic Web-based representation of integrated genomic and phenomic knowledge. Journal of Biomedical Informatics 41(5), 717–729 (2008)
18. Diseasome Dataset, http://www4.wiwiss.fu-berlin.de/diseasome/
19. The DrugBank Database, http://www.drugbank.ca/

Designing ABA-Based Software for Low-Functioning Autistic Children

Silvia Artoni[1], Maria Claudia Buzzi[1], Marina Buzzi[1], Fabio Ceccarelli[2],
Claudia Fenili[1], Beatrice Rapisarda[1], and Maurizio Tesconi[1]

[1] CNR-IIT, Pisa, Italy
{Silvia.Artoni,Claudia.Buzzi,Marina.Buzzi,Maurizio.Tesconi,
Claudia.Fenili,Beatrice.Rapisarda}@iit.cnr.it
[2] University of Firenze, Florence, Italy
febius.cecca@gmail.com

Abstract. The ABCD SW (Autistic Behavior & Computer-based Didactic software) project aims to design and develop didactic software for children in the low-functioning autism spectrum, according to the principles of Applied Behavior Analysis (ABA). ABA therapy is based on scientific principles: teaching by discrete levels, errorless interaction, teacher prompting, reinforcement, fading, shaping and analysis of data collected during the educational sessions to monitor the child's progress. In this paper we describe the ABA didactic software component, illustrating and discussing design choices, showing system architecture and user interfaces, and describing future developments.

Keywords: Didactic Software, Autism, ABA methodology, Usability, Software Design.

1 Introduction

Autism is defined by the Diagnostic and Statistical Manual of Mental Disorders (DSM-IV TR) [1] and the International Statistic Classification of Mental and Behavioral Disorders [18] as certain delays or anomalies appearing in children at around 3 years of age in at least one of the following areas: 1) social interaction, 2) communicative and social use of language, 3) symbolic or imaginative play. Autism Spectrum Disorder (ASD) includes Autism, Asperger syndrome and Pervasive Developmental Disorder-Not Otherwise Specified. The severity and variety of symptoms vary significantly from individual to individual, so personalized intervention provides an educational approach that can be tailored to each child's needs.

Of the many studies that address educational methods for teaching autistic children, several show the effectiveness of Applied Behavioral Analysis (ABA) [14, 15, 17]. ABA intervention analyzes the child's behavior and attempts to model it by modifying what happens before (its antecedents) or after (its consequences) an undesired behavior. In the ABA model each task is divided into elementary steps of

F.V. Cipolla-Ficarra et al. (Eds.): ADNTIIC 2011, LNCS 7547, pp. 230–242, 2012.

increasing difficulty, each step part of a sequence of trials leading to accomplishing the task successfully and autonomously.

Successful intervention also relies on the coherence of the program in each environment where the child spends time, at school and at home. Intensive and early ABA intervention (30-40 hours/week) greatly facilitates the child's learning [1, 2, 4].

In a previous paper, we proposed an ABA eLearning Environment for autistic children [3] comprising three main SW components for 1) implementing didactic software (SW) modules, 2) recording trial evaluation data (SW for recording a child's progress) and 3) analyzing collected data. These software components are independent, and synchronization occurs via database.

The *Didactic SW* component implements the sequence of ABA programs (as described in Section 3). Since during ABA therapy sessions with children training with didactic SW alternates with working at the table, both data related to computer-driven or classic ABA therapy (at the table) with a subject must be recorded in the database (*SW for recording child's progress* component). Data analysis is asynchronous and triggered throughout a specific user interface (*Data Analysis SW* component).

In this paper we describe the design phase of software that implements basic didactic programs for autistic children, specifically designed for Applied Behavior Analysis. The analysis and design phases of this main component involved therapists, caregivers and parents.

The paper is organized in five sections. After this brief introduction, Section 2 illustrates related studies focusing on design and implementation of software for teaching autistic children. Section 3 summarizes the principles of the ABA method, showing an example of a program. Section 4 describes in detail the study set-up, design process, system architecture and user interfaces. The paper ends with a discussion of future work.

2 Related Work

Several studies specifically refer to the development of systems for ASD persons. Monibi and Hayes implemented a library of virtual cards for autistic children's activities on a Nokia N800 (Mocoto prototype). The card library can be extended with pictures or digital images, and it is possible to customize the activities (e.g., size and number of cards, audio cues, etc.) [12].

To enhance the social skills of persons with ASD, el Kaliouby et al. built a suite of wearable technologies (cameras, microphones, sensors) for capturing, analyzing, and sharing their interactions in an engaging way [10].

As described in [3] and in the next section, ABA therapy is based on Augmentative and Alternative Communication (AAC) and Discrete Trial Training (DTT). Sampath et al. proposed an AAC system for bidirectional communication between child and caregivers: a gateway on a handheld device was built, allowing conversion between pictures and spoken language [16].

Kientz et al. [11] developed two systems to facilitate efficient child monitoring: Abaris, building indices into videos of therapy sessions and allowing easy data seeking and CareLog, for collecting and analyzing behavioral data (unplanned incidents also called "problem behaviors").

Hailpern et al. [7] investigated the use of computers to assess the behavior of nonverbal children. Defining a set of dependent variables for use in video annotation, they made it possible to analyze the interactions of nonverbal children, capturing feedback related to attention, engagement and vocal behavior.

De Leo and Leroy involved special-education teachers in designing SW to facilitate communication with severely autistic children via smart phones [6].

Many digital products are available for augmentative communication (e.g., GoTalk, Tango, Dynavox, Activity Pad), but teachers and therapists have experienced low usability and flexibility with these products, and training is required for set-up and customization, making it difficult for parents to use it at home. Furthermore, they are expensive [8].

Existing tools support the child's therapy (tools for AAC and DTT, and for monitoring child's progress and behavior), but to our knowledge do not specifically automate ABA therapy (i.e., implement ABA programs as described in the next section), which is the primary goal of our software.

We believe that technology can enhance the lives of children with autism, for instance by creating more sophisticated eLearning tools. Despite considerable research on tools to enhance children's learning and support caregivers, to our knowledge the few free products available for teaching ABA are limited in function or work poorly, while the most stable products are commercial. Considering the high incidence of autism [13], this gap should be closed.

3   ABA-Based Didactic SW

As previously mentioned, ABA intervention is based on Augmentative and Alternative Communication (AAC) and Discrete Trial Training (DTT). AAC is commonly employed in learning disabilities and neurological pathologies to increase the user's perceptions, providing an alternative method for communicating (images, signs, etc.). DTT is a one-to-one instructional approach (sequence of elementary trials) used to teach skills in a planned, controlled, and systematic manner in order to allow the child to operate independently. The sequence of trials progresses (program by program) through discrete levels with increasing levels of difficulty. The main ABA programs are Matching, Receptive and Expressive. To ask the child to do a program, therapists use a discriminative stimulus (SD) as a command. More details on ABA therapy can be found in [3] and [4].

3.1   An Example of ABA Method: The Category COLORS

Table 1 shows details of programs usable for the category "Colors". This category is composed of several articles: red, yellow, blue, green, orange, purple, etc. The matching program for the category *Colors* has four subprograms: matching an image of a color with another image of the same color (image/image); matching a word corresponding to the name of a color with an image of the color (word/image); matching a word corresponding to the name of a color with another word corresponding to the name of the color (word/word); matching an image of a color with the word corresponding to the name of the color (image/word).

Table 1. Programs, discriminative stimulus and child response

PROGRAMS	SDs	Child response
A – MATCHING: - image/image - word/word - image/word - word/image	"put together"	The child drags with his/her finger or uses the mouse to move one element over its copy
B – RECEPTIVE:	SD: "Touch *color_name*" SD: "Touch" (a *colored* square is shown)	Touches the image (a *colored* square) of the *color*
C – EXPRESSIVE:	SD: "What is it?	1. Says the "*color_name*" or 2. Touches the written label in a choice of three elements (if the subject is unable to speak)

Figure 1 shows two examples of matching programs: on the left the ABA program *matching image/image* of the article *red*, on the right the ABA program *matching word/word* of the article *green*.

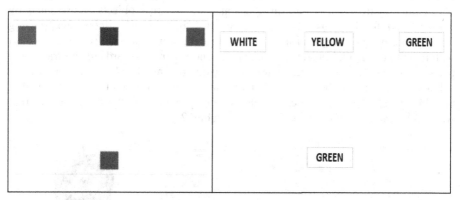

Fig. 1. Program matching image/image (on the left) and Program matching word/word (on the right)

A kind of generalization consists in changing the discriminative stimulus (SD), as shown in Table 2:

Table 2. Generalization: alternative discriminative stimuli

PROGRAMS	Alternative SDs
A – MATCHING:	"match"
	"combine"
	"add on"
	"place with the right color"
	"couple"
B – RECEPTIVE:	"find (...)"
	"is the color (...)"
	"looking for (...)"
	"Press on (...)"
C – EXPRESSIVE:	"What color is it?"
	"What is this?"
	"What do you call this color?"
	"Is the color ..."

3.2   The Role of Images

Images have a central role in the world of an autistic child since the method of "learning through seeing" is usually the most effective [9]; learning and communication development are often supported by the visual channel.

For this reason, material supplied to the children during the therapy sessions is mostly visual and must fulfil the requirements of clarity, simplicity and precision in the communication. Therefore, images must be clearly legible, large, well-defined, on a neutral background, and in a central position on the page; the windows are minimal (minimal number of elements, no background images, etc.) since any other element can be a distraction. Images chosen for the exercises display different degrees of abstraction: from those closest in appearance to the real objects (represented by photographs) to the most abstract (represented by objects' silhouettes), passing through intermediate stages of more or less abstract drawings. The trials usually start with a photo of the real object (e.g., an apple) and progress towards the abstraction: a color photo, a black and white version, a realistic drawing, a stylized one, and finally a black silhouette of the object. Different apples with different colors is another possible generalization. Images are the stimuli provided to the child in the trial, whereas an example of abstraction is shown in Fig. 2.

Fig. 2. Abstraction of the stimulus of the trial: color photos, b/w photo and silhouette (category food, article apple)

Furthermore, for each object we can have various sequences of abstractions: considering colors, we might have for instance a colored square, then a stylized colored square (strokes), color spots, the tip of a brush full of color, etc. (see Fig. 3). The reason is that the child needs to learn to recognize an object in its various representations.

Fig. 3. Abstraction of the stimulus of the trial: drawings (category colors, article red)

4   Study Set-up

The *Didactic software* is specifically designed for teaching very young autistic children (2-6 years old), although older persons with comparable abilities could also benefit. To simplify child-computer interaction (especially for younger children) and allow a method "similar" to physical ABA therapy, touch-screen devices and vocal synthesis to announce the commands of the (educational) program trials have been chosen. If a touch-screen device is unavailable, it is possible to interact with the program by using a mouse.

Although the sequence of DTT levels in an ABA program is well-defined, the therapist needs the flexibility to jump to the previous or next level according to the child's response, so we discarded possibility of automating the progression of levels. Our choice was to provide the therapist with maximum control and freedom of action and avoid rigid protocols that might hinder the course of therapy. For efficiency's sake we preselect the next DTT level when no prompt/help has been provided to the child in the previous trial (assuming an independent successful trial has been carried out by the subject) in order to make selection faster, but offer the therapist the opportunity to select a different level. Autistic subjects are often attracted to/distracted by details, so ABA therapy is physically carried out at an empty table. Analogously, the SW has two separate interfaces: one for controlling the therapy's flow (selecting category, article, and level) that is used by the therapist, and the other where the trial is visualized for the therapy itself, devoted to the child. The idea is to use an extended screen (dotted orange circle in Fig. 4) incorporating a *touch screen* for the therapy and a *mini-laptop/tablet* for the control.

The logical architecture diagram of the Didactic ABA-based SW is shown in Fig. 4.

The *Therapist UI* allows the setup of the child's UI, selecting the program, article and trial level. The child executes trials through the *child UI*, interacting with the touch screen. Parents, therapist and any persons who wish to contribute to the project may add articles via the *Social UI* (a Web interface). Approval of therapists is required to effectively store an element in the database. The *Social UI* also allows insertion of labels and words for various language versions (Internationalization).

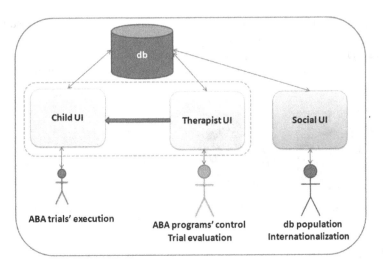

Fig. 4. Logical scheme of the ABA eLearning Environment: didactic SW component

Concerning images, we decided to use a vectorial representation for simple objects. In fact, SVG images can be scaled without introducing the graininess typical of zooming on bitmapped files. This feature is important for future programs that may include teaching the concept of opposites (small/large, tall/short, etc.) using object manipulation. In some cases, specific customization of images might be required by children's special needs. The system offers caregivers tools (user interfaces) for customizing images and inserting new ones according to the elements (e.g., child's learning curve), and acquisition programs that are offered to children.

Following participatory design principles, our system was designed with the active participation of ABA therapists, psychologists and parents of autistic children. The inclusion of autistic children in the design would be an interesting experience, but since the design focuses on a challenging target (very young low-functioning children), alternative strategies are required for their direct involvement. To refine the system design, a pilot test with ABA tutors has been carried out to verify their usability (various UIs are proposed). Next, a user test with seven autistic children is scheduled from September 15, 2011 to June 14, 2012 to evaluate the didactic effectiveness of the software. The next section describes an overview of the system architecture.

4.1   System Architecture: Design, Modeling, Tools

The architecture of the application was designed with ICONIX (en.wikipedia.org/wiki/ICONIX), a method for software development that predates both the Rational Unified Process (RUP), Extreme Programming (XP) (http://en.wikipedia. org/wiki/Extreme_Programming) and Agile software development (http://agilemanifesto.org/). It is a UML Use Case driven process that uses only four UML based diagrams in a four-step process that turns use case text into source code. Using the robustness analysis, which reduces the ambiguity in use case descriptions, ICONIX makes design and testing easier (http://en.wikipedia.org/wiki/ICONIX).

For implementation we chose Java, a popular platform-independent language that provides powerful graphic libraries, with the adoption of the Batik open-source library for the use and manipulation of SVG (Scalable Vector Graphics) objects. SVG is a markup language for describing two-dimensional graphics applications and images, and a set of related graphics script interfaces. SVG allows the representation of graphic objects in a vectorial format, as bidimensional vector (W3C, http://www.w3.org/Graphics/SVG/).

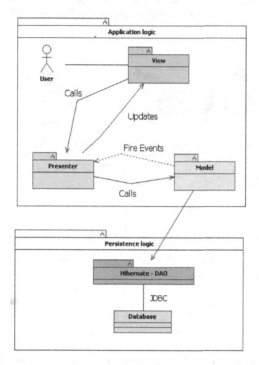

Fig. 5. System architecture

To allow the persistence of information at the session level, we used the Hibernate open-source platform (http://www.hibernate.org/). Hibernate allows developing Java applications by providing a service of Object-Relational Mapping (ORM), managing the representation and the maintenance of entity in a relational database linked to a system of Java objects. In this way Hibernate easily renders the instances of the classes persistent, allowing one to carry out CRUD (Create, Read, Update, Delete) operations on the database (see Fig. 5) The selected database is mySQL, which is interfaced by JDBC (Java DataBase Connectivity).

4.2   User Interfaces

The User Interface (UI) is one of the main components of the system. Different UIs are available for the various participants: child, therapists, researchers and parents. Therapists use the UI for ABA therapy with the children and to analyze data. To ensure the children's and family's privacy, researchers can only access a child's data in an anonymous form, after receiving the parents' consent. Parents use the same UIs as therapists when performing therapy with their children, and have a Web UI to enable (authorize) therapists to insert and manage their child's data and eventually donate their child's trial data.

Due to the complexity of ABA therapy, it is crucial to allow caregivers simple and rapid interaction when selecting a specific article in a category, in order to apply an appropriate program (for instance matching color/color) on the correct ABA sequence of trials. Figure 6 shows the look&feel of the main Therapist UI for ABA program selection.

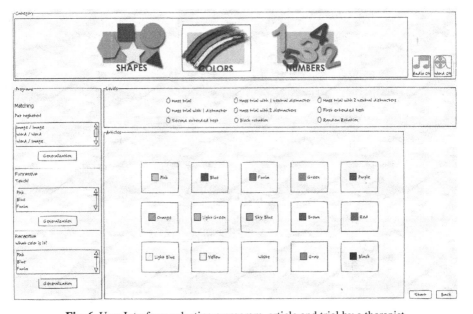

Fig. 6. User Interface: selecting a program, article and trial by a therapist

Selection of the trials proposed to the child is organized by levels: in the upper part of the interface the category is chosen; on the left side it is possible to select a program (between matching, receptive or expressive) and related subprograms; in the central part are the ABA levels (mass trials, etc.) in the upper area, and the graphic icons of the articles are presented in the lower one. Furthermore, on the right part of the UI there are two buttons for turning audio and text on/off as needed. A multimodal interface that delivers information via multiple channels can deliver content more effectively. It is important to note that in the UI used by the child, words are always in capital block letters. Lowercase represents a generalization.

The parent (or caregiver) may add a child using the UI shown in Fig. 7.

Regarding child interaction, analogous to the face-to-face ABA therapy carried out at an empty table, only a blank UI is presented, with the article under acquisition placed in the selected program. It is very important to design the child's UI avoiding any possible visual auto-stimulation (see Fig. 1).

Analogously, parents and therapists have a user interface for adding a new category, and then new articles. Generic contributors may also add articles, but their actual insertion in the database is subject to approval.

The child interacts with the touch-screen where the trial selected by the therapist is visualized. Figure 8 shows a trial: category food, article pineapple, mass trial with two neutral distracters.

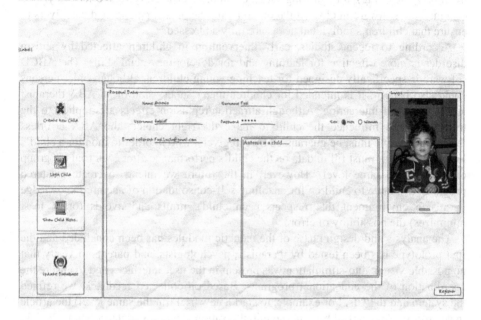

Fig. 7. User interface for parents: adding a child

Fig. 8. Child user interface: mass trial with two neutral distracters

5   Conclusion and Future Work

In this paper we have presented the design and development of ABA-based software for low-functioning autistic children, developed within the framework of the ABCD SW project, aimed at creating eLearning environments (didactic programs and monitoring learning) for teaching autistic children efficiently and effectively. We designed the software in close collaboration with therapists, parents and caregivers to ensure that children's individual needs are fully addressed.

According to recent studies, early intervention in children affected by autism disorder is more effective for learning and for developing social skills. The ABCD software is specifically designed for teaching young children, although older persons could also benefit. It is intended for children under supervision of an ABA therapist and not for self-interaction. Although attraction/repulsion effects are applied to the trial articles to influence the child to make the right choice, the ABA errorless teaching principle must be guaranteed by caregivers, who in order to monitor a child's learning progress must fill in data on the child's performance after each trial (or group of trials in the same level). However, in the future we intend to create mastered programs available to children for enabling self-consolidation of acquired knowledge in a safe environment that respects each child's limits and avoids (or at least minimizes) the possibility of error.

The analysis and design phase of the didactic modules has been concluded and the first prototype has been tested by therapists, psychologists, and parents to verify that no possible visual auto-stimulation was present in the user interfaces and to ensure the coordination of the educational programs. Based on collected feedback, we refined the system and the UIs. For example, to start a new trial (on the same level) the article in acquisition was moved back to the initial position. This was replaced with a FadeIn effect, to avoid potential visual stimulation for some children.

At this time we have only implemented basic ABA programs (as shown in Table 1). Advanced programs might include opposites, ordering sequences, puzzles, etc. and will be integrated in the system in the future.

The next step is to carry out a test with autistic children with various user profiles (abilities and needs). This pilot test will involve autistic children in the design of the system in a "driven" modality: considering the young age of participants, different UIs for the same trial will be proposed in order to understand preferences and monitor interaction. Outcomes will be used to further tune and refine the system. At the moment the degree of adaptation is selected by therapists according to the child's abilities. Two buttons are available for (dis)activating audio (voice synthesizer) and written discriminative stimuli: Audio ON, Word ON (see Fig. 7 upper right corner).

In the new school year (from September 15, 2011 to June 15, 2012) the system will be tested in kindergarten and primary schools adhering to the ABCD projects. We have established a double evaluation of children participating in the user test, in September 2011 and June 2012, carried out by a psychologist (with different scales according to children profiles and diagnosis). In this way we aim to measure the child's abilities and skills before and after the 9-month ABA intervention, to scientifically assess the children's progress. Children involved in these tests have already been selected with the support of the Lucca Association for Autistic Syndromes (LASA). Since ABA therapy should be applied both at home and at school, an initial collaboration agreement has been already signed, and others are in preparation with managers of the children's schools.

This software is only one part of the whole project. Another important part involves recording the data of a child's learning progress. ABA is a structured method, measureable, based on a rigorous scientific approach, and requires therapists to record data from each trial of the programs carried out by each child. This is a crucial part of the whole eLearning environment. The next step of our study is to design a usable data collection SW program on mobile devices.

Acknowledgments. We thank the Regione Toscana, which funded this project within the framework of the "FAS 2007 2013 Delibera CIPE 166/2007 PAR FAS Regione Toscana Action Line 1.1.a.3" (Feb 2011-Gen 2013).

References

1. American Psychiatric Association. DSM-IV-TR. Diagnostic and Statistical Manual of Mental Disorders, 4th edn. (2001)
2. Anderson, S.R., Romanczyk, R.G.: Early Intervention for Young Children with Autism: Continuum-Based Behavioral Models. The Journal of The Association for Persons with Severe Handicaps 24(3), 162–173 (1999)
3. Artoni, S., Buzzi, M.C., Buzzi, M., Fenili, C.: Didactic Software for Autistic Children. In: Cipolla Ficarra, F.V., de Castro Lozano, C., Pérez Jiménez, M., Nicol, E., Kratky, A., Cipolla-Ficarra, M. (eds.) ADNTIIC 2010. LNCS, vol. 6616, pp. 73–80. Springer, Heidelberg (2011)
4. Artoni, S., Buzzi, M.C., Buzzi, M., Fenili, C., Mencarini, S.: Accessible Education for Autistic Children: ABA-Based Didactic Software. In: HCI 2011, vol. (8), pp. 511–520 (2010)
5. Corsello, C.M.: Early intervention in autism. Infants & Young Children 18(2), 74–85 (2005)
6. De Leo, G., Leroy, G.: Smartphones to facilitate communication and improve social skills of children with severe autism spectrum disorder: special education teachers as proxies. In: IDC 2008, pp. 45–48 (2008)
7. Hailpern, J., Karahalios, K., Halle, J., Dethorne, L., Coletto, M.: A3: HCI Coding Guideline for Research Using Video Annotation to Assess Behavior of Nonverbal Subjects with Computer-Based Intervention. ACM Trans. Access. Comput. 2(2), Article 8 (2009)
8. Hayes, G., et al.: Interactive visual supports for children with autism. Springer Personal and Ubiquitous Computing, 18 p. (2010), doi:10.1007/s00779-010-0294-8

9. Hodgdon, L.A.: Visual strategies for improving communication: practical supports for school and home. QuirkRoberts, Troy (1995)
10. el Kaliouby, R., Goodwin, M.S.: iSET: Interactive Social-Emotional Toolkit for Autism Spectrum Disorder. In: Proceedings of International Conference on Interaction, Design and Children - IDC 2008, pp. 77–80. ACM Press, New York (2008)
11. Kientz, J.A., Hayes, G.R., Westeyn, T.L., Starner, T., Abowd, G.D.: Pervasive Computing and Autism: Assisting Caregivers of Children with Special Needs. IEEE Pervasive Computing 6(1), 28–35 (2007)
12. Monibi, M., Hayes, G.R.: Mocotos: Mobile Communications Tools for Children with Special Needs. In: IDC 2008, pp. 121–124 (2008)
13. Myers, S.M., Johnson, C.P.: The Council on Children With Disabilities: Management of Children With Autism Spectrum Disorders. Pediatrics 120, 1162–1182 (2007), doi:10.1542/peds
14. Rosenwasser, B., Axelrod, S.: The contribution of applied behavior analysis to the education of people with autism. Behavior Modification 25(5), 671–677 (2001)
15. Rosenwasser, B., Axelrod, S.: More contributions of applied behavior analysis to the education of people with autism. Behavior Modification 26(1), 3–8 (2002)
16. Sampath, H., Sivaswamy, J., Indurkhya, B.: Assistive systems for children with dyslexia and autism. ACM Sigaccess Accessibility and Computing (96) (2010)
17. Weiss, M.J.: Expanding ABA intervention in intensive programs for children with autism: The inclusion of natural environment training and fluency based instruction. The Behavioural Analyst 2(3), 182–186 (2001)
18. World Health Organization, The ICD-10.Classification of Mental and Behavioural Disorders. World Health Organization, Geneva (1992)

What Are Your Children Watching on YouTube?

Marina Buzzi

Istituto di Informatica e Telematica, CNR
via Moruzzi, 1 56124 I-Pisa, Italy
Marina.Buzzi@iit.cnr.it

Abstract. YouTube is a popular video repository offering family entertainment channels. However, pornography is flooding the Internet and children can accidently access unsafe videos. Specifically, porno audio content inserted into popular cartoons is present in YouTube, with the risk of exposing children to disturbing experiences. To evaluate the diffusion of this phenomena, a questionnaire was proposed to 100 parents of children 2 to 13 years old. Results were also integrated with data collected from several interviews. This study aims to 1) assess the parents' degree of knowledge of YouTube user interface mechanisms for signaling and filtering inappropriate content 2) understand the parents' perception of children's safety. Results showed that one-third of the sample acknowledge that their children have accessed inappropriate content and many parents believe they can monitor their children "sufficiently" while carrying out other activities. Only 1/3 of parents check the video category and keywords, while 2/3 of participants know that is possible to signal questionable content but do not know how to do it. The possibility of knowing the nature of retrieved content before accessing it was judged an interesting and useful feature for improving the safety level of YouTube for children.

Keywords: YouTube, Children, Safe Content, User Interface, Pornography.

1 Introduction

Web 2.0 has opened up new frontiers for individuals: first of all, it enables collaboration, facilitates and encourages connections in social networks, and provides simple tools for sharing user generated content. However, this abundance of expression, contents, interactive tools, games, and videos may hamper children's safety. Specifically, pornography is a plague that has dramatically spread throughout the Internet. YouTube offers easy-to-use graphic user interfaces and short videos, so even children 2-3 years old are able to activate the next video from the playlist. Preventing children from viewing or listening to inappropriate content (porn or violence), especially at an early age (2-6 years), is crucial for the child's healthy psychological growth due to the great plasticity of young brains [6]. In particular, visual material (videos, images, gestures) associated with audio reinforces learning. Concerning teens, although exposure to sexual content is not related to negative outcomes in sexual development, it appears that for some it can cause emotional distress [12].

F.V. Cipolla-Ficarra et al. (Eds.): ADNTIIC 2011, LNCS 7547, pp. 243–252, 2012.
© Springer-Verlag Berlin Heidelberg 2012

In this paper we describe a survey conducted with a questionnaire proposed to more than one hundred parents, with the aim of understanding how children interact with YouTube under adult supervision. The paper is organized into five sections. Section 2 introduces related work. In Section 3, to better understand how children and parents interact with YouTube, we describe a survey in the form of a questionnaire distributed to three schools (kindergarten, elementary and middle schools), and to our colleagues with children in this age range. The aim of the questionnaire was to understand how parents and children use YouTube, whether they monitor their children's use or they check movie keywords, and their knowledge of user interface (UI) mechanisms for asking videos to be removed, if they own an account. In Section 4 the survey results are discussed, also referring to the effectiveness of YouTube UI mechanisms to deliver safe content. The paper ends with conclusions and proposes future work.

2   Related Work

User-generated content represents an enormous amount of information available on the Internet. The control of this content is a challenge that has led to concerns for legislation as various threats to security and privacy are configured [3].

Depending on user age (children vs teens) different control strategies may be applied. However, the educational and psychosocial benefits of Internet communication far outweigh its potential dangers, so parents cannot forbid their teens access to social networks. Listening to different opinions in a multiethnic environment enhances the development of cognitive processes. This education is complementary and consistent with school educational programs [10]. In this new learning process, schools should mitigate parental fears about Internet threats by fueling the responsible and creative use of Internet applications [8]. Promoting e-safety education via peers might be an effective strategy for creating a broader, cohesive whole-school approach [2].

With small children even more attention is required: i.e., the parent should control the child's actions step-by-step or in some kind of automatic way. However, automatic techniques do not guarantee total accuracy, i.e., some questionable content may be delivered or safe content erroneously filtered), so nothing is more effective than parent supervision of child-Internet interaction. A survey of resources and tools for automatic parent control was carried out by Thierer [9]. European guidelines for safe use of the computer by children indicate placing the computer a in public zone of the house (not in the child's room) to favor a more effective control (http://www.saferinternet.org/).

Ybarra et al. conducted a study with teens, showing that the use of techniques for preventing access to inappropriate content (filtering, blocking, and monitoring), considerably reduced the risk of exposure to undesirable sexual material (86% lower odds among 10- to 12-year-olds and 88% among 13- to 15-year-olds) [12].

New Internet communication tools are spreading rapidly. Social networks are increasing in use among teens. George and Scerri argued that monitoring what children are viewing on the Internet is impossible, since pornographic content in not limited to Adults-Only sites but is spread throughout the Net and can be easily retrieved with a search or accidently downloaded by anyone, anytime, without requiring age or identity verification [5].

Around 50% of children in Europe have accessed pornographic content either deliberately or accidentally on the Internet [7]. Kijkwijzer proposed adopting a content classification and graphically tagging content suitable for different ages with different icons: 1) for all 2) for children over 6 years old (6), 3) for children over 12 years old (12), and 4) for children over 16 years old (16). Analogously the nature of the content may rapidly be identified with six graphic icons: violence, sex, horror/fear, drugs or abuse of alcohol, discrimination and bad language content [7].

Since ISP policies contain certain weaknesses and legislation varies across countries, Ali discusses threats to children on the Internet and provides basic recommendations for their protection, relative to several domains and aspects. Specifically, he argues that to protect children in on-line access, greater cooperation is required between the public and private sectors and citizens (the children's parents) [1].

Google is focusing more and more attention on security and safety with specific programs for increasing awareness of parents and security for children. In Italy a specific program was started on Oct 28, 2010 in collaboration with the Communications Police, also including a series of videos teaching practical security sessions.

The "Safety Mode" of YouTube allows automatically filtering content marked as inappropriate at the browser level; however, it is not totally accurate. The Safety Mode is effective for removing questionable videos from the playlist or from proposed videos.

In [4], an example in which audio porn content was substituted for the original audio of a famous Disney cartoon is discussed. Although users commented on the video and asked for its removal, after several months it is still online and has not been more appropriately retagged with different keywords. For triggering the video removal, YouTube uses a threshold based on numbers of users flagging the content as inappropriate. A set of basic guidelines for improving the safety of YouTube access for children has been proposed.

3   The Survey

To investigate the causes of user disappointment and quantify the presence of this kind of phenomenon, a questionnaire concerning the use of YouTube and the knowledge of its UIs was distributed to parents of children aged 2-13 years, either when they accompanied the child to school or given directly by teachers to students. The questionnaire was distributed in paper format to encourage all parents to respond, whether they owned a computer or not, and to obtain a realistic approximation of the diffusion of YouTube.

The questionnaire directed to parents was composed of specific questions and one text field for free comments/suggestions. The first part characterizes the sample by gathering data on participants (sex, age, Internet skill) and their children (number and age). The questions composing the second part are reported in Table 1.

Table 1. Main questions composing the survey

1. How much do you use YouTube on average?
2. Have you accidentally accessed any content (audio or video) not suitable for children (pornographic or violent)?
3. How frequently do your children use YouTube on average?
4. Do you always monitor your children when they are watching videos on YouTube?
5. How long do you leave children alone when they are watching YouTube videos?
6. Have your children accidentally accessed inappropriate content (porn or violence), also in only audio format?
7. Do you know **that it is possible** to report an inappropriate video to remove from YouTube?
8. Do you know **how** to report an inappropriate video to remove from YouTube?
9. Have you **ever reported** an inappropriate video to be removed from YouTube?
10. Do you know the function of the flag (located under the video on the right) on the YouTube interface?
11. Do you know that by moving the mouse over the flag a phrase appears that explains its functions?
12. When you access a video on YouTube do you check its category (such as Film & Animation) and the keywords used to describe it (tags)?
13. In your opinion, would it be useful for any YouTube videos to know the targeted audience: adults, adolescents or for all (analogously to the cinema)?
14. Do you have an account on YouTube (user, password)?
15. Have you ever uploaded a video to YouTube?
16. Do you know YouTube policy on uploading videos (i.e., which content may be loaded, legal conditions, terms and responsibilities for upload of inappropriate content, copyright, etc.)?

3.1   Results

One hundred and six parents participated in this study. Data from the survey provided a characterization of the sample. The subjects comprised 57 women and 49 men, with age ranging from 20-50+ years, as shown in Fig. 1. The sample was slightly unbalanced with respect to gender, mainly since the questionnaires were distributed at school to be filled out by parents, and mostly women were recruited.

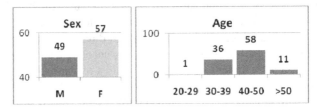

Fig. 1. Sample characterization: Sex (left) and age of parents (right)

Considering that each parent may have one or more children, the distribution of survey participants' children's ages is shown in Fig. 2.

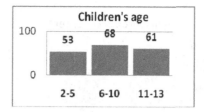

Fig. 2. Sample characterization: children's age

A first characterizing factor is how parents and their children use YouTube. Figure 3 shows the rate of watching YouTube both for parents (left bar) and children (right bar) according this scale: 6-7, 3-5 and 1-2 *times/week*, 2-4 *times/month*, and never. The 35% of the sample declared their children never access YouTube at home. However, some of these children (especially the older ones) may have accessed YouTube sporadically, for example at a friend's house.

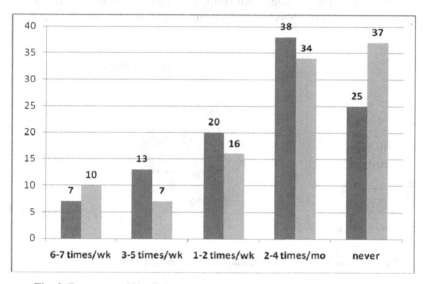

Fig. 3. Frequency of YouTube use: parents (left bar) and children (right bar)

Some kind of content inappropriate for children had accidently been accessed by 47% of the responders (Fig.4). Thirty-six parents (i.e. one-third of the sample) declared that their children have accessed inappropriate content. However, this is probably underestimated since, as discussed later in this section, 1) not all parents monitor their children and 2) not all parents stating that they monitor their children actually do so completely, but often leave them alone for a few minutes.

More than one-half of the total sample (51%) declared they monitor their children while watching YouTube channels (Fig. 5, left). However at the cross-question "How long do you leave children alone when they are watching YouTube videos?" it was revealed that actually about 28% of participants leave their children alone for a few minutes and 8% for half an hour.

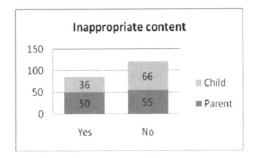

Fig. 4. Access to inappropriate content: child (top) and parents (bottom)

Specifically, thirty parents declared they monitored their children in spite of leaving them alone in front of YouTube for a few minutes, and 9 participants left them unsupervised even longer (Fig. 5, right). This false sense of security is linked to the concept of "proximity = safety" we verified with a few targeted interviews: "*If I'm home with them, they are protected*", "*What can happen in a few minutes?*".

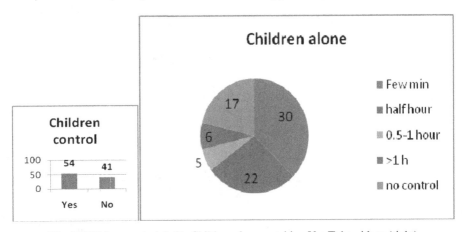

Fig. 5. Children control (left), Children alone watching YouTube videos (right)

Concerning mechanisms for reporting inappropriate content, Fig. 6 shows the three degrees of knowledge that emerged from questionnaire answers (questions 7, 8, 9 in Table 1):

1) to know that it is possible ask for video removal (*knowledge*) (question 7)
2) to know that it is possible and exactly "how" to ask for video removal (*awareness*) (question 8)
3) to have actually asked for video removal (*usage*) (question 9).

Although 58% of users declared knowing that it is possible to signal inappropriate content only 36% stated they knew the mechanism for asking for video removal and only less than 3% actually used it. Furthermore, at the cross question "Do you know the function of the flag?" only 30% of participants (32 users) declared knowing the function of the flag. These low percentage might even overestimate this data in the general average population since 80% of participants consider themselves to be technically skilled.

Additional interviews revealed that unskilled persons are afraid of making erroneous searches. An example of a parent declaration is reported:

"YouTube is a very powerful tool and like all powerful tools requires enormous control. I came across "ambiguous" content several times, luckily before my son noticed them. I confess that I have never done anything to remove them, I thought I had made a poorly conducted search! I think there is a sort of resignation to the fact that there is a lot of junk content on the net, and so you do not know that at least it is possible act to limit them."

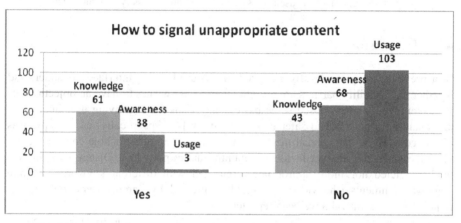

Fig. 6. How to signal questionable content: knowledge, awareness and actual usage

Keywords and video categories were not used much. Of the whole sample, only 34 parents regularly checked the category and keywords of retrieved movies, representing 32% of the total sample (Fig. 7).

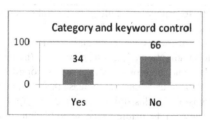

Fig. 7. Frequency of YT use: parents (left bar) and children (right bar)

One question asked whether would be useful to categorize content by audience age. In this case most (94%) of the participants agreed that there should be a clear icon showing minimum age (see Fig. 8). Two of six persons who did not agree to this mechanism's introduction, in targeted interviews explained that in their opinion, it would be unsuccessful or in any case insufficient for protecting children from accidently accessing content, since a simple Web search with Google easily brings up porn content.

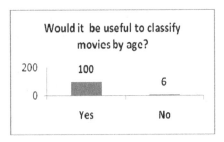

Fig. 8. Perception of the usefulness of a mechanism to classify content by age

4   Discussion

In a previous study we briefly analyzed the YouTube user interface, to understand whether any usability barriers are present when a user wishes to have an objectionable video removed, and proposed some basic suggestions for improving user interaction and enabling a customized safer content delivery [4]. Specifically, an example was discussed to show that current mechanisms for signaling questionable content are not effective since the analyzed video containing audio-porn in a Disney cartoon was neither deleted nor more appropriately retagged with different keywords. Despite negative comments (the video was highly criticized by parents/users) only a few requests for its removal have been reported.

To better investigate why users did not flag this questionable video as inappropriate using the UI element, in this work, we carried out a survey of parents of 2- to 13-year-old children to actually evaluate the usability of YouTube user interfaces for signaling inappropriate content. For reader convenience, the proposed guidelines are reported below (more details are available in [4]):

1. Give more visibility to Safety and Safety mode links, for instance changing their position from the bottom to the top of the page
2. Require video authors to specify the target audience (all, children, teens, adults). This is useful both for assumption of legal responsibility (by the author) and for tagging content. This data may be crossed with results of opinion mining, video analysis and other sophisticated techniques to increase their accuracy.
3. Introduce a mechanism for classifying the video's target audience by user. For instance, a user vote on the nature of the video ("adults only" or "no children") by adding a specific icon to the UI would also be effective for audio content.
4. Use redundant techniques for matching info provided by authors with those collected by user feedback.
5. Alert users to the nature of the video content in a visual way, for instance by icons (for all, older than 14 years, for adults, etc.).
6. Provide a button for immediately blocking undesirable content (even when the YouTube Safe Mode filter is activated but not effective). By providing an immediate result, this feature would significantly contribute to user satisfaction.

Fig. 9. Basic guidelines (source [4])

From the proposed survey the following points emerged:

- One-third of the sample acknowledged that their children have accessed inappropriate content.
- Many parents believe they can monitor their children "sufficiently" while engaged in other activities. Specifically 46% of parents declaring they supervised their children (25/54 users) let them stay alone in front YouTube for a few minutes, while 19% did so for half an hour (10/54 users).
- Only 1/3 of parents checks the video category and keywords. However, this measure is not effective i.e. not sufficient to guarantee access to safe content, since these subjective user-generated data are beyond the Provider's control.
- Nearly 2/3 of parents know that is possible to signal questionable content but do not know how to do so.
- Only 30% of participants "declared knowing" how to asking for video removal.
- Almost all parents (94%) consider it useful to introduce an icon classifying movies by audience age.

Although techniques for content filtering are available, interviews revealed that parental control functions offered by the computer OS (operating system) are very rarely used. Only users with technical skill are actually able to apply these features.

5   Conclusion

It might be not safe to let children remain even a few minutes alone in front of YouTube since they can easily navigate the playlist and proposed videos, accidently accessing inappropriate content. This suggests that user interface should integrate more mechanisms for content filtering depending on receiver demographics.

According to the World Wide Web Consortium (Web Accessibility Initiative) simple, understandable, clear and interoperable interfaces are needed to ensure accessibility of Web Applications and satisfying interaction. Thus, introducing differentiated ways for removing or filtering questionable content is important for matching the abilities and skill of different users.

To augment children's safety, a video repository such as YouTube by default should only deliver content suitable for all audiences, while questionable content would be explicitly requested. Dynamically adapting content to user age, preferences and skill should provide ad-hoc customization, according to age or personal sensibility, valuable for all users.

This study confirms our previous hypothesis. To provide a safer environment for young children, the user interface should incorporate mechanisms for tagging and the video repository should filter user-generated porn content based on user preferences. Specifically, it is suggested to tag porno-content both at the video upload (carried out by the author) and also by taking advantage of collaborative feedback expressed by users, gathered by means of a simple interaction with the user interface.

A mechanism for immediately blocking undesirable content would provide safer experiences for our children. Additionally the targeted audience of each video, informing the user of the nature of the retrieved content before accessing it would be useful.

In future work, a user interface for video distribution will be designed, in order to incorporate the proposed guidelines and evaluate these features with a set of parents of young children.

Acknowledgments. We thank all the parents who participated in this study (including our colleagues at CNR-Pisa) for the time they took to fill out the proposed questionnaires, and all the staff of the Scuola Materna of San Colombano (Lucca), the Scuola Elementare "Don Milani", Pisa, and the Istituto Comprensivo "L. Fibonacci", Pisa.

References

1. Ali, M.: Protecting Children in Cyber Space. WTIS Day: PTA Essay Competition (2009), http://mpra.ub.uni-muenchen.de/17150/
2. Atkinson, S., Furnell, S., Phippen, A.: Securing the next generation: enhancing e-safety awareness among young people. Computer Fraud & Security (7), 13–19 (2009) ISSN 1361-3723, doi:10.1016/S1361-3723(09)70088-0
3. Arino, M.: Content Regulation and New Media: A Case Study of Online Video Portals. In: Proc. EuroCPR Conference, Seville, pp. 25–27 (2007)
4. Buzzi, M.: Children and YouTube: access to safe content. In: CHItaly Proceedings of the 9th ACM SIGCHI Italian Chapter International Conference on Computer-Human Interaction: Facing Complexity, pp. 125–131. ACM Press, New York (2011)
5. George, C., Scerri, J.: Web 2.0 and User-Generated Content: legal challenges in the new frontier. Journal of Information, Law and Technology 2, 235–254 (2007), http://ssrn.com/abstract=1290715
6. Guzzetta, Baldini, S., Bancale, A., Baroncelli, L., Ciucci, F., Ghirri, P., Putignano, E., Sale, A., Viegi, A., Berardi, N., Boldrini, A., Cioni, G., Maffei, L.: Massage Accelerates Brain Development and the Maturation of Visual Function. The Journal of Neuroscience 29(18), 6042–6051 (2009)
7. Joyce, A. (in collaboration with the Insafe team): Raising Awareness: Safe Use of Mobile Phones by Children and Young People (2007), http://www.saferinternet.org/
8. Sharples, M., Graber, R., Harrison, C., Logan, K.: E-safety and Web 2.0 for children aged 11–16. Journal of Computer Assisted Learning 25(1), 70–84 (2009)
9. Thierer, A.: Parental Controls & Online Child Protection: A Survey of Tools & Methods, http://www.pff.org/parentalcontrols/
10. Tynes, B.M.: Internet Safety Gone Wild?: Sacrificing the Educational and Psychosocial Benefits of Online Social Environments. Journal of Adolescent Research 22, 575 (2007), doi:10.1177/0743558407303979
11. Valcke, M., Bonte, S., De Wever, B., Rots, I.: Internet parenting styles and the impact on Internet use of primary school children. Computers & Education 55(2), 454–464 (2010)
12. Ybarra, M.L., Finkelhor, D., Mitchell, K.J., Wolak, J.: Associations between blocking, monitoring, and filtering software on the home computer and youth-reported unwanted exposure to sexual material online. Child Abuse & Neglect 33(12), 857–869 (2009)

Can Your Friends Help You to Find Interesting Multimedia Content on Web 2.0?

Alejandro Corbellini[1,2], Daniela Godoy[1,2], and Silvia Schiaffino[1,2]

[1] ISISTAN Research Institute, UNICEN University,
Tandil, Bs. As., Argentina
[2] CONICET, National Council for Scientific and Technical Research, Argentina
{alejandro.corbellini,silvia.schiaffino,
daniela.godoy}@isistan.unicen.edu.ar

Abstract. Social tagging constitutes one of the defining characteristics of Web 2.0 as it allows users to collectively classify and find diverse resources, such as Web pages, songs or pictures, using open-ended tags. The data structures underlying these systems, also known as folksonomies, suffered an explosive growth on account of the widespread success of social tagging. Thus, it is becoming increasingly difficult for users to find interesting resources as well as filter information streams coming from this massive amount of user-generated content on Web 2.0. In addition, most resources lacks easily extractable content to apply traditional content-based profiling approaches. In this paper we present an approach to build tag-based profiles for multimedia resources (such as songs, pictures or videos) using the social tags associated to resources as a means to describe them and, in turn, user interests. Experimental results show that the tags assigned by members of the community can help to predict the interestigness of a given resource for a user in an effective way.

Keywords: Social Tagging Systems, Folksonomies, Web 2.0.

1 Introduction

Social tagging systems, also known as folksonomies, emerged in the last years as a novel social classification on the Web that contrasts with traditional pre-defined taxonomies or directories usually seen on the Web. This scheme relies on the convergence of tagging efforts of a large community of users to a common categorization system that can be effectively used to organize and navigate large information spaces. In fact, the term *folksonomy* is a blend of the words *taxonomy* and *folk*, and stands for conceptual structures created by the people [6].

Multimedia resources such a songs, videos or pictures are collectively created, annotated and categorized in sites such as *Last.fm*[1], *Flickr*[2] or *YouTube*[3], among others. In these sites, users annotate resources using a freely chosen set of keywords or open-ended tags. In fact, it is argued that the power of tagging lies in the ability for

---

[1] http://www.last.fm/
[2] http://www.flickr.com/
[3] http://www.youtube.com/

F.V. Cipolla-Ficarra et al. (Eds.): ADNTIIC 2011, LNCS 7547, pp. 253–261, 2012.

people to freely determine the appropriate tags for resources without having to rely on a predefined lexicon or hierarchy.

The downside of tagging is the constantly expanding size of communities using social sites and the completely unsupervised nature of tags that lead to a huge volume of resources to be explored and analysed. In consequence, the discovery of relevant resources becomes a time consuming and difficult task for users. Tag-based user profiling techniques have emerged to help users in selecting appropriate tags to resources, finding relevant information and locating like-minded users [11, 2].

In traditional information retrieval and filtering systems, long-term interests are expressed in user profiles, which are usually learned starting from the textual content of documents exemplifying the user interests. In folksonomies, however, most of the resources have a non-textual content, including music, pictures and video. In the absence of textual content, meta-data can be used to build profiles. Particularly, in tagging systems the most important meta-data associated to resources are the tags or annotations assigned by users.

In this paper, a tag-based profiling approach that exploits social tags as a source for modelling user interests is presented. This approach assumes that users are likely to be interested in additional content annotated with similar social tags to the ones assigned to resources they showed interest in before. Thus, a learning algorithm is used to train a classifier (or user profile) that recognizes potentially interesting resources. This profile can be also applied to filter incoming information from tagging systems (e.g. RSS feeds).

The rest of this paper is organized as follows. Section 2 introduces the proposed approach for user profiling based on social tagging activity. Section 3 describes the empirical study carried out to validate the approach with a dataset from *Lastfm* site. Section 4 reviews related research in the area. Finally, concluding remarks are stated in Section 5.

2   Our Approach

A folksonomy can be defined as a tuple $F := (U, T, R, Y, \pi)$ which describes the users U, resources R, and tags T, and the user-based assignment of tags to resources by a ternary relation between them, i.e., $Y \subseteq U \times T \times R$ [6]. In this folksonomy, π is a user-specific sub-tag/super-tag-relation possible existing between tags, i.e., $\pi \subseteq U \times T \times T$.

The collection of all tag assignments of a single user constitute a *personomy*, i.e., the personomy P_u of a given user $u \in U$ is the restriction of F to u, i.e.,

$$P_u := (T_u, R_u, I_u, \pi_u) \text{ with } I_u := \{(t, r) \in T \times R | (u, t, r) \in Y\}, \ T_u := \pi_1(I_u),$$

$$R_u := \pi_2(I_u), \text{ and } \pi_u := \{(t_1, t_2) \in T \times T | (u, t_1, t_2) \in \pi\}, \text{ where } \pi_i \text{ is the}$$

projection on the ith dimension. In social tagging systems, tags are used to organize shared information within a personal information space.

The interests of a user are extracted from the user own personomy. This is, the resources the user annotated in the past are assumed to reflex the user preferences. To describe these resources, content in the form of text is sometime not available, but meta-data is. In social tagging systems the richer meta-data information about resources is the tags assigned to resources by the user community. Using social tags for user profiling allows users to capitalize on the associations made by persons who have assigned similar tags to other resources.

Section 2.1 describes the pre-processing techniques applied to tags in order to reduce syntactic variations. Section 2.2 introduces the learning technique employed to learn a user profile starting from the resources in the user personomy and the tags associated to them.

2.1   Tags Pre-processing

Each resource in the user personomy is considered in the proposed approach as an example of the user interests and it is described with the tags other users assigned to the resource. This is known as the full tagging activity (FTA) associated to resources, i.e., all tags assigned by members of the community to the.

Even though the success of tagging systems was greatly due to the possibility of freely determine a set of tags for a resource without the constraint of a controlled vocabulary, lexicon, or pre-defined hierarchy; the free-form nature of tagging also leads to a number of vocabulary problems. In this paper we deal with two common variations [17]:

- inconsistently grouping of compound words consisting of more than two words. Often users insert punctuation to separate the words, for example *ancient-egypt*, *ancient_egypt*, and *ancientgypt*;
- use of symbols in tags, symbols such as #, -, +, /, :, _, &, ! are frequently used at the beginning of tags to cause some incidental effect such as forcing the interface to list some tag at the top of an alphabetical listing.

To prevent syntactic mismatches due to these reasons original raw tags were filtered to remove symbols such as #, -, +, /, :, _, &, ! , which at the same time allows joining compound words. After these pre-processing step tags are weighted according to the number of users that assign the tag to the resource so that the more frequently a tag is used to annotate a resource the more important it is to describe the resource content. Figure 1 shows an example of an album in *Last.fm* and the tag cloud associated to this resource, that summarized its full tagging activity.

Fig. 1. Example of representing an album in Last.fm using the tag cloud

2.2   One-Class Classification

In order to profile a user annotating multimedia resources, such as songs or pictures, the tags or annotations in the user personomy are taken as examples. The annotated resources in a personomy constitute positive examples of the user interests that can be easily collected from folksonomies. On the contrary, to identify representative negative examples or non-interesting resources is more complex since users might not tag a potentially interesting resource because of multiple reasons.

Since only positive examples of the user interests are available, the task of determining whether a resource is interesting for a user basing learning exclusively on these examples can be seen as a one-class classification problem. One-class classification differs in one essential aspect from conventional classification as it assumes that only information of one of the classes, the target class, is available. The boundary between the two classes has to be estimated from data of only the normal, genuine class. Then, the task is to define a boundary around the target class, such that it accepts as many of the target objects as possible, while it minimizes the chance of accepting outlier objects.

One-class classification based on SVMs (Support Vector Machines) are used in this paper because they showed superior performance than other classifiers in a comparative study [5]. SVMs are a useful technique for data classification, which has been shown to be perhaps the most accurate algorithm for text classification, it is also widely used in Web page classification. Schölkopf et al. [14] extended the SVM methodology to handle training using only positive information and Manevitz and Yousef [8] applied this method to document classification and compare it with other one-class methods.

For training one-class SVM classifiers, the origin is considered the only member of the negative class as well as a certain number of data points of the positive class. SVM approach proceeds by determining the hyperplane that separates most of the negative data from the origin of the hypersphere containing the examples of the target class, separating a certain percentage of outliers from the rest of the data points. Then the standard two-class SVM techniques are employed. Figure 2 depicts this procedure. In this work we used LibSVM[4] [1] implementation of one-class SVM.

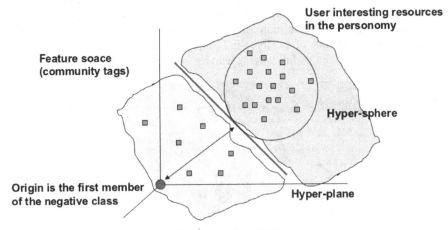

Fig. 2. One-class SVM

---

[4] http://www.csie.ntu.edu.tw/~cjlin/libsvm/

3   Experimental Results

In this paper, we use the *Last.fm* dataset described in [13] that collects neighbour and friend relationships in addition to tagging activity. In this site, friends are contacts in the social networks, while neighbours are users recommended by the system as potential contacts based on their music playing histories. The dataset also contains annotations in the form of triples (user,item,tags) and group membership information that was crawled from *Last.fm* site. The entire dataset contains 99.405 users, 52.452 of these users are considered active, i.e. have at least one annotation. The 10.936.545 triples annotate 1.393.559 items with 281.818 tags, belonging to 66.429 groups.

To represent a resource into the profile of a user the full tagging activity of the resource was used, including the tags assigned by all the community. In addition, smaller groups conformed by users having some relationship with the target user were considered in this study. Other relationships available in the dataset that were used for experimentation are:

- *friends*: extracted from a fraction of *Last.fm* social network, friendship relationships are symmetric;
- *group members*: users that belonging to the same groups as the user in consideration;
- *neighbours*: neighbourhood of users with similar tastes, neighbourhood relationship is not symmetric.

For experimentation 100 users were randomly selected from those having a minimum of 10 friends, group memberships and neighbours in the dataset and also at least 100 annotated resources. Evaluation was carried out using a holdout strategy that split data into a 66% for training and a 34% for testing. This is, each personomy was divided into a training set used to learn the one-class classifier and a testing set used to assess its validity. To make the results less dependent of the data splitting, the average and standard deviation of 5 runs are reported for each user, with error-bars indicating standard deviations.

Figure 3 shows the accuracy of classifiers for detecting interesting examples in the testing sets. This is, how many times the classifier deemed a resource as relevant and it effectively was. It can be observed in the figure that classifiers built using the full tagging activity of the community reach a good performance, only improved using tagging activity of users belonging to the same groups than the target users. Friends instead are not good predictors of the user interests. Likewise, classification of resources using neighbour tags was the worst performing scheme.

The performance reached for the different classifiers can be explained by the reduction in the dimensionality space during learning when information provided for less users than the entire community is considered. Table 1 summarizes the number of unique tags involved in learning the classifiers in each case. Also, the minimum, maximum and average number of tags used for the classifiers are reported in the table. Table 2 shows the number of users in the community, friends per personomy, number of groups the user belong to and neighbours suggested by *Last.fm*.

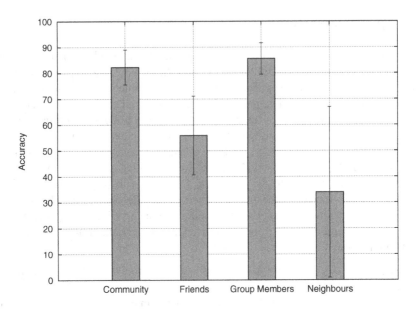

Fig. 3. Classifiers accuracy in identifying interesting resources

It is worth noticing that when classifiers are learned using the tags assigned by other users in the same groups as the target user, accuracy improves in spite of the slight reduction in the number of tags. This implies that the complexity of the learning problem is diminished, consequently reducing the times of training and classification.

Table 1. Summary of tag dimensions according to the users considered

Node	Community	Friends	Group members	Neighbours
# unique tags	45778	4027	40328	172
# minimum	1090.0	67	808.0	2
# maximum	21808.0	2178.0	7908.0	84
Mean ± SD	9155.6±7058.08	447.44±635.00	4480.8±2455.93	19.11±24.00

Table 2. Summary of number of user relationships

	# minimum	# maximum	Mean ± SD
# community	-	-	99405
# friends	113	873	381.33±244.89
# groups	52	300	106.77±72.58
# neighbours	59	60	59.55±0.49
# resources	108	3546	692.22±1031.82

4   Related Works

Tag-based profiling approaches enable personalize resource recommendation in social tagging systems [2, 11]. User profiles consisting of weighted tags vectors are obtained using the tags frequency of occurrence in the user resources as well as the inverse user frequency as a measure of their relative importance [12, 3, 16].

Firan et al. [4] compared tag-based user profiles with more conventional profiles based on song and track usage in the music search portal *Last.fm*. The results showed that tag-based profiles significantly improve the quality of recommendations. Au Yeoung at al. [18] investigated an algorithm which performs graph-based clustering over the network of user tagged documents to identify interest topics and extract tag vectors. In [15], tag clustering is used to group tags with similar meanings as the basis for a personalization algorithm for recommendation in folksonomies. Both users and resources are modelled as weighted tag vectors and tag clusters are intermediary between them. Vectors describing resources are used to detect relevant resources for a given cluster of tags, whereas similarity among a user vector and a tag clusters allows to recommend resources.

Graph representations were also proposed to model the relationships among tags in a user profile. Michlmayr et al. [9] compared tag-based profiles consisting of a single vector of weighted tags with graph representations in which nodes correspond to tags and edges denote co-occurrence or other relationships among them. *Add-A-Tag* [10] algorithm, extends this model to include temporal information by updating the weights of edges in the graph using an evaporation technique known from ant algorithms for discrete optimization. The idea of using semantic relationships among tags in tag-based profiles has also been explored in [7], in which the semantic distance between two tags is calculated based on co-occurrence statistics and common sense reasoning.

User profiles in these works model the user preferences in terms of the tags a user employed to annotate its resources in the past. Instead, in this research a user profile models the type of resources a user is interesting in based on the social tags attached to them, i.e. using a collective description of the resource. Thus, the proposed approach does not rely on the degree of coincidence between user tags and tags assigned by other members of the community to the resources.

5   Conclusions and Future Work

In this paper a tag-based profiling approach that exploits social tags for identifying relevant resources from folksonomies according to the interests of individual users was presented. One-class classifiers were used to learn the user interests from resources in the user personomy and the tags collectively assigned to them. Thus, collective knowledge extracted from folksonomies contributes to automatic, personal Web document classification.

Experimental results obtained with a dataset from *Last.fm* site showed that tag-based classifiers accurately recognize interesting resources. In these experiments, the use of other relationships among users were also explored in order to reduce the tag space, thereby diminishing the complexity and times involved in learning classifiers. The results demonstrate that friends and neighbours do not provide enough information to efficiently classify novel resources. In contrast, information about user membership to one or more groups allows to limit the number of users classifiers are learned from and, at the same time, to improve the accuracy of classifiers.

In future works we are planning to experiment with other types of social networks existing on the Web in which relationships among users are of different nature. For example, followers/followee relation in micro-blogging networks as well as friends and groups in Facebook, among others. We will also experiment with more semantic representation of tagging activities. Instead of simply sintactic modification to tags as the one used in this paper, semantic ones will be aoolied with the help of dictionaries and other lexical resources.

Acknowledgments. This work has been partially funded by CONICET through project PIP No. 114-200901-00381.

References

1. Chang, C.-C., Lin, C.-J.: LIBSVM: a library for support vector machines(2001), Software, http://www.csie.ntu.edu.tw/~cjlin/libsvm
2. Dattolo, A., Ferrara, F., Tasso, C.: The role of tags for recommendation: a survey. In: 3rd International Conference on Human System Interaction (HSI 2010), pp. 548–555. IEEE Press, Rzeszow (2010)
3. Diederich, J., Iofciu, T.: Finding communities of practice from user profiles based on folksonomies. In: 1st International Workshop on Building Technology Enhanced Learning Solutions for Communities of Practice (TEL-CoPs 2006) (2006)
4. Firan, C., Nejdl, W., Paiu, R.: The benefit of using tag-based profiles. In: 2007 Latin American Web Conference (LA-WEB 2007), pp. 32–41. IEEE Press, New York (2007)
5. Godoy, D.: Comparing One-Class Classification Algorithms for Finding Interesting Resources in Social Bookmarking Systems. In: Lacroix, Z., Vidal, M.E. (eds.) RED 2010. LNCS, vol. 6799, pp. 88–103. Springer, Heidelberg (2012)
6. Hotho, A., Jäschke, R., Schmitz, C., Stumme, G.: Information Retrieval in Folksonomies: Search and Ranking. In: Sure, Y., Domingue, J. (eds.) ESWC 2006. LNCS, vol. 4011, pp. 411–426. Springer, Heidelberg (2006)
7. Huang, Y.-C., Hung, C.-C., Yung-Jen Hsu, J.: You are what you tag. In: AAAI Spring Symposium on Social Information Processing (AAAI-SIP), pp. 3–41 (2008)
8. Manevitz, L.M., Yousef, M.: One-class SVMs for document classification. Journal of Machine Learning Research 2, 139–154 (2002)
9. Michlmayr, E., Cayzer, S.: Learning user profiles from tagging data and leveraging them for personal(ized) information access. In: Workshop on Tagging and Metadata for Social Information Organization, Banff, Alberta, Canada (2007)
10. Michlmayr, E., Cayzer, S., Shabajee, P.: Add-A-Tag: Learning adaptive user profiles from bookmark collections. In: 1st International Conference on Weblogs and Social Media (ICWSM), Boulder, Colorado (2007)

11. Milicevic, A.K., Nanopoulos, A., Ivanovic, M.: Social tagging in recommender systems: A survey of the state-of-the-art and possible extensions. Artificial Intelligence Review 33(3), 187–209 (2010)
12. Noll, M.G., Meinel, C.: Web Search Personalization Via Social Bookmarking and Tagging. In: Aberer, K., Choi, K.-S., Noy, N., Allemang, D., Lee, K.-I., Nixon, L.J.B., Golbeck, J., Mika, P., Maynard, D., Mizoguchi, R., Schreiber, G., Cudré-Mauroux, P. (eds.) ASWC 2007 and ISWC 2007. LNCS, vol. 4825, pp. 367–380. Springer, Heidelberg (2007)
13. Schifanella, R., Barrat, A., Cattuto, C., Markines, B., Menczer, F.: Folks in folksonomies: social link prediction from shared metadata. In: 3rd ACM International Conference on Web Search and Data Mining (WSDM 2010), pp. 271–280. ACM Press, New York (2010)
14. Schölkopf, B., Platt, J.C., Shawe-Taylor, J.C., Smola, A.J., Williamson, R.C.: Estimating the support of a high-dimensional distribution. Neural Computation 13(7), 1443–1471 (2001)
15. Shepitsen, A., Gemmell, J., Mobasher, B., Burke, R.: Personalized recommendation in social tagging systems using hierarchical clustering. In: ACM Conference on Recommender Systems (RecSys 2008), Lausanne, pp. 259–266 (2008)
16. Stoyanovich, J., Yahia, S.A., Marlow, C., Yu, C.: Leveraging tagging to model user interests in del.icio.us. In: AAAI Spring Symposium on Social Information Processing (AAAI-SIP), pp. 104–109 (2008)
17. Tonkin, E., Guy, M.: Folksonomies: Tidying up tags? D-Lib. 12(1) (2006)
18. Au Yeung, C.M., Gibbins, N., Shadbolt, N.: A study of user profile generation from folksonomies. In: Social Web and Knowledge Management, Social Web 2008 Workshop at WWW 2008 (2008)

Author Index

Alharbi, Saad   104
Alma, Jacqueline   1
Amandi, Analía   92, 197
Armentano, Marcelo   197
Artoni, Silvia   230

Berdún, Luis   197
Budàn, Paola D.   15
Buzzi, Maria Claudia   26, 230
Buzzi, Marina   230, 243

Campo, Marcelo   140, 208
Ceccarelli, Fabio   230
Clusella, María M.   15
Corbellini, Alejandro   114, 253
Costaguta, Rosanna   85, 134
Crasso, Marco   208

Diaz-Pace, J. Andrés   176
Digión, Leda B.   165
Donini, Francesco   26
Durán, Elena   134

Fares, Rubén   85
Fenili, Claudia   230
Ficarra, Francisco V. Cipolla   1, 71, 124, 151
Ficarra, Miguel Cipolla   1, 71
Ficarra, Valeria M.   71, 124

Garino, Carlos García   58, 186
Gebrehiwot, Abraham   26
Generoso, Adriana   15

Godoy, Daniela   114, 253
Gradišnik, Mitja   219

Kratky, Andreas   151

Lucchesi, Cristian   26
Lunardelli, Alessio   26

Mateos, Cristian   38, 58, 208
Mirasso, Anibal   58
Mitre, María G.   15
Mori, Paolo   26

Nicoletti, Matías   176

Pacini, Elina   58
Podgorelec, Vili   48, 219

Rapisarda, Beatrice   230
Ribero, Melisa   58
Rodríguez, Guillermo   140
Rodríguez, Juan Manuel   38

Salinas, Sergio Ariel   186
Santillán, María A.   15
Schiaffino, Silvia   114, 176, 253
Silva Logroño, Juan Francisco   197
Soria, Alvaro   140
Sosa, Mabel   165

Tesconi, Maurizio   230

Yannibelli, Virginia   92

Zunino, Alejandro   38, 186, 208